IMAGES
of America

RUBIDOUX

ON THE COVER: The Heber Parks residence is shown in 1916. From left to right are (in the trees to the left) unidentified, Mary, and Clara; Heber Parks (in the rear by the car); and Margaret (running down the driveway). The girls were all Heber's grandchildren. (Courtesy Ida Parks Condit family.)

IMAGES
of America

RUBIDOUX

Kim Jarrell Johnson

ARCADIA
PUBLISHING

ISBN 978-0-7385-4764-0

Published by Arcadia Publishing
Charleston, South Carolina

Printed in the United States of America

Library of Congress Catalog Card Number: 2007922172

For all general information contact Arcadia Publishing at:
Telephone 843-853-2070
Fax 843-853-0044
E-mail sales@arcadiapublishing.com
For customer service and orders:
Toll-Free 1-888-313-2665

Visit us on the Internet at www.arcadiapublishing.com

Contents

In memory of Don and Nell Jarrell, my parents, with whom I spent many childhood hours in Rubidoux shopping in Western Auto, Grants, TG&Y, Berner Judds dress shop, Mayfair Market, and Stater Brothers. In memory of my grandmother Eula Jarrell. I enjoyed many fried chicken dinners in her home in Rubidoux. In memory of Frank Kuma, longtime Mission Boulevard business owner, Rubidoux booster, and dear family friend.

INTRODUCTION

Rubidoux is an unincorporated town tucked up against the bank of the Santa Ana River in the northwestern corner of Riverside County. It is located west of the city of Riverside and south of the Riverside/San Bernardino County line. It is the most urbanized unincorporated community in Riverside County.

Before Europeans arrived, Native Americans sparsely populated the Rubidoux area; it was at the junction of several tribal territories: Serrano, Gabrielino, Luiseno, and Cauhilla. Since the land did not belong to any particular tribe, it became a place where all the tribes took advantage of the Santa Ana River and the abundant animal and plant life on its banks.

The area has been known by several names through the years. First it was known as the Rancho Jurupa when the land was owned by the Mission San Gabriel. It continued to be called Rancho Jurupa under its first and second private owners, Juan Bandini and Benjamin Wilson. When Louis Robidoux purchased 6,700 acres of the 32,000-acre Rancho Jurupa in 1847, his portion became known as the Robidoux Rancho. In 1870, land on the opposite side of the Santa Ana River from the Robidoux Rancho was purchased to start a colony. The new town site was named Riverside. The area of the former Robidoux Rancho soon became known as West Riverside, even though it predated the new town by many years. That name stuck until the 1950s, when the local chamber of commerce decided to bring the town that had developed west of Riverside out of its shadow and give it its own name. They reached back in history and, with a U instead of an O, named the community Rubidoux, the name it is known by today. The different spellings of Robidoux/Rubidoux cause confusion. The general rule is if something is named for Louis Robidoux it uses the old spelling, and if it is named for the town, it uses the new spelling. Interestingly, many of Robidoux's modern descendants use the "Rubidoux" spelling.

Rubidoux's early history was inextricably tied to the whims of the Santa Ana River. Before the river was controlled with levees constructed in the 1950s, it ranged across a much wider area than it does today. The river had two channels at the base of the low mountain that became known as Mount Rubidoux. But while the river provided much to the Robidoux Rancho, with its rich bottomland and life-giving water, it could also cause great hardship. In 1862, a great flood occurred. The Robidoux home became an island as floodwaters washed around it. After the waters receded, the fertile land along the river had been replaced by useless sand. This would be the first of many known floods that impacted the Rubidoux area.

Louis Robidoux became one of the first subdividers in Southern California as he sold off portions of his rancho, 50 or 100 acres at a time. The first to take advantage of this opportunity was Cornelius Boy Jensen, who bought property south of what is now Mission Boulevard near the intersection of Riverview Drive. He was soon followed by Arthur Parks. His property was located north of Mission Boulevard and west of today's Rubidoux Boulevard.

Rubidoux as a town dates to the 1920s when the first subdivisions occurred. Businesses began cropping up along Mission Boulevard west of present-day Wallace Street. East of Wallace Street was still river bottom. Some of those early commercial buildings, though fast disappearing, are still located along Mission Boulevard. Rubidoux, then known as West Riverside, continued to grow through the 1930s, 1940s, and 1950s. It became a small town with markets, hardware stores, a five-and-dime, a dress shop, restaurants, and other typical stores of the day. Travel courts and motels were scattered along Mission Boulevard to cater to the traveling public who used this route from Los Angeles to the desert and San Diego long before the freeways were built. Longtime residents of the area remember that as Rubidoux's heyday. It was a time of parades, Christmas displays, and middle-class families shopping in "their" town.

The flight of businesses from downtowns that began in the 1960s impacted Rubidoux as well. Housing tracts in other areas of Jurupa began to draw middle-class families away from Rubidoux who were looking to move up to larger homes. By the late 1970s, some people began to say that Rubidoux should be bulldozed to allow for a clean start.

A new century has brought new life to Rubidoux. In an effort to revitalize the area, the redevelopment process has been used to bring road improvements and several government buildings to Mission Boulevard. It is hoped that these improvements will bring new life to an old community.

Two smaller communities, Belltown and Crestmore, lie adjacent to Rubidoux. Their stories are included in this book as well.

Belltown began in 1907 as a subdivision of land northwest of the Santa Ana River in the West Riverside area. N. R. Bell filed the subdivision and named it after himself. Located south of Fourth Street (now Twenty-fourth Street) and east of C Street (now Hall Avenue), it consisted of just 12 large lots. The subdivision apparently wasn't successful because it was re-subdivided two more times, making the majority of the lots smaller each time. By 1924, the configuration of Belltown was basically as seen today. Mexican immigrants, who came to this area during and after the Mexican Revolution, primarily populated Belltown. It was a small community centered around Our Lady of Guadalupe Church and Belltown School, both on Hall Avenue. Prior to World War II, Belltown was home to many Mexican families as well as just two or three families each of Italians and African Americans. One Italian family had vineyards and a winery on Hall Avenue. After World War II, Belltown became home to many African American families. Now, in a new century, Belltown has returned to its original roots with the majority of families being of Mexican descent.

In 1926, Irvine and May Keith Biggar filed a subdivision map named Biggar's Crestmore Heights. It was located south of the Riverside/San Bernardino County line and west of today's Rubidoux Boulevard. Just north of this subdivision, in San Bernardino County, was the 1907 subdivision of the City of Crestmore, which is where the Biggars got the idea for the name. Later this small area also became known as Crestmore. This 60-lot subdivision was laid out along roads with romantic-sounding Spanish names: Andalusia, Barcelona, Castellano, Salamanca, and Valencia.

Crestmore's claim to fame was the Riverside Cement Company on Rubidoux Boulevard, which is a California Point of Historical Interest and a Riverside County Landmark. This company was founded in 1906 under the name Southern California Cement Company. It was one of the first construction materials producers in the region and was innovative in the cement industry by creating new ways to reduce dust pollution and to analyze raw and finished products. In 1907, while its cement plant was under construction in Crestmore, the Riverside-Portland Cement Company constructed a railroad line from Riverside to Crestmore. This was to provide a line for supplies to be shipped to the plant and as a transportation facility for employees. The new railroad was called the Crescent City Railway Company. The line was located along what is now Market Street and serviced both Crestmore and Belltown.

Crestmore continues today as a small, hillside enclave of larger lots with most of the homes having been built between 1920 and 1960. Many homeowners keep horses or other animals in this area, which still retains a rural atmosphere.

One

EARLY DAYS

The story of Rubidoux's early days is full of adventure, as pioneers from all over the world came to Rubidoux to work the land, raise their families, and participate in local life and the greater world around them. Early pioneer Louis Robidoux was one of the first three county supervisors in the new county of San Bernardino. Arthur Parks was a self-taught lawyer from England who would go on to be justice of the peace, road supervisor, and school board member. Cornelius Jensen, a ship captain from the Isle of Sylt near Denmark, served nine terms on the Riverside County Board of Supervisors. These men and other early pioneers lived the life typical of that time, living on large pieces of the old ranchos, raising animals and crops.

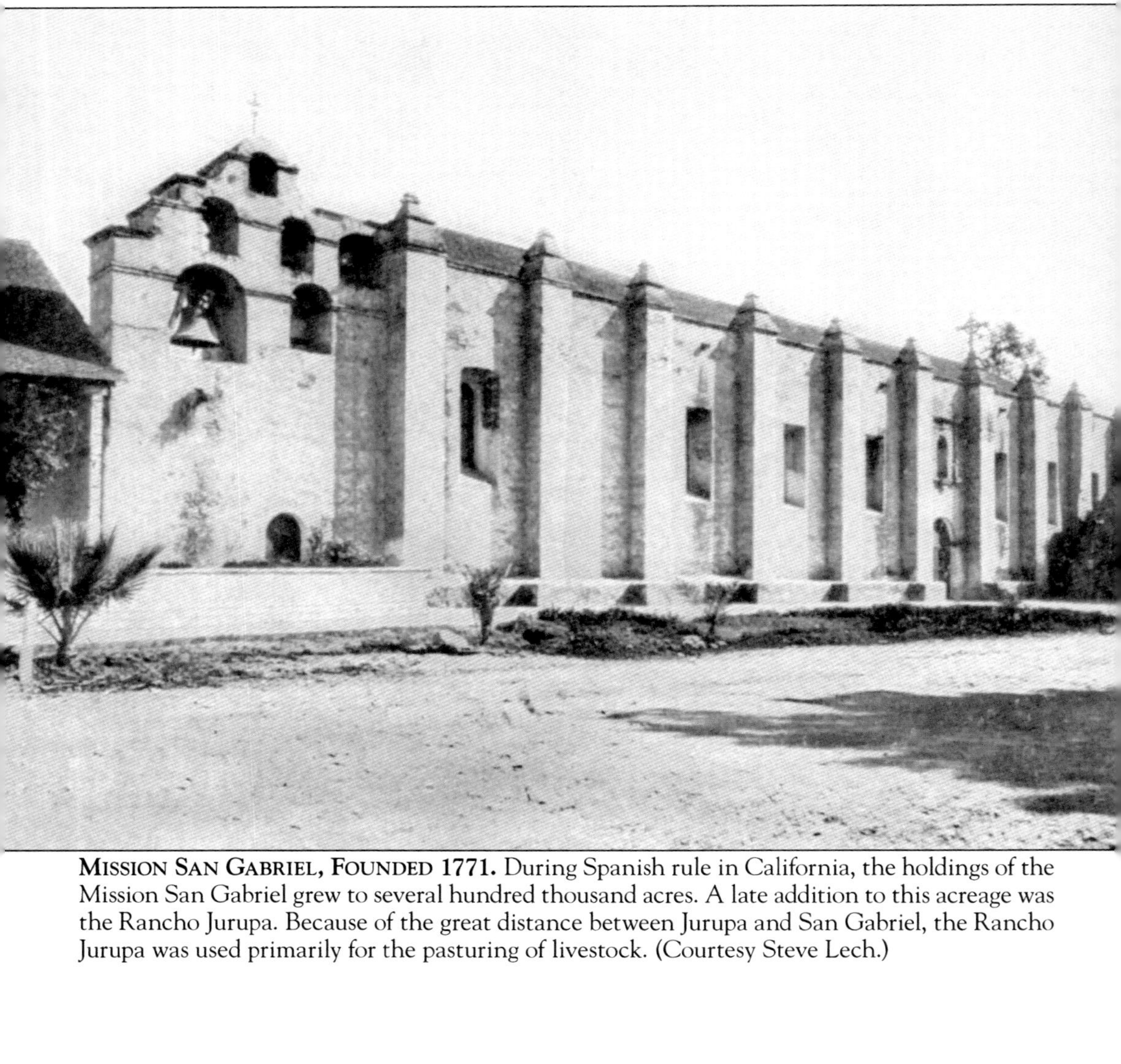

MISSION SAN GABRIEL, FOUNDED 1771. During Spanish rule in California, the holdings of the Mission San Gabriel grew to several hundred thousand acres. A late addition to this acreage was the Rancho Jurupa. Because of the great distance between Jurupa and San Gabriel, the Rancho Jurupa was used primarily for the pasturing of livestock. (Courtesy Steve Lech.)

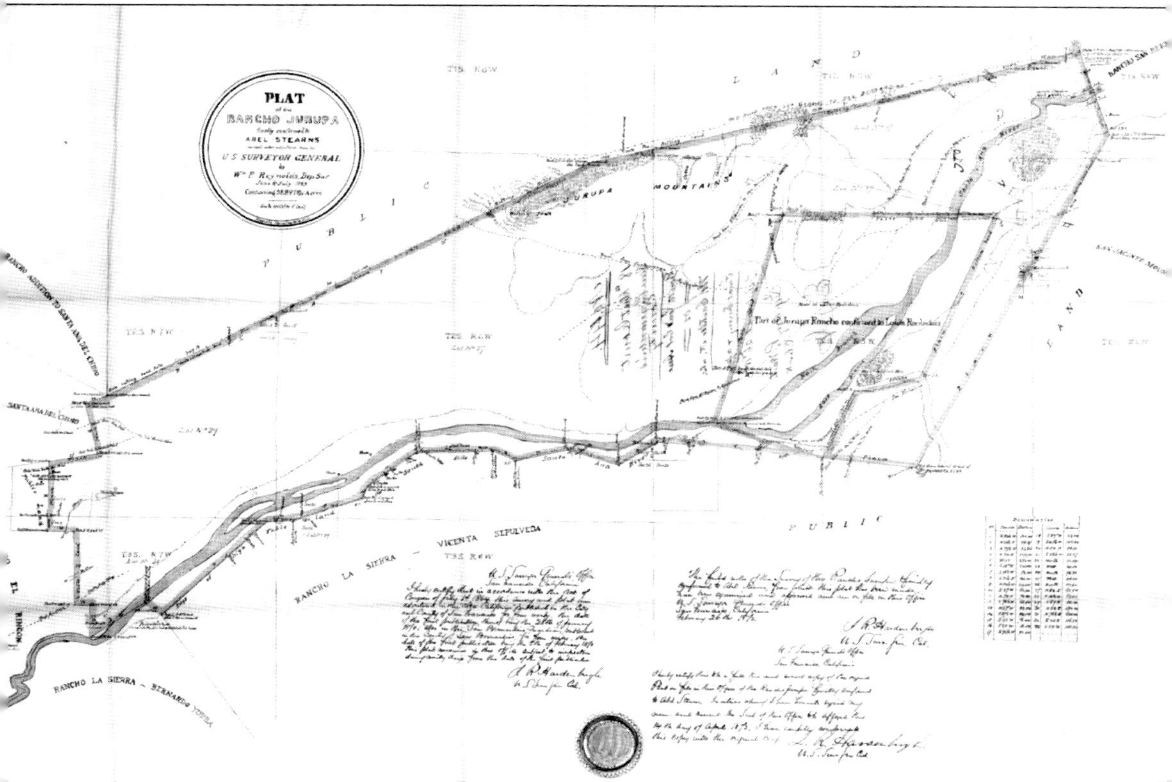

RANCHO JURUPA MAP. This is a map of the Rancho Jurupa as it was confirmed after California became a part of the United States. The square portion of land on the right side of the map is the land purchased by Louis Robidoux, which became known as the Robidoux Rancho. (Courtesy Chuck Cox.)

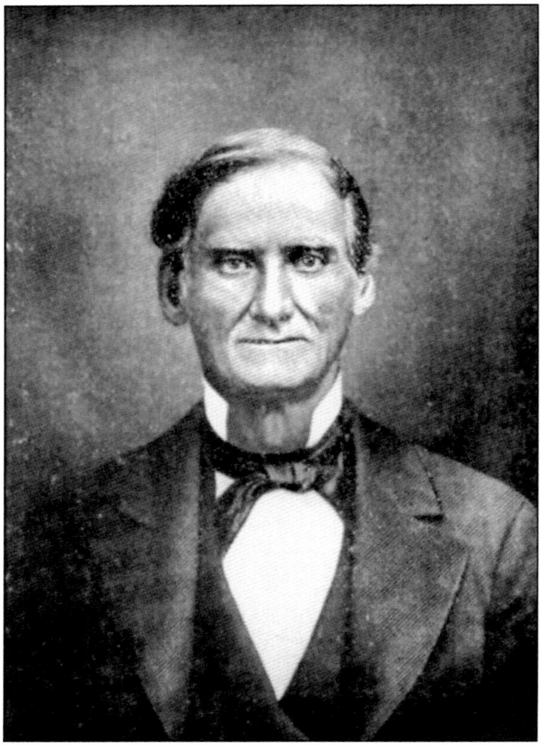

JUAN BANDINI. On September 28, 1838, the Mexican government granted the 32,000-acre Jurupa Rancho to Juan Bandini. Bandini was born in Peru and came to California about 1820. He built a home on his new rancho, but it was located overlooking the Santa Ana River near present-day Hamner Avenue. In his 1840 book *Two Years before the Mast,* Richard Henry Dana described Bandini as an elegant figure who danced and waltzed beautifully, spoke with a refined voice, and carried himself with the bearing of a man of high birth. (Courtesy Steve Lech.)

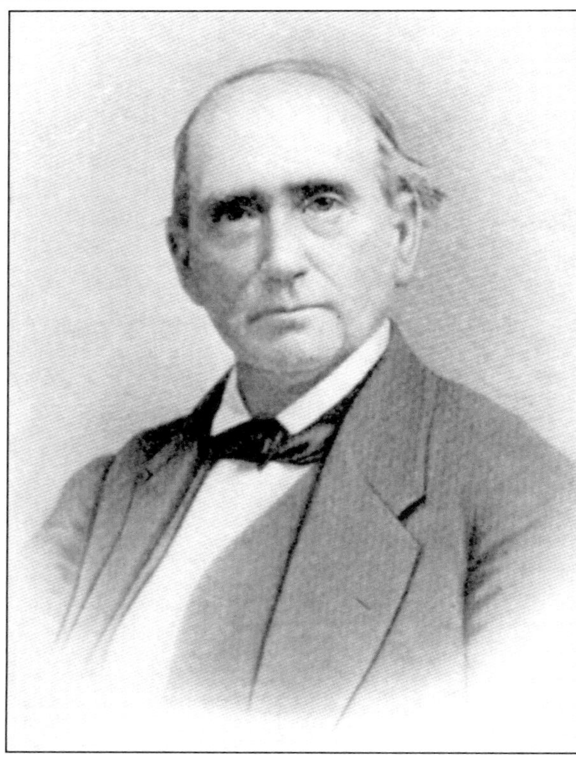

BENJAMIN WILSON. Wilson became the owner of what would become the community of Rubidoux when he bought 6,700 acres of the Rancho Jurupa from Juan Bandini in about 1843. He is believed to have built the first home in Rubidoux, an adobe home near the Santa Ana River and Mount Rubidoux. Wilson later moved to Los Angeles and became its first mayor. (Courtesy Steve Lech.)

LOUIS ROBIDOUX. Robidoux was born near St. Louis in 1796. He grew up on the American frontier and became a fur trader and later a storekeeper. After living in Santa Fe, New Mexico, where he met and married Guadalupe Garcia, Robidoux came to California. In approximately 1844, Robidoux bought Wilson's portion of the Jurupa Rancho, and after the purchase, the area became known as the Robidoux Rancho. Robidoux and his wife raised seven children on the rancho. He was a well-known and well-respected man in inland Southern California, and when the County of San Bernardino was formed, he became one of its first supervisors. (Courtesy Steve Lech.)

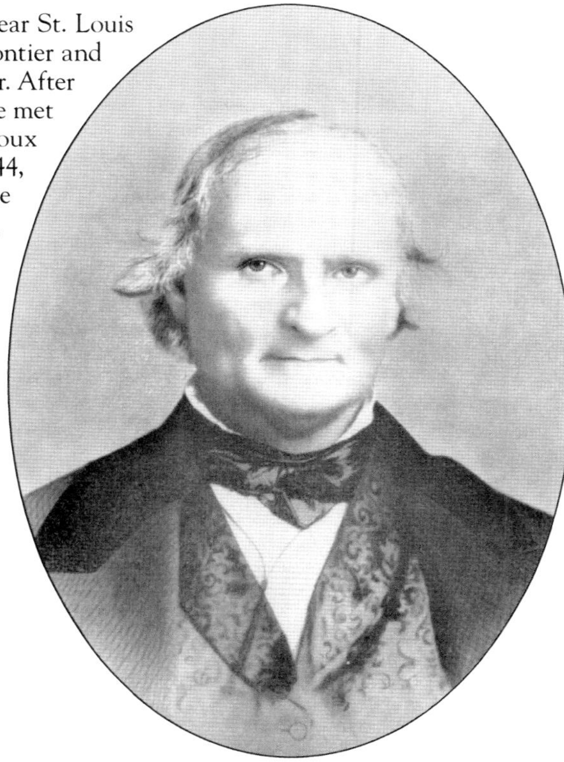

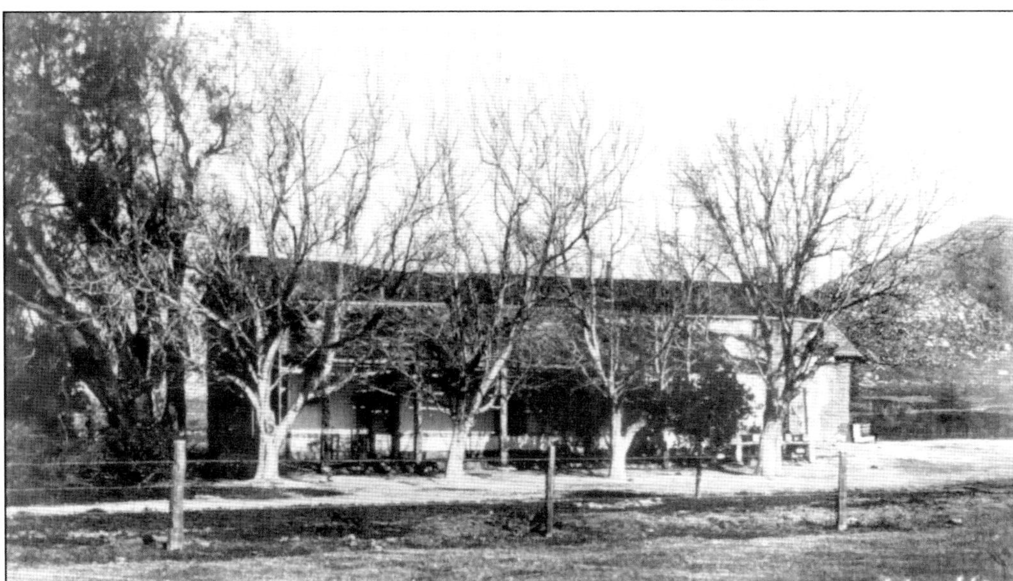

ROBIDOUX'S HOME. The adobe home built by Benjamin Wilson was part of the Rancho bought by Louis Robidoux. Robidoux expanded the home to house his growing family as well as enterprises such as wine and perfume making. This picture of the house, taken about 1890, has Rattlesnake Hill in the background. The house faced the Santa Ana River. It was located near what is now the northeast corner of Rubidoux and Mission Boulevards in Rubidoux. (Courtesy Steve Lech.)

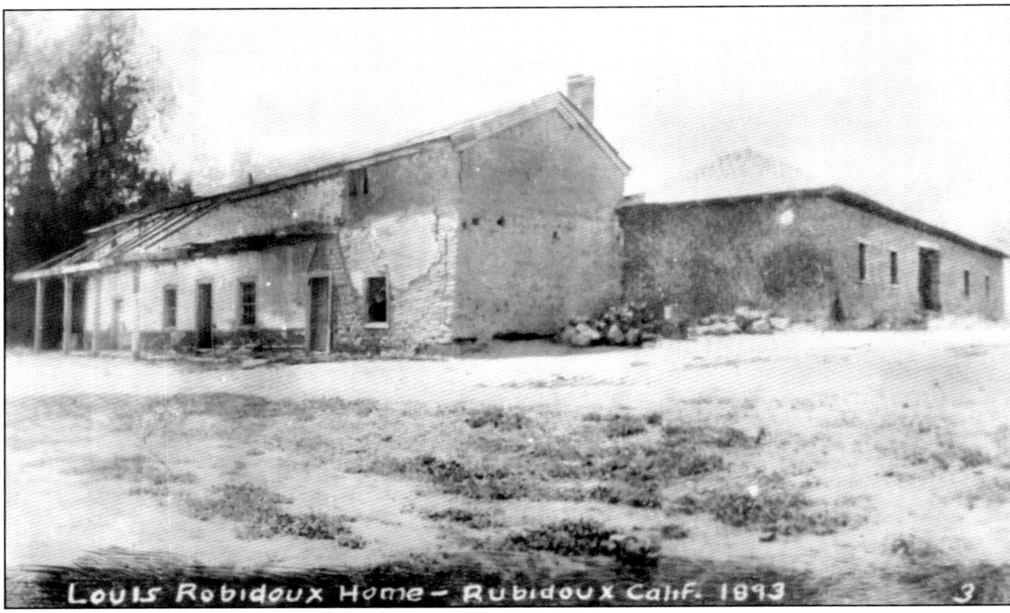

LOUIS ROBIDOUX HOME. This photograph, *c.* 1897, shows the Robidoux winery, right, in relationship to the house, on the left. The Robidoux house was at the crossroads of several important trails. Thus the family was always kept abreast of area news and became well-known for their hospitality. (Courtesy Steve Lech.)

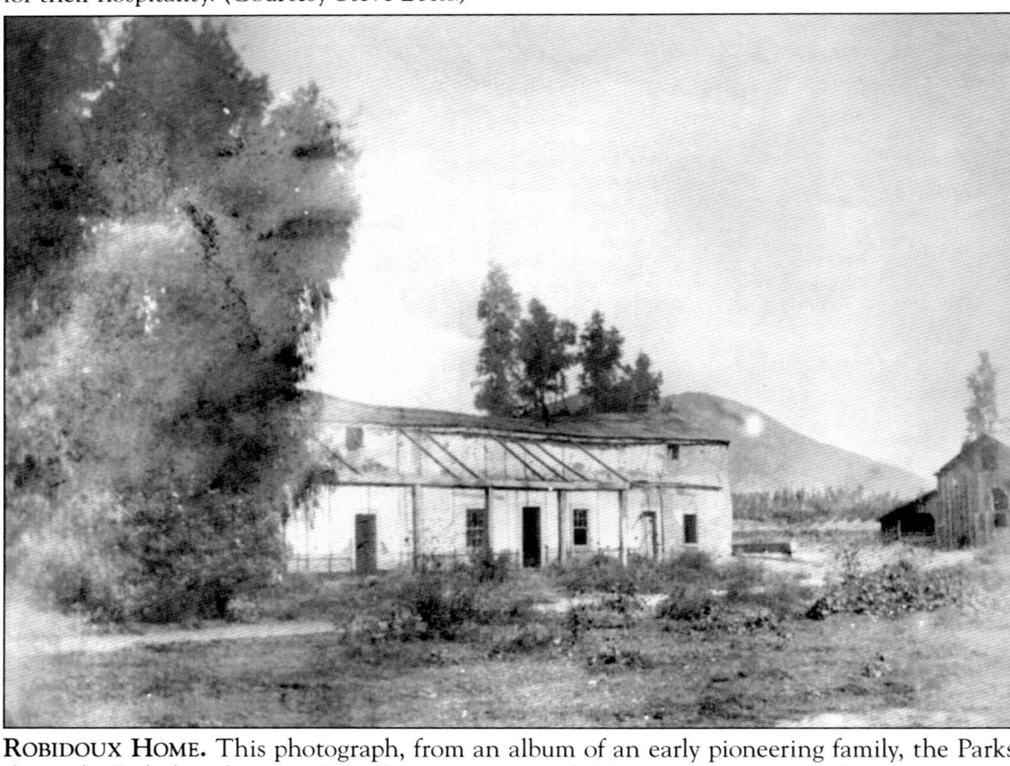

ROBIDOUX HOME. This photograph, from an album of an early pioneering family, the Parks, shows the Robidoux home *c.* 1910. (Courtesy Riverside Metropolitan Museum.)

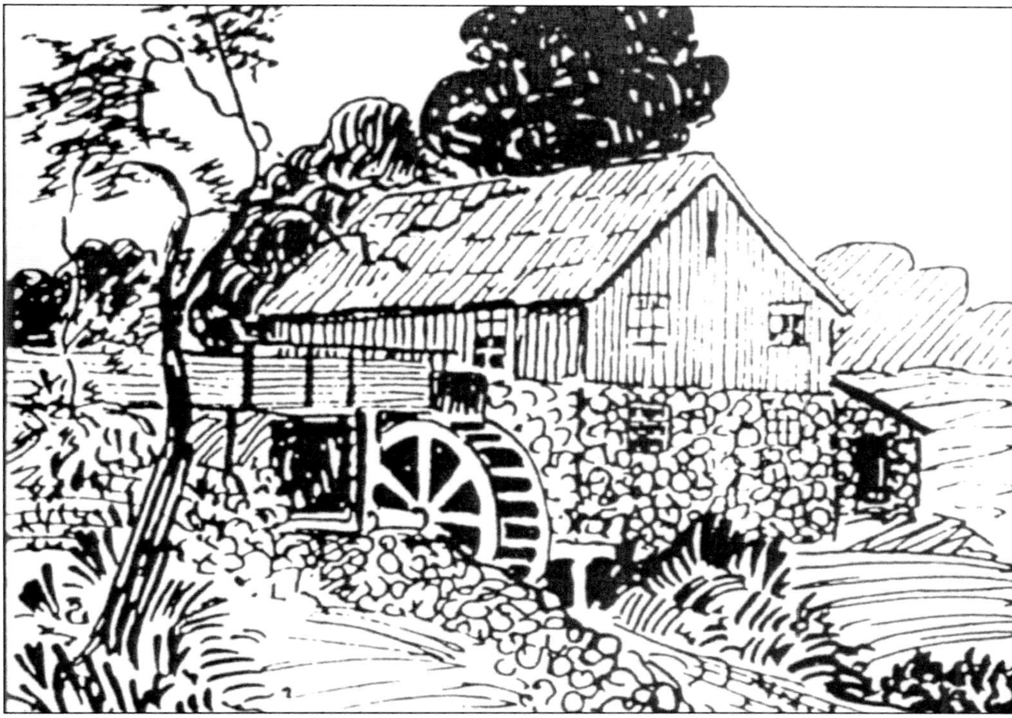

ROBIDOUX'S GRISTMILL. Robidoux built what was probably the only functioning mill in Southern California at that time on the Robidoux Rancho. The mill supplied flour to the Mormon Battalion, commanded by Gen. Stephan Kearney, when it occupied Los Angeles in 1847. Water for the mill came from the Santa Ana River. Prior to 1862, the river ran much closer to the mill's location. This sketch of the gristmill is based on the memories of Heber Parks, who saw the ruins of the mill when he moved to Jurupa as a boy in 1868. (Courtesy Riverside County Library System, Glen Avon Library.)

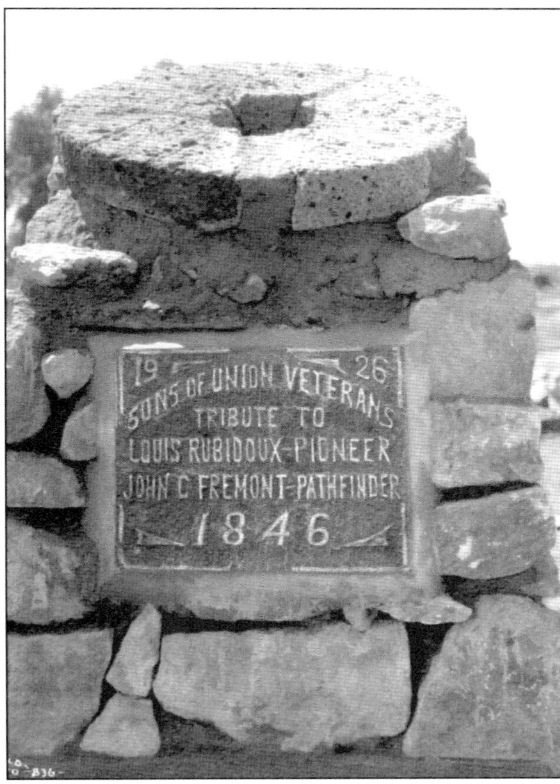

GRISTMILL MONUMENT. The mill was located near today's Molino Way and Fort Street where this historical monument is located. The monument includes one of the gristmill stones. Another stone is located at Riverside's Mission Inn. (Courtesy Riverside Metropolitan Museum.)

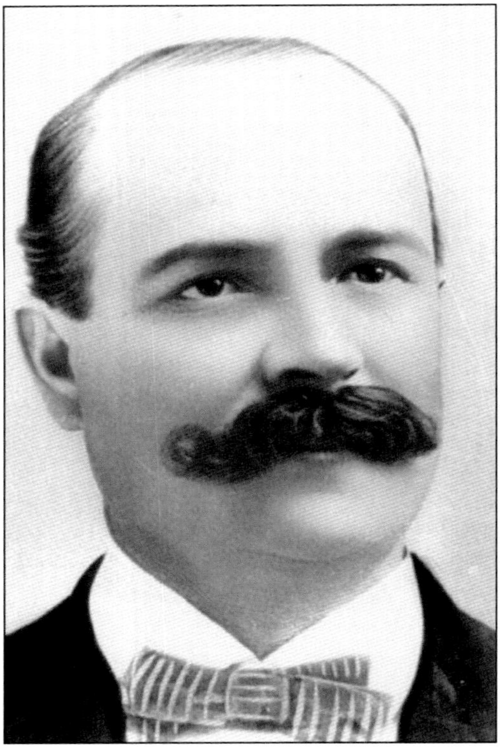

Abundo Robidoux. Louis Robidoux's youngest son was born at the Robidoux home in 1851. This photograph shows him as an adult. (Courtesy Ben Rubidoux.)

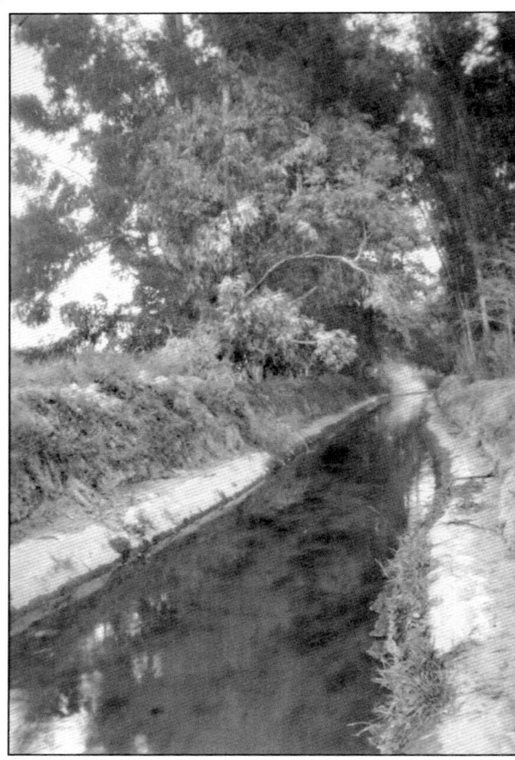

Jurupa Ditch. The Jurupa Ditch may date to as early as 1843–1845 when Benjamin Wilson reportedly dug a ditch to carry water for irrigation. After buying Wilson's property, Louis Robidoux probably continued to use the same ditch to irrigate his land and to provide water to his gristmill. Following Robidoux's death in 1868, new owners, including Cornelius Jensen, formed a water association and filed the first formal claim for water rights from the Santa Ana River. In 1902, its owners incorporated as the Jurupa Ditch Company. This company continues to provide water to its shareholders to this day. Portions of the ditch are now piped underground. One of the best places to see the ditch today is along the south side of Riverview Drive from Limonite Avenue to the end of Riverview Drive. (Courtesy Riverside Metropolitan Museum.)

ARTHUR PARKS. On February 16, 1867, Arthur Parks bought 50 acres of land from Louis Robidoux for $500. In May of that year, he bought another 60 acres from Robidoux's son Pasqual for the same price. Parks's land was located north of Mission Boulevard in the vicinity of Avalon Street. He was an ex-Mormon from England who came to Jurupa by way of Utah and San Bernardino. Parks became a self-taught lawyer and served as justice of the peace, road supervisor, clerk of elections, and as a school board member. (Courtesy Ida Parks Condit family.)

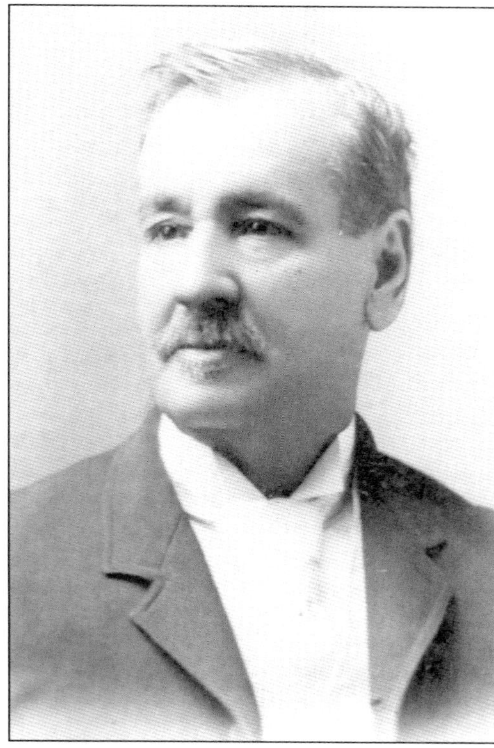

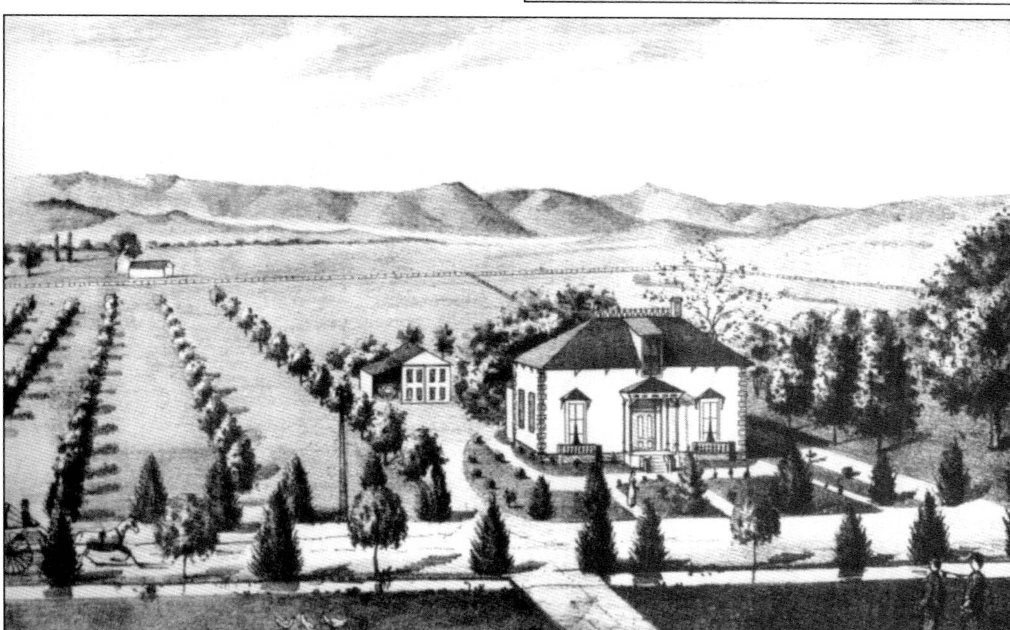

ARTHUR PARKS HOME. This drawing shows the home and property of Arthur Parks, c. 1883. Parks originally built a small adobe home in 1867. A large, wooden addition was added to the front of the house about 1875. The home was located at what is now 5560 Thirty-fourth Street. It was demolished in 1974. (Courtesy Riverside County Library System, Glen Avon Library.)

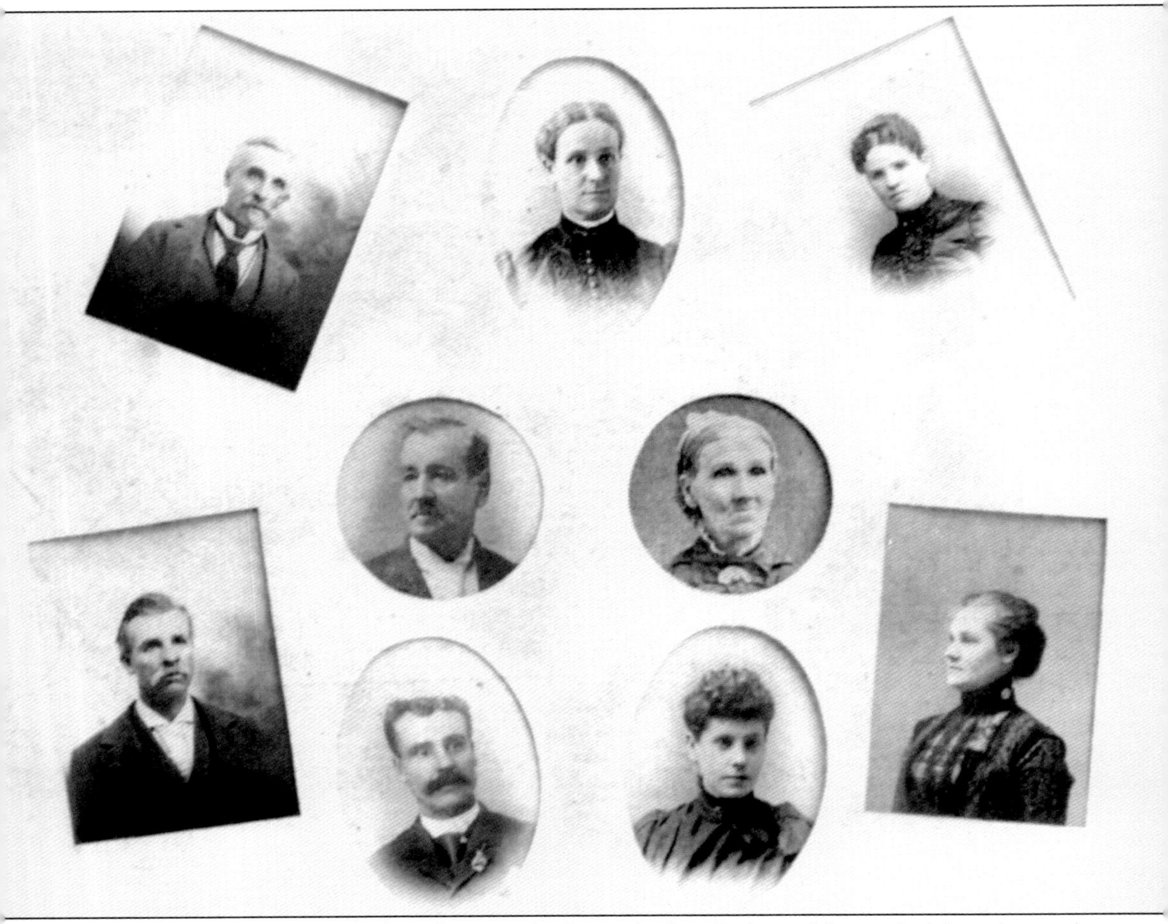

ARTHUR PARKS FAMILY. This photograph shows Arthur Parks and his wife, Mary Anne, (in the center) with their seven surviving children. Clockwise from top left are Heber, Betsy, Olive, Celena, Linda, Orlando, and Arthur J. (Courtesy Ida Parks Condit family.)

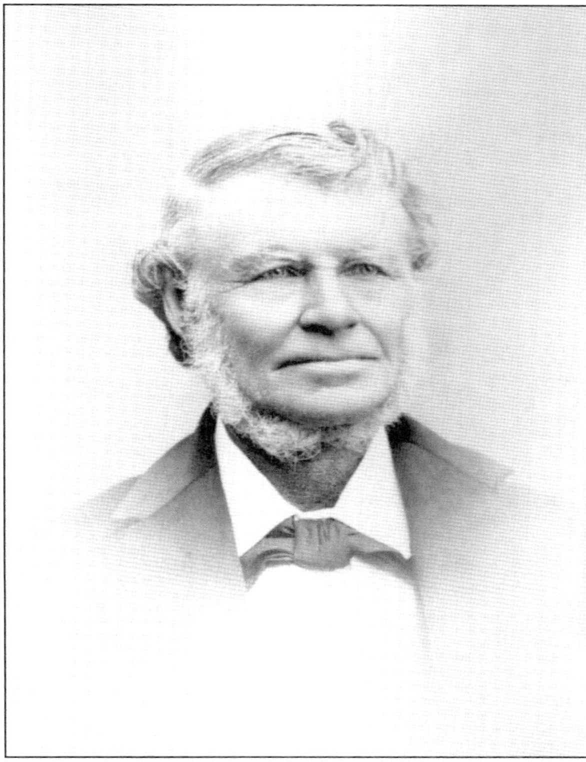

CORNELIUS BOY JENSEN, C. 1865. Born on the Island of Sylt off the coast of Denmark in 1815, Jensen was a sea captain, serving on a ship that came to San Francisco in 1848. After his crew abandoned the ship because of gold fever, Captain Jensen stayed in California, becoming a store owner in gold country and later in Agua Mansa (San Bernardino County) where he moved in 1851. He was well-known and respected both in Agua Mansa and at his home in Jurupa. He served a total of nine single-year terms as county supervisor between 1856 and 1877. (Courtesy Riverside Metropolitan Museum.)

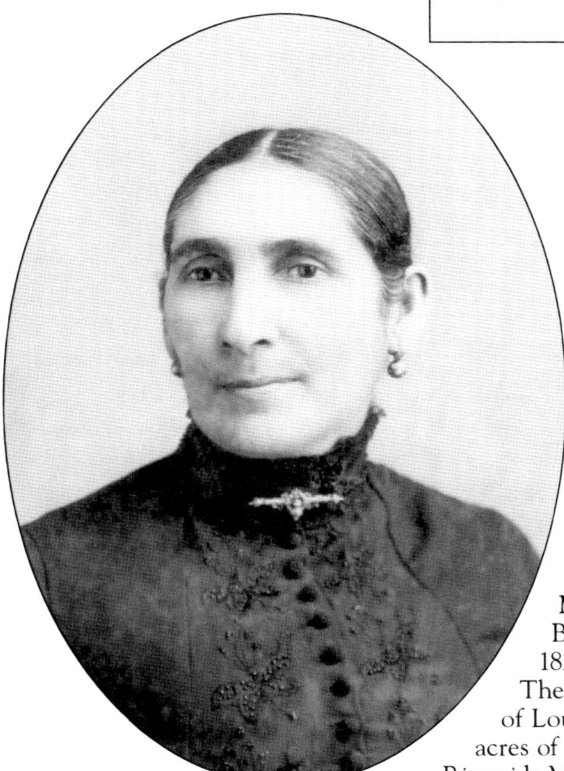

MERCEDES ALVARADO JENSEN, C. 1865. Born in 1837, Mercedes married Cornelius in 1854 at the Catholic church in Agua Mansa. The wedding celebration was held at the home of Louis Robidoux. The couple purchased 100 acres of the Robidoux Rancho in 1865. (Courtesy Riverside Metropolitan Museum.)

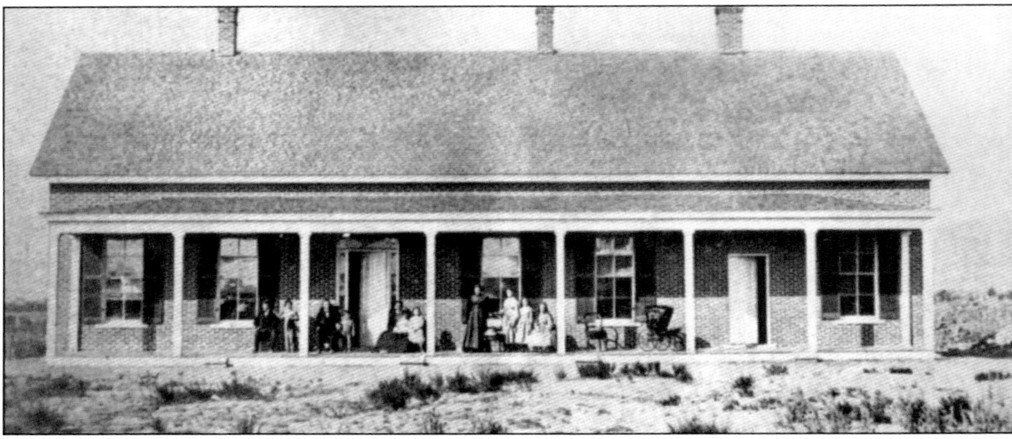

Cornelius Jensen Home. The Jensen home, built in 1868–1870, was unique in many ways. It was the first kiln-fired brick building constructed in what is now Riverside County. It was made in an architectural style found in Jensen's birthplace on the Island of Sylt. However, probably because of his wife's influence, it had a front porch, which is uncommon on Sylt but very common in California. Thus, the house became a marriage of the cultures of the Danish sea captain and his Californio wife, Mercedes. Bricks for the Jensen home were manufactured on site by Chinese laborers from clays available on the ranch. The beams were hauled by a team of oxen from the sawmills in the San Bernardino Mountains. On the Jensen ranch, which grew to over 300 acres, grapes were grown for wine and raisins, and groves of apricots and oranges were planted. Jensen also raised sheep, cattle, and horses, primarily on property he owned in other areas. (Courtesy Jensen family.)

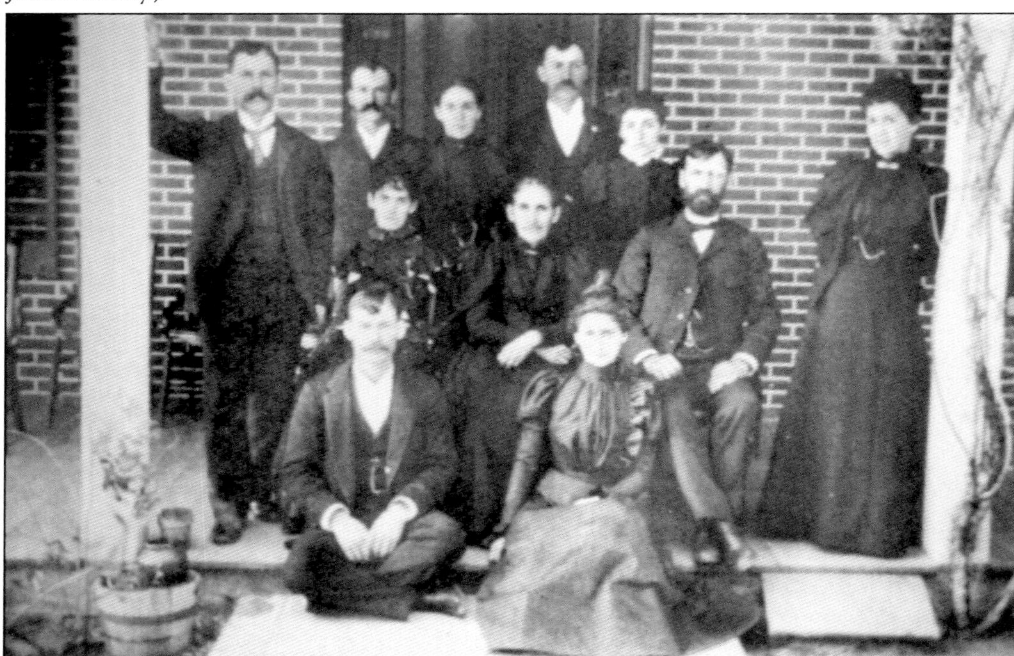

Jensen Family. The Jensen family is shown on January 1, 1898. Pictured from left to right are (first row) Robert and Mary; (second row) Connie, mother Mercedes, and Jose; (third row) Cornelius Jr., John, Tomasa, Henry, Erolinda, and Francisca. (Courtesy Jensen family.)

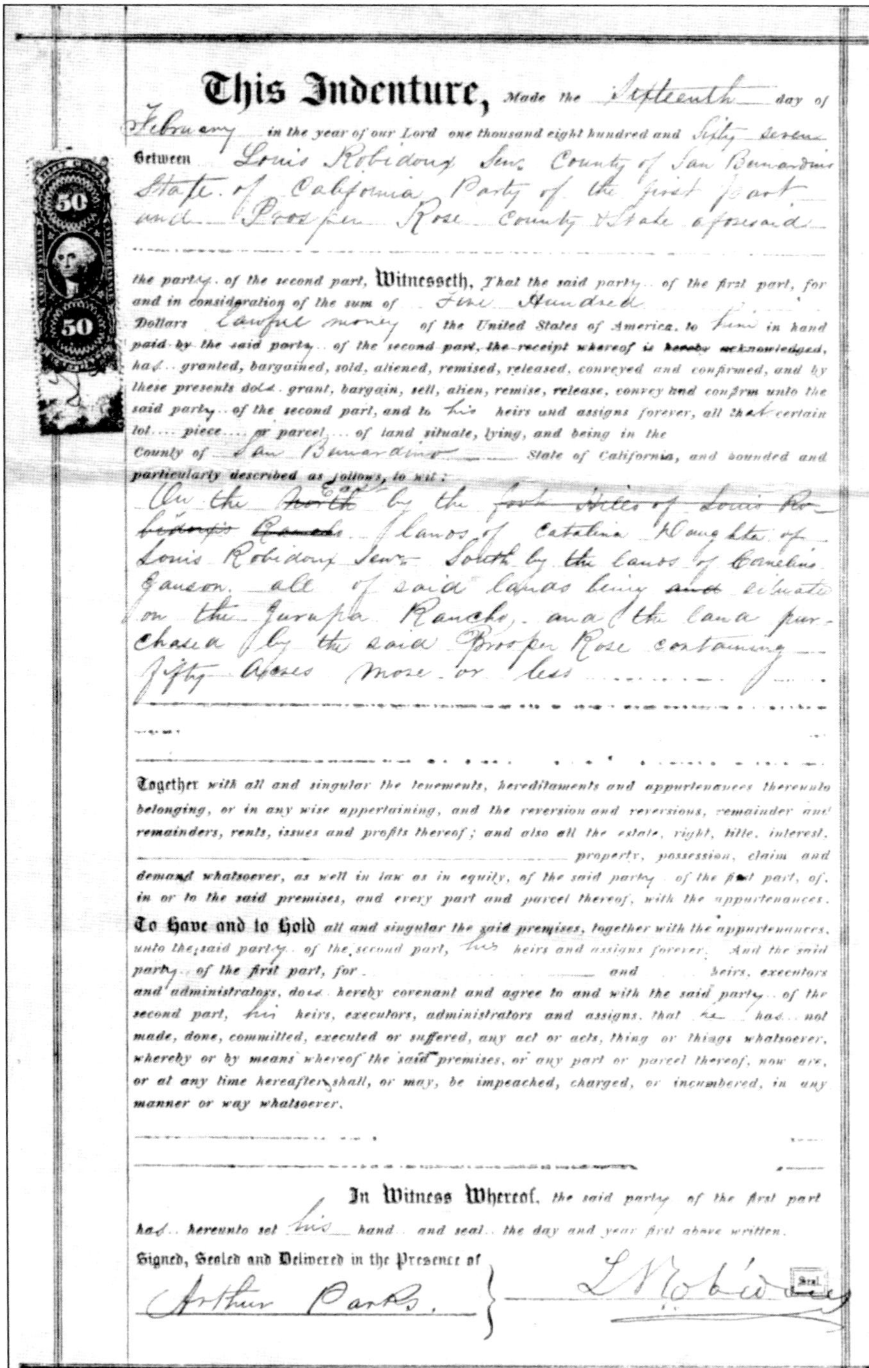

This Indenture, Made the Sixteenth day of February in the year of our Lord one thousand eight hundred and Sixty Seven Between Louis Robidoux Senr County of San Bernardino State of California Party of the first part and Prosper Rose County & State aforesaid

the party of the second part, **Witnesseth,** That the said party of the first part, for and in consideration of the sum of Five Hundred Dollars lawful money of the United States of America, to him in hand paid by the said party of the second part, the receipt whereof is hereby acknowledged, has granted, bargained, sold, aliened, remised, released, conveyed and confirmed, and by these presents does grant, bargain, sell, alien, remise, release, convey and confirm unto the said party of the second part, and to his heirs and assigns forever, all that certain lot.... piece.... or parcel.... of land situate, lying, and being in the County of San Bernardino State of California, and bounded and particularly described as follows, to wit:

On the East by the lands of Catalina daughter of Louis Robidoux Senr South by the lands of Cornelius Jauson all of said lands being situate on the Jurupa Rancho, and the land purchased by the said Prosper Rose containing fifty Acres more or less

Together with all and singular the tenements, hereditaments and appurtenances thereunto belonging, or in any wise appertaining, and the reversion and reversions, remainder and remainders, rents, issues and profits thereof; and also all the estate, right, title, interest, property, possession, claim and demand whatsoever, as well in law as in equity, of the said party of the first part, of, in or to the said premises, and every part and parcel thereof, with the appurtenances.

To Have and to Hold all and singular the said premises, together with the appurtenances, unto the said party of the second part, his heirs and assigns forever. And the said party of the first part, for and heirs, executors and administrators, does hereby covenant and agree to and with the said party of the second part, his heirs, executors, administrators and assigns, that he has not made, done, committed, executed or suffered, any act or acts, thing or things whatsoever, whereby or by means whereof the said premises, or any part or parcel thereof, now are, or at any time hereafter shall, or may, be impeached, charged, or incumbered, in any manner or way whatsoever.

In Witness Whereof, the said party of the first part has hereunto set his hand and seal the day and year first above written.

Signed, Sealed and Delivered in the Presence of

Arthur Parks. L Robidoux [Seal]

Bancroft's Blank, No. 462—DEED, WARRANTY AGAINST GRANTOR. H. H. Bancroft & Company, Booksellers and Stationers, San Francisco, Cal.

EARLY SALES CONTRACT. This early contract is dated February 16, 1867. It carries the signatures of two early Jurupa pioneers—Arthur Parks and Louis Robidoux. The contract also refers to "Cornelius Jansen," probably Cornelius Jensen, another early pioneer. (Courtesy Riverside County Regional Park and Open-Space District.)

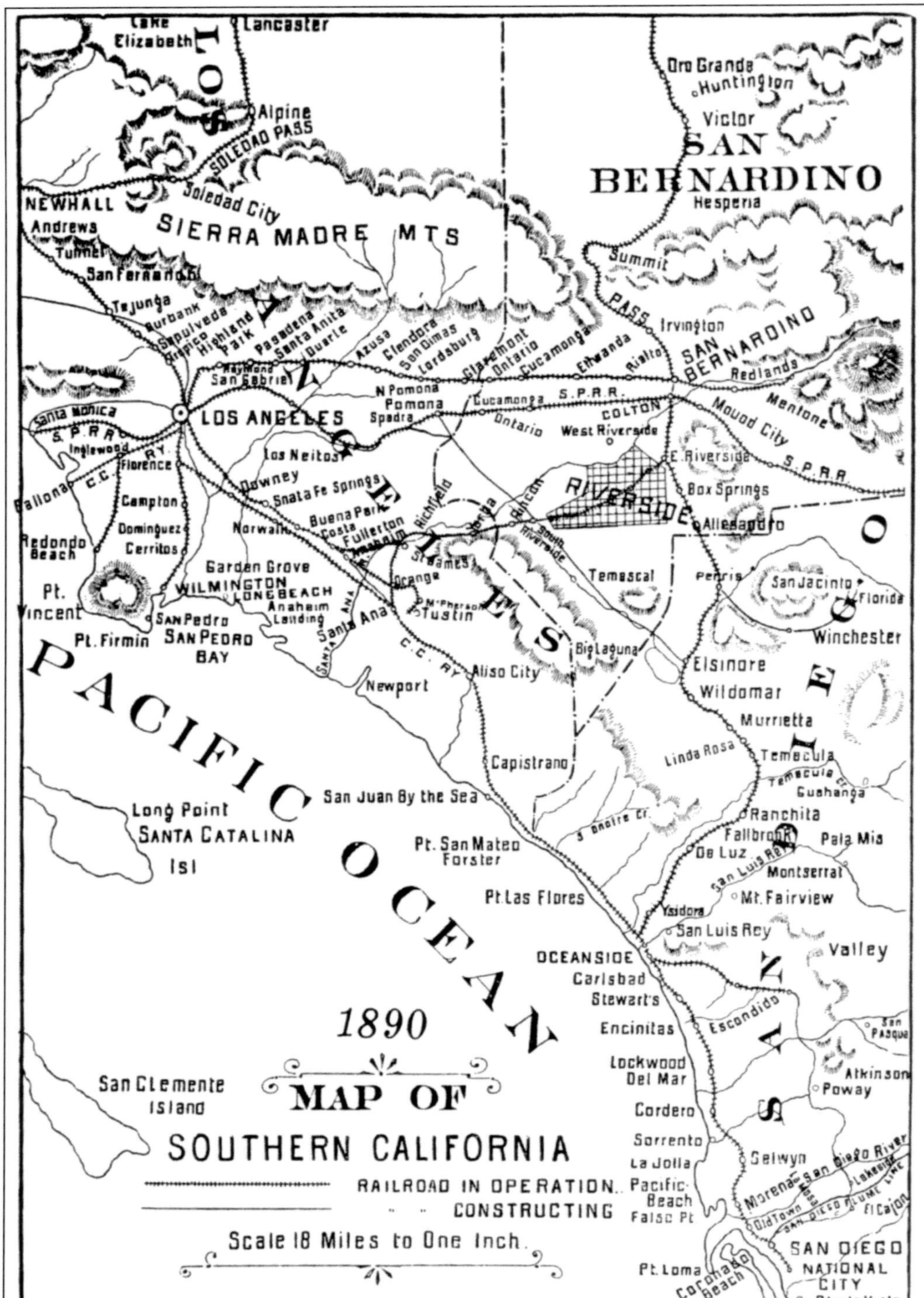

MAP, 1890. This 1890 map of Southern California shows West Riverside, just above the city of Riverside. (Courtesy author.)

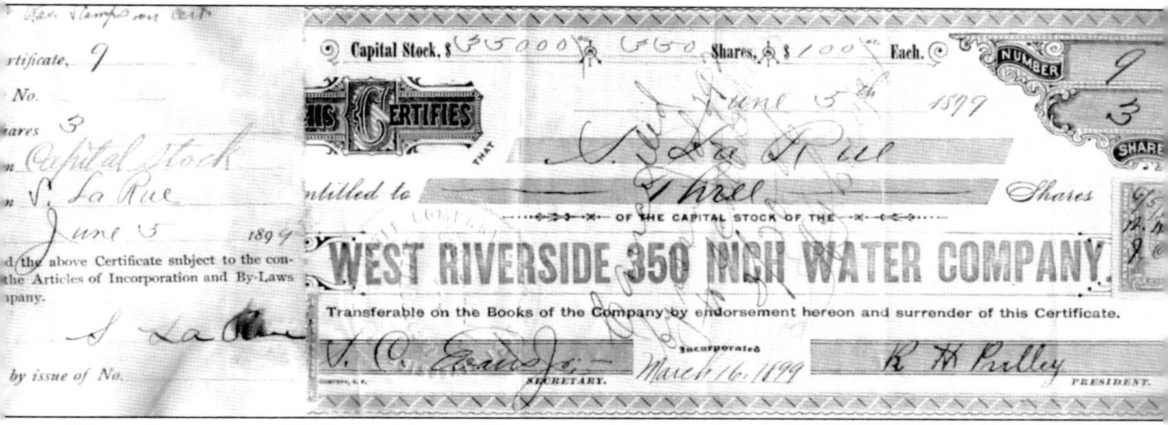
rtificate, 9
No.
ares 3
n Capital Stock
n S. La Rue
June 5 1899
d the above Certificate subject to the con- the Articles of Incorporation and By-Laws npany.
S. La Rue
by issue of No.

Capital Stock, $35000 350 Shares, $100 Each.

NUMBER 9

3 SHARES

THIS CERTIFIES THAT S. La Rue June 5th 1899

entitled to Three Shares

OF THE CAPITAL STOCK OF THE

WEST RIVERSIDE 350 INCH WATER COMPANY.

Transferable on the Books of the Company by endorsement hereon and surrender of this Certificate.

SECRETARY. Incorporated March 16, 1899 PRESIDENT.

WEST RIVERSIDE 350 INCH WATER COMPANY. This irrigation water company was founded March 16, 1899, and had the rights to deliver 350 inches of water in the Jurupa Canal. Shares were sold to property owners, each share entitling them to a certain amount of water. This share certificate was issued to Scott LaRue, an early settler for whom LaRue Street is named. (Courtesy Chuck Cox.)

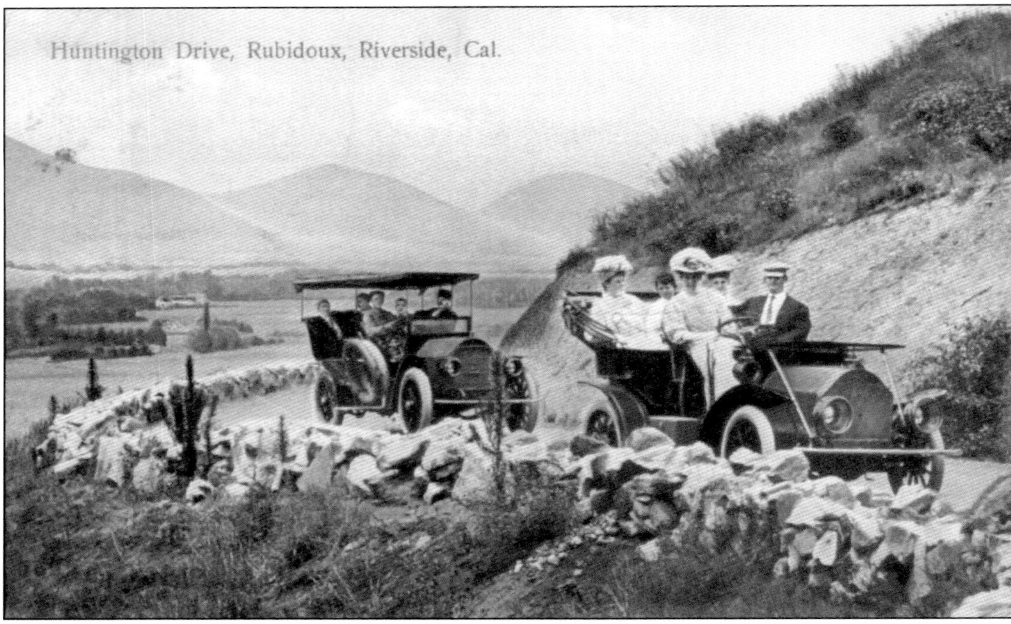

VIEW OF JURUPA. This postcard from the early 1900s shows two cars full of tourists taking a day trip up Mount Rubidoux. This view from Huntington Drive shows West Riverside in the distance, including what appears to be Louis Robidoux's home. (Courtesy Steve Lech.)

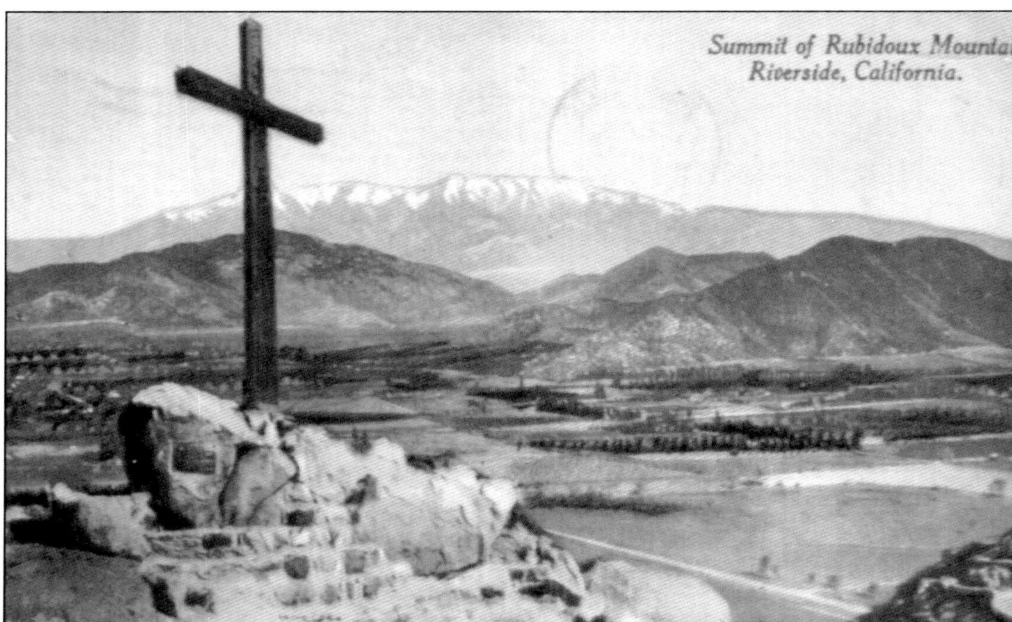

VIEW FROM THE TOP OF MOUNT RUBIDOUX. Postmarked 1912, this postcard shows a beautiful view of rural West Riverside from the summit of Mount Rubidoux. (Courtesy Lolly Miller.)

Two

Santa Ana River

The story of the Santa Ana River in the Rubidoux area is the story of life-giving water. It is what made the land of the Jurupa Rancho desirable to its settlers. It helped water crops in the rich land along the river and helped sustain herds of cattle and flocks of sheep. But living next to a river also had dangers. Flooding, although infrequent, was devastating. The earliest recorded flood, in 1862, brought great hardship to the Rubidoux Rancho. Later floods poured water and mud into downtown Rubidoux. The creation of a levee system, the first in Riverside County, and other flood control projects upriver from Rubidoux finally brought protection from the river.

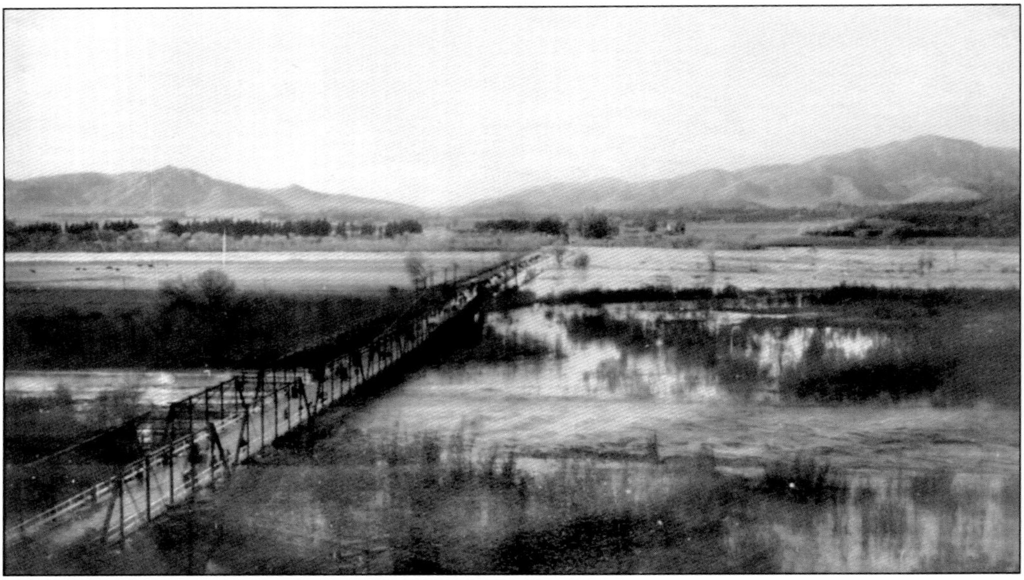

FLOOD, 1910. This photograph shows the flood level of the Santa Ana River on January 1, 1910. While the 1910 flood was not one of the big ones, it still carried a significant amount of water. (Courtesy Riverside Metropolitan Museum.)

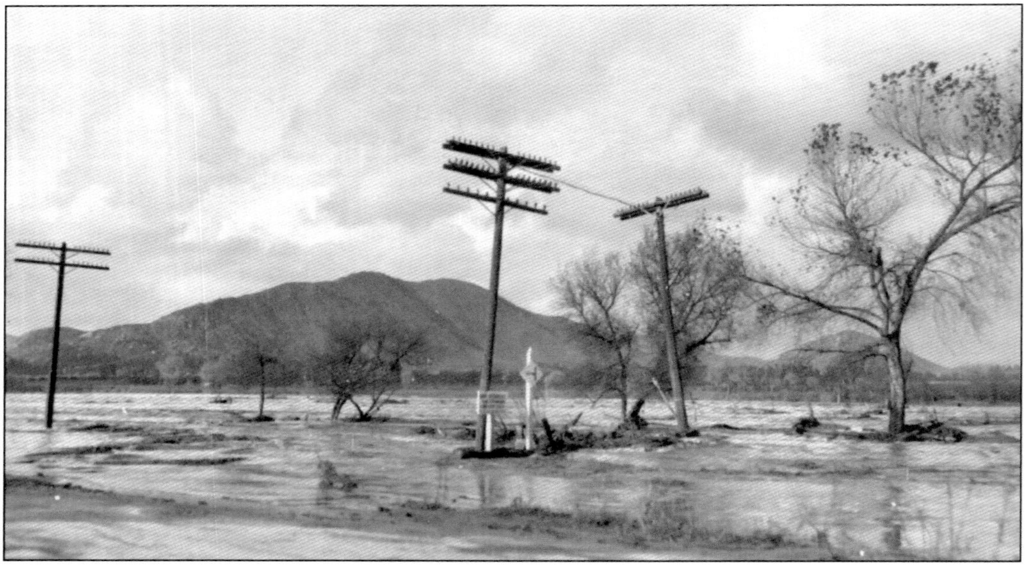

FLOODED COUNTY ROAD. Prior to being known as Mission Boulevard, the main road through Rubidoux was known as "County Road," probably because it was a county-maintained road. This photograph shows the road flooded during January 1910. (Courtesy Riverside Metropolitan Museum.)

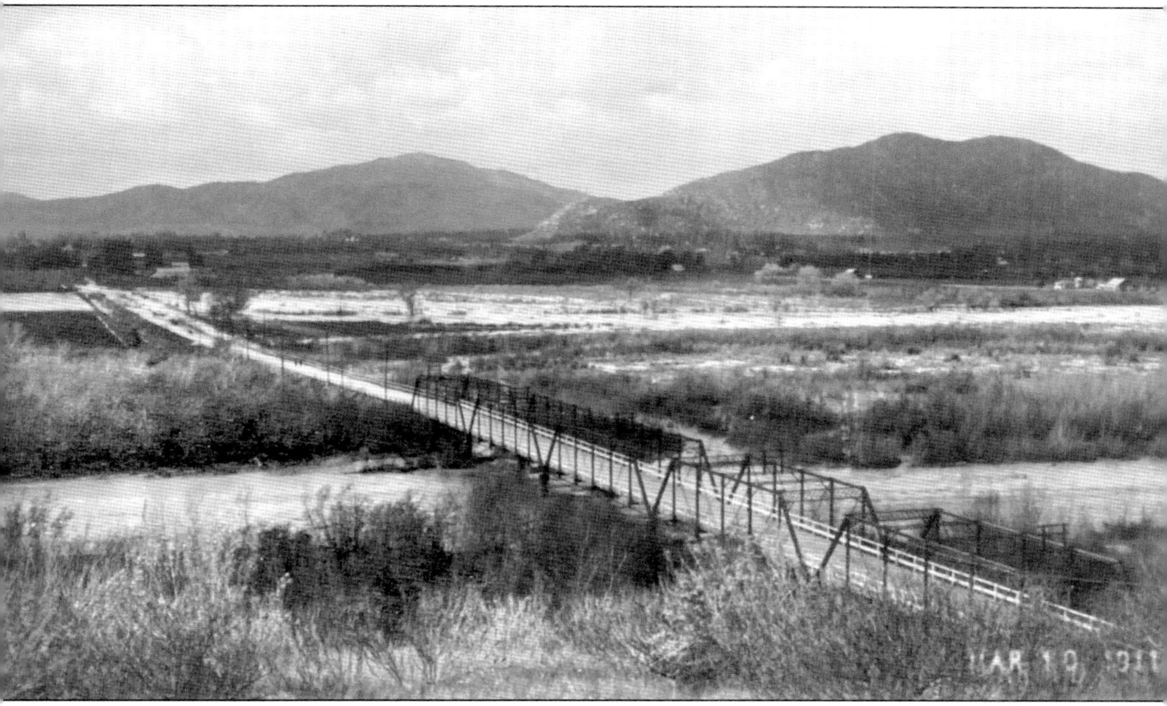

SANTA ANA RIVER AT MISSION BOULEVARD, 1911. The Santa Ana River carved two channels along the riverbed through the West Riverside area before the levee was built to control flooding along the river. The first channel ran along the base of Mount Rubidoux where the present river runs. The second channel ran in the vicinity of today's Wallace Street. (Courtesy Riverside Metropolitan Museum.)

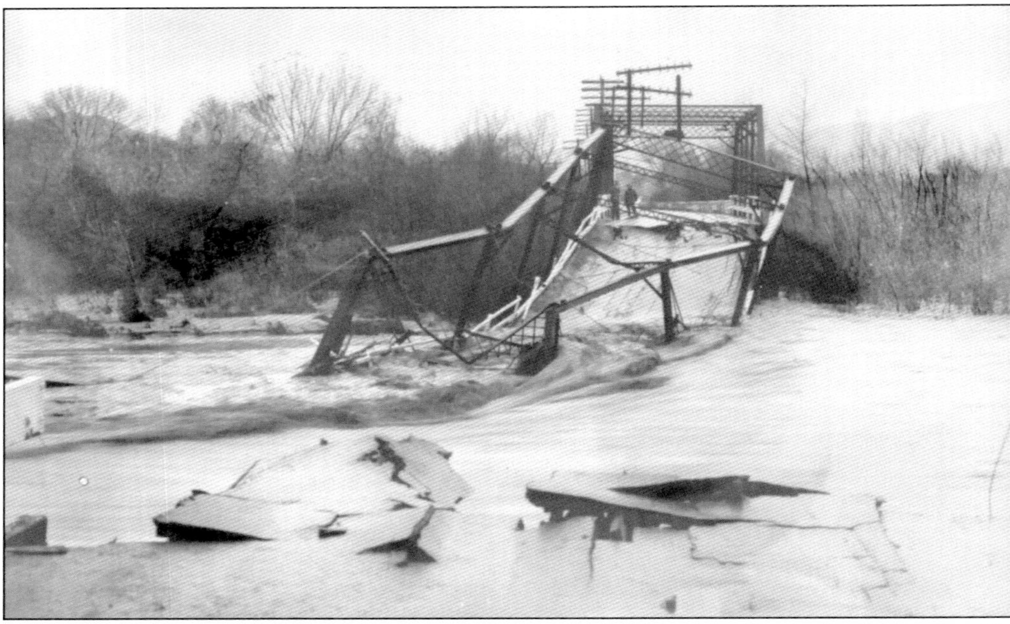

Flood, 1916. The 1916 flood of the Santa Ana River was the first major flood to be captured on film but was just another in the long history of Santa Ana flooding. This shows the bridge that crossed the river from Riverside to the Jurupa area after it was washed out. (Courtesy Steve Lech.)

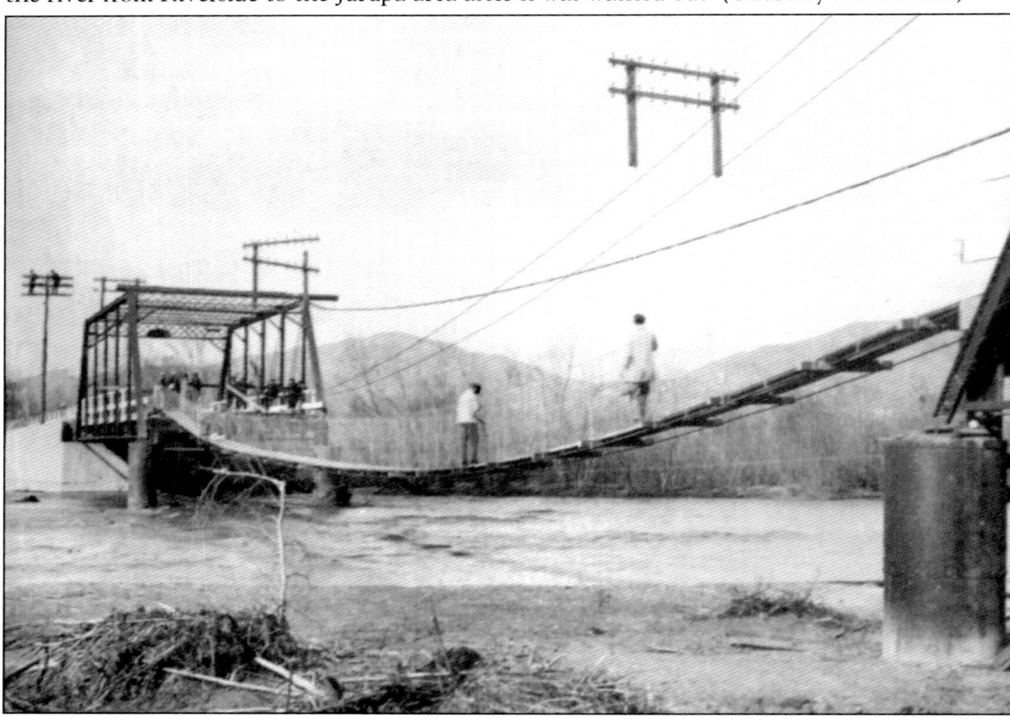

Temporary Bridge, 1916. A temporary pedestrian bridge was constructed to cross the Santa Ana River, allowing Rubidoux residents a way to still get into Riverside. (Courtesy Ida Parks Condit family.)

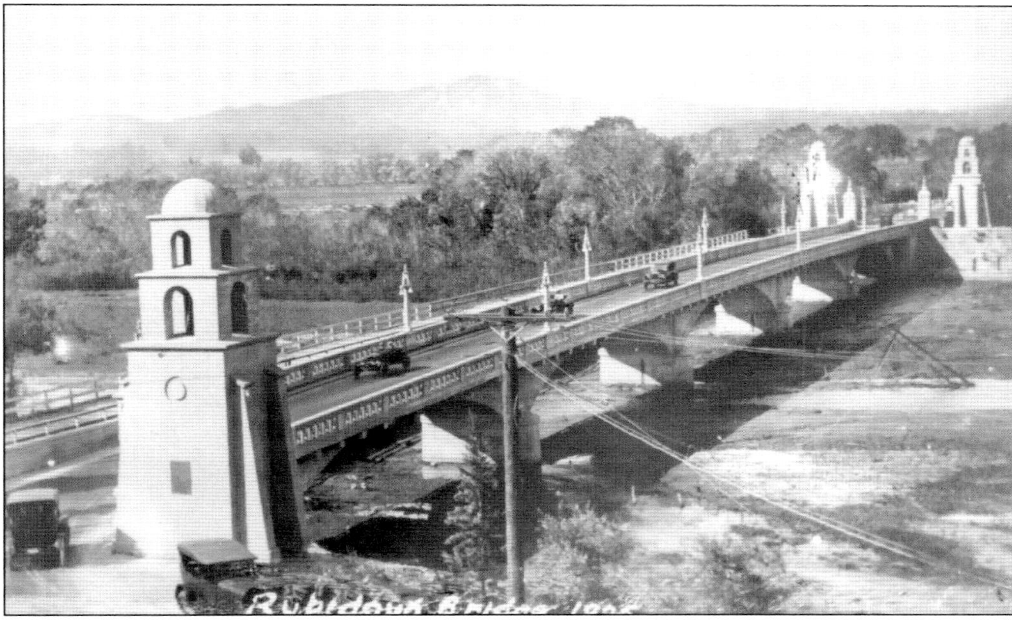

NEW SANTA ANA RIVER BRIDGE. A newer, more picturesque bridge was constructed to cross the river in 1923. It included two mission-style towers at each end of the bridge and a railing that had the raincross motif, the symbol of the city of Riverside. (Courtesy Riverside County Library System, Louis Robidoux Library.)

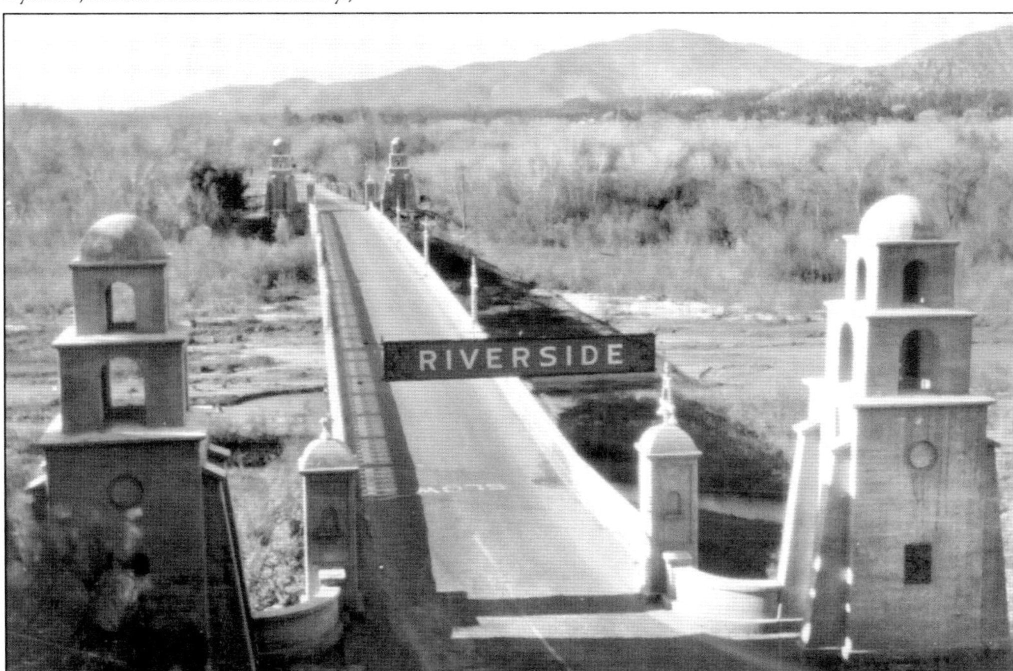

SANTA ANA RIVER BRIDGE. This view looks across the bridge toward West Riverside in the mid-1920s. Note how overgrown and undeveloped the land on the far side of the bridge is. (Courtesy Steve Lech.)

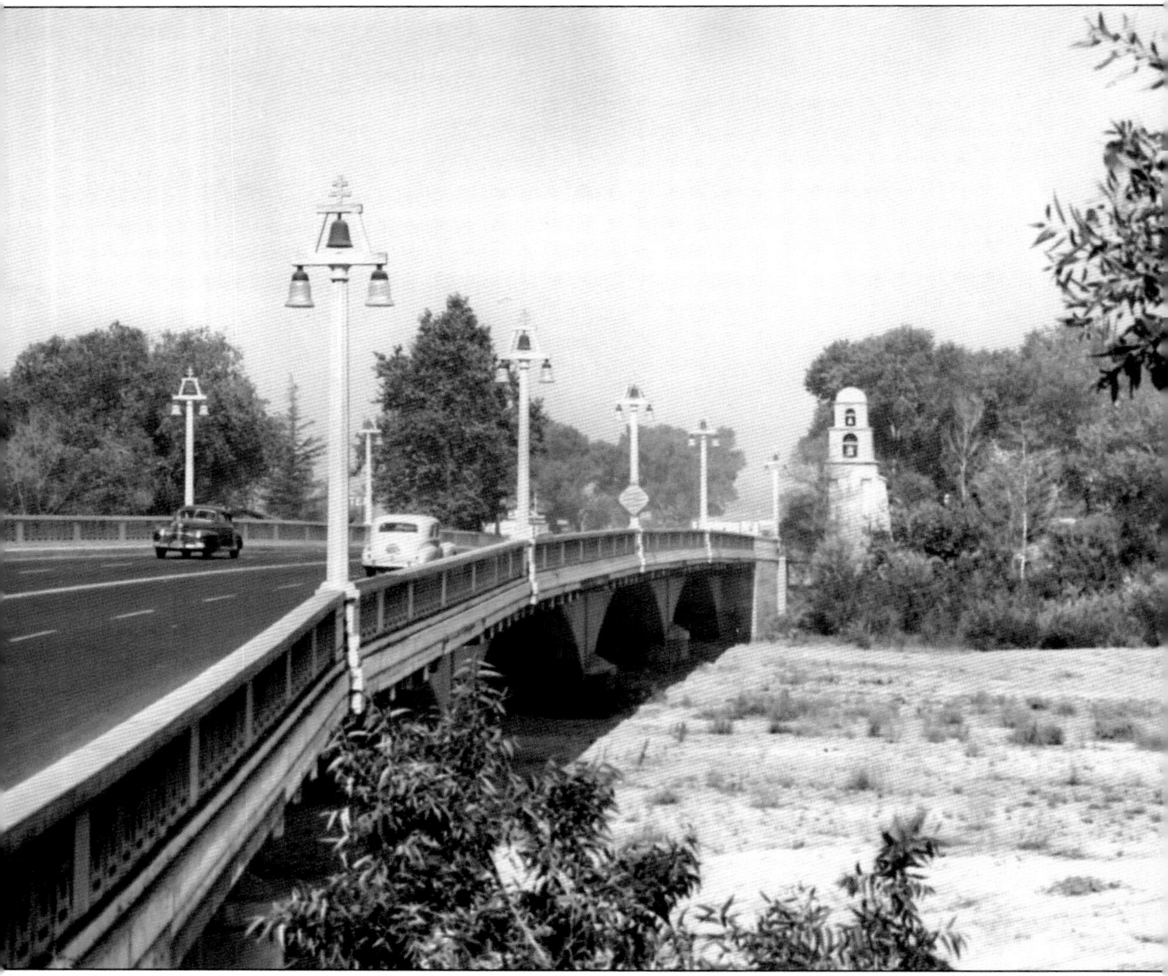

WIDENED BRIDGE. As more and more traffic used the bridge between Jurupa and Riverside, the two lanes it provided became outdated. In 1931, the bridge was widened to four lanes. (Courtesy Jurupa Mountains Cultural Center.)

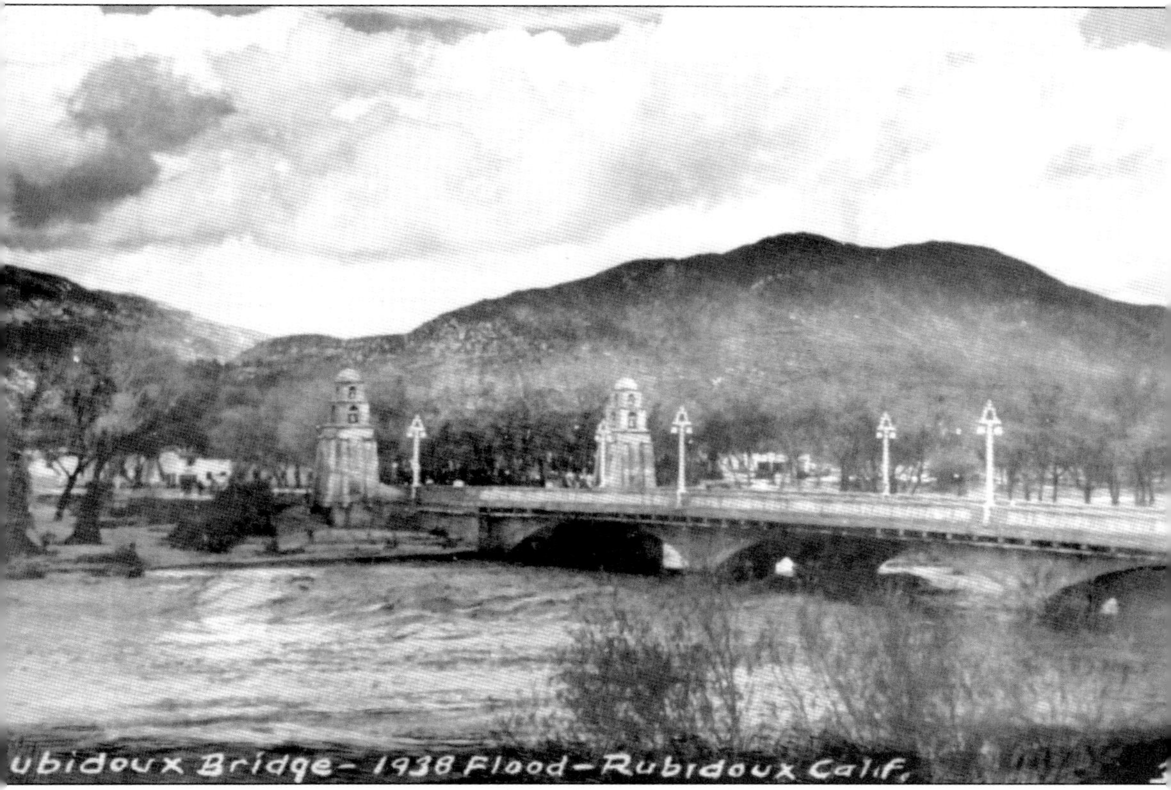

FLOOD, 1938. The Santa Ana River Bridge is shown during the 1938 flood. The bridge to West Riverside was the only bridge on the Santa Ana River to survive, but it was closed to traffic for two weeks. The flood took 159 lives in Southern California; 116 of them were in Riverside County. The devastation caused by this flood prompted the formation of the Riverside County Flood Control and Water Conservation District as well as the building of the levees along the river seen today in the Rubidoux area. (Courtesy Flabob Airport.)

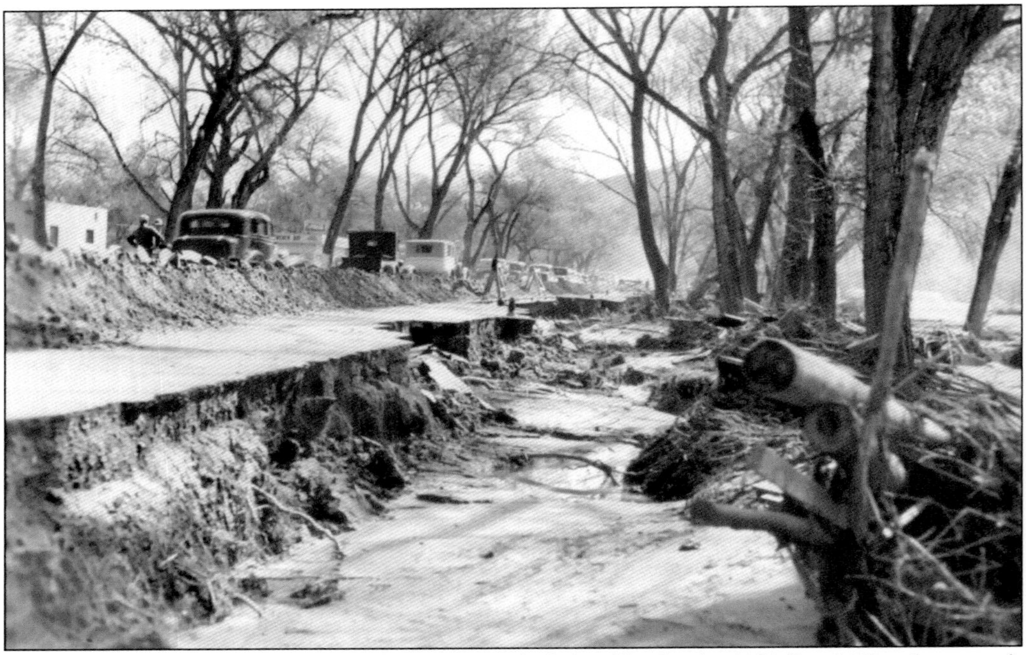

MARCH 1938 FLOOD. West Riverside was particularly hard hit by the 1938 flood. The photograph above shows flood damage along Mission Boulevard. The image below shows workers removing a flood-damaged vehicle. Because of the sudden nature of this flood, many vehicles, including a state fire truck, were caught in the floodwaters and mud. (Courtesy Riverside County Flood Control and Water Conservation District.)

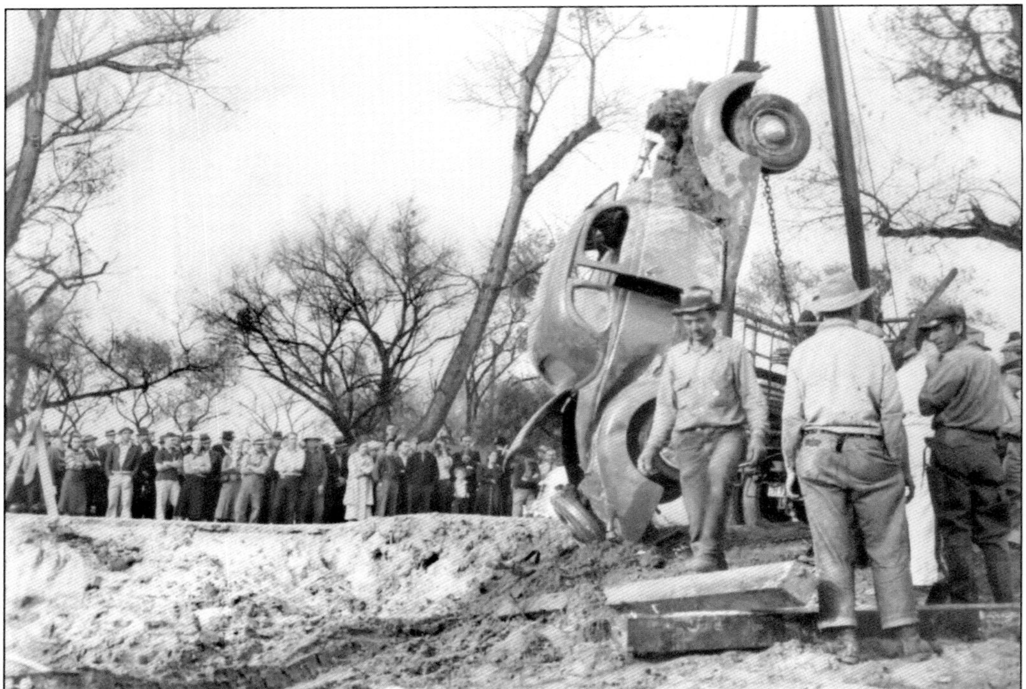

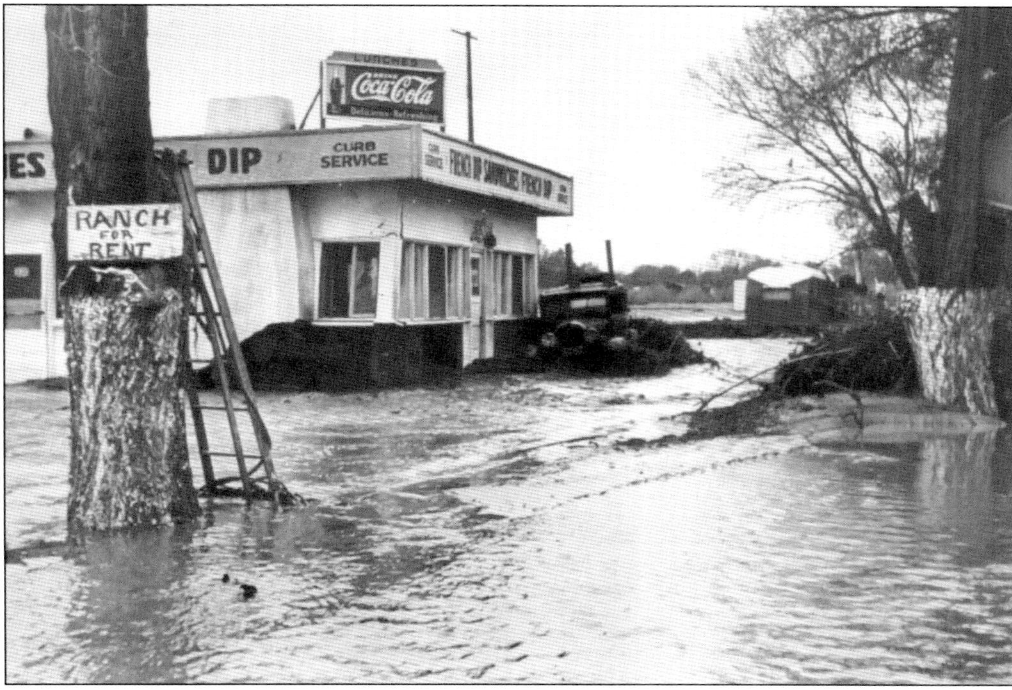

Flood Damage. As the floodwaters poured through West Riverside, many businesses along Mission Boulevard, including these two cafés, were damaged by both high water and mud. (Courtesy Riverside County Flood Control and Water Conservation District.)

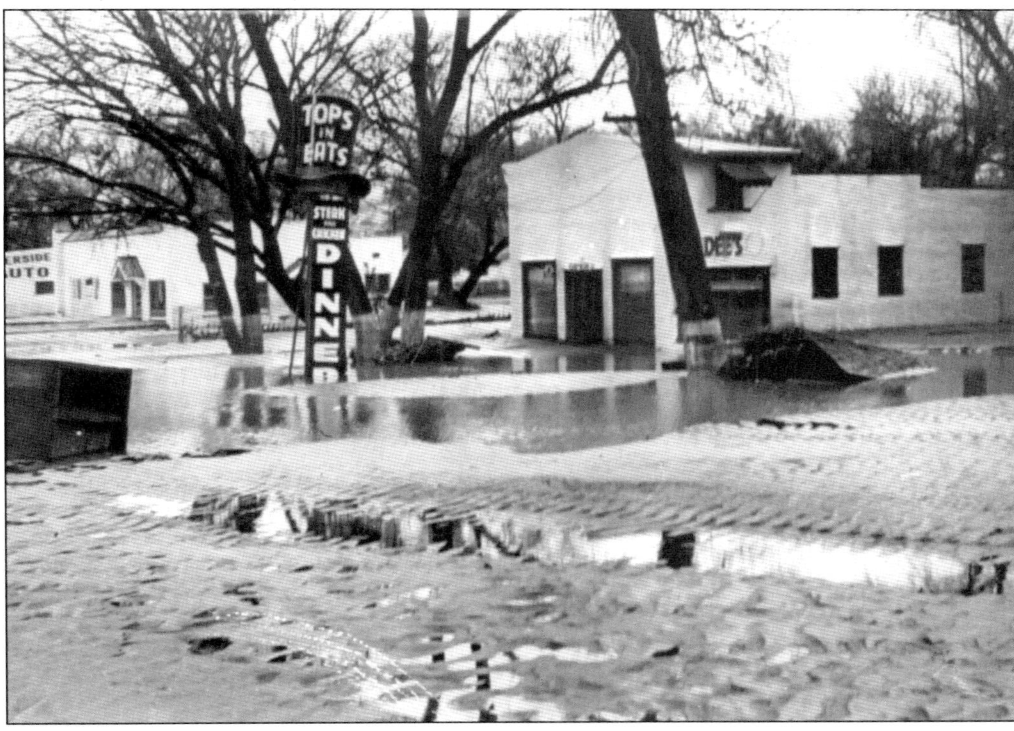

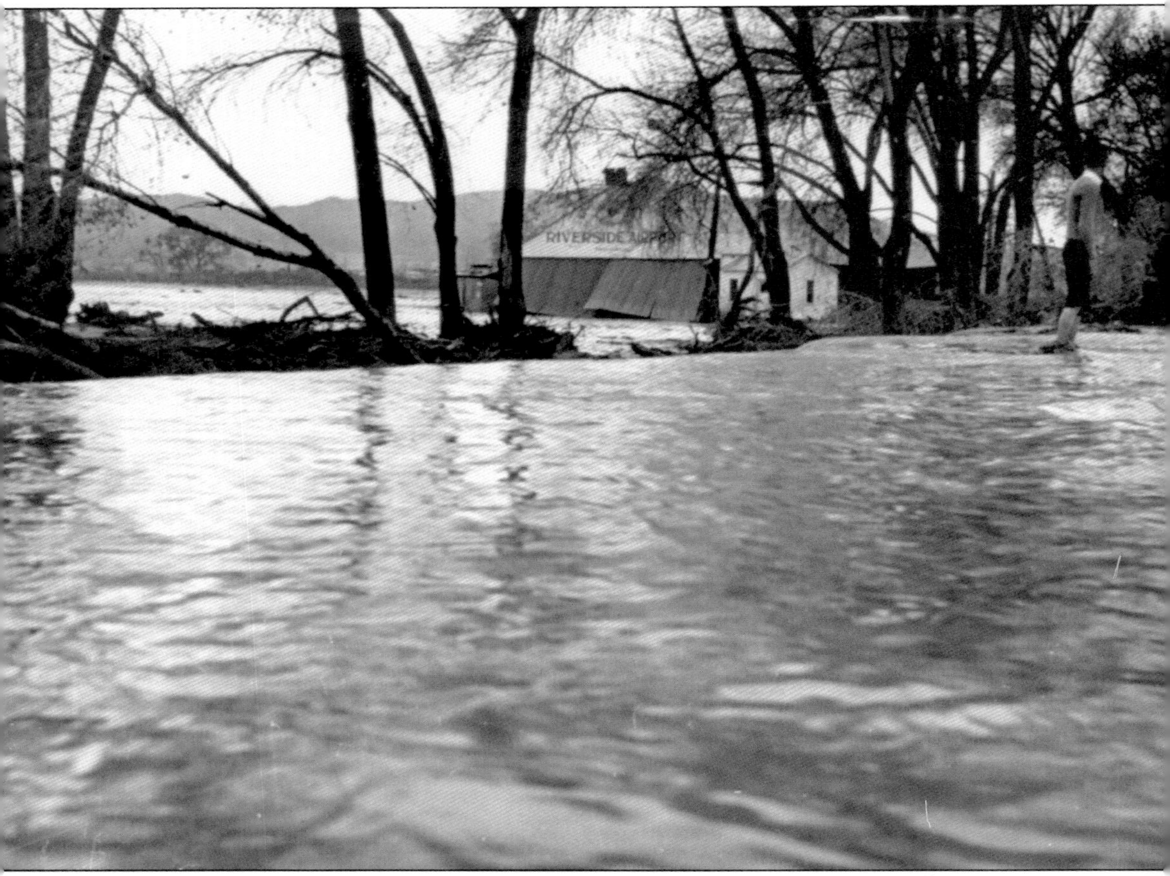

FLOODED AIRPORT. This photograph shows the flooding at the Riverside Airport in West Riverside. Most of the landing field was wiped away in this flood, spelling the end of the airport. (Courtesy Riverside County Flood Control and Water Conservation District.)

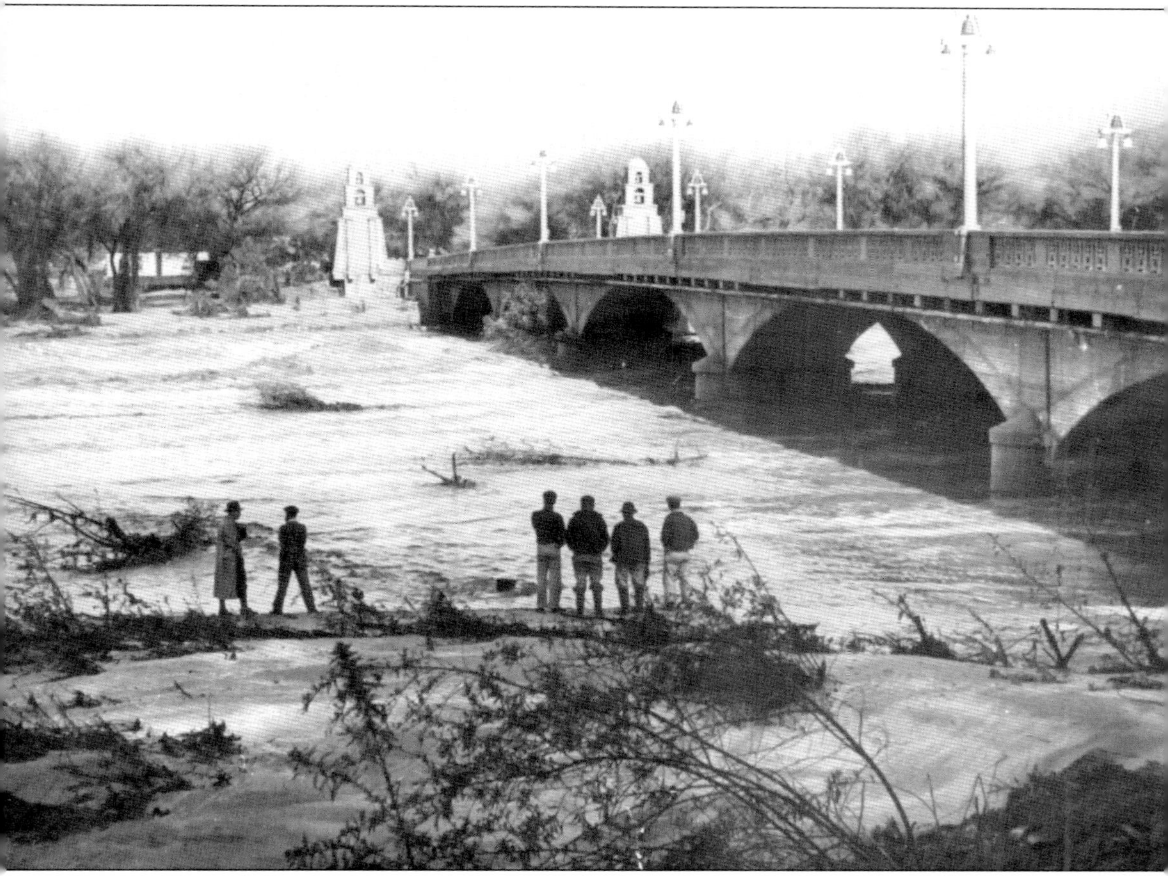

VIEW OF BRIDGE. People are gathered on the riverbank to see the Santa Ana River during the 1938 flood. In the back left corner of the photograph, a large hangar at the Riverside Airport is visible. This photograph illustrates how close the airport was to the river. (Courtesy Riverside County Flood Control and Water Conservation District.)

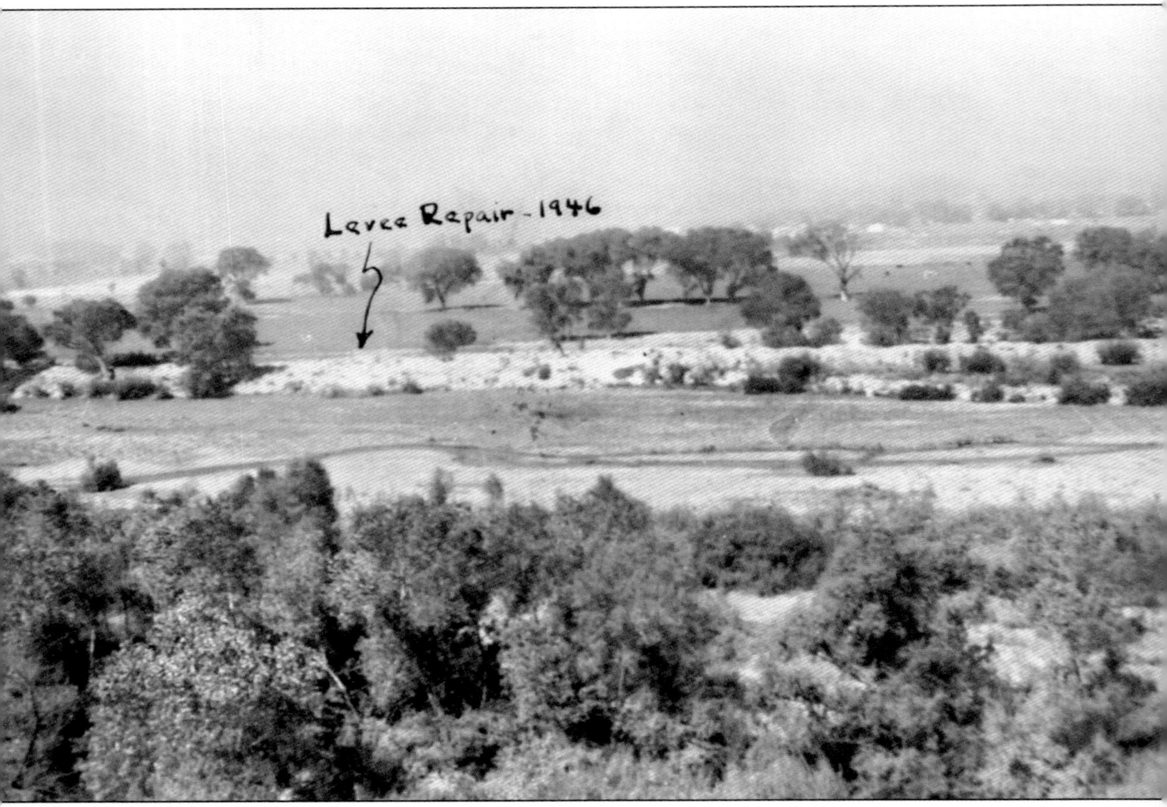

SANTA ANA RIVER, 1947. This photograph shows the riverbed and levee system in place in 1947 and the picturesque fields and trees found on the West Riverside side of the river. This photograph is from the Flood Control District files and was taken to show where the levee had been repaired the previous year. (Courtesy Riverside County Flood Control and Water Conservation District.)

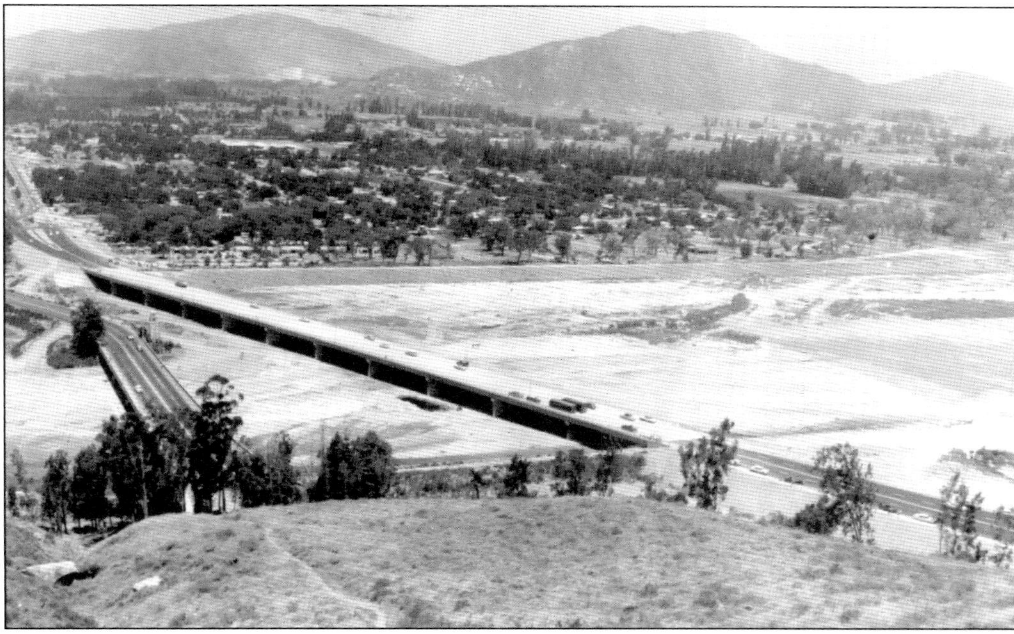

TWO BRIDGES, 1958. The 1923 bridge became outdated because it did not span a wide enough distance across the river and did not provide enough clearance under its length to allow for high-water events. A new bridge was constructed upriver. This photograph shows the old and new bridges side by side. (Courtesy Riverside County Flood Control and Water Conservation District.)

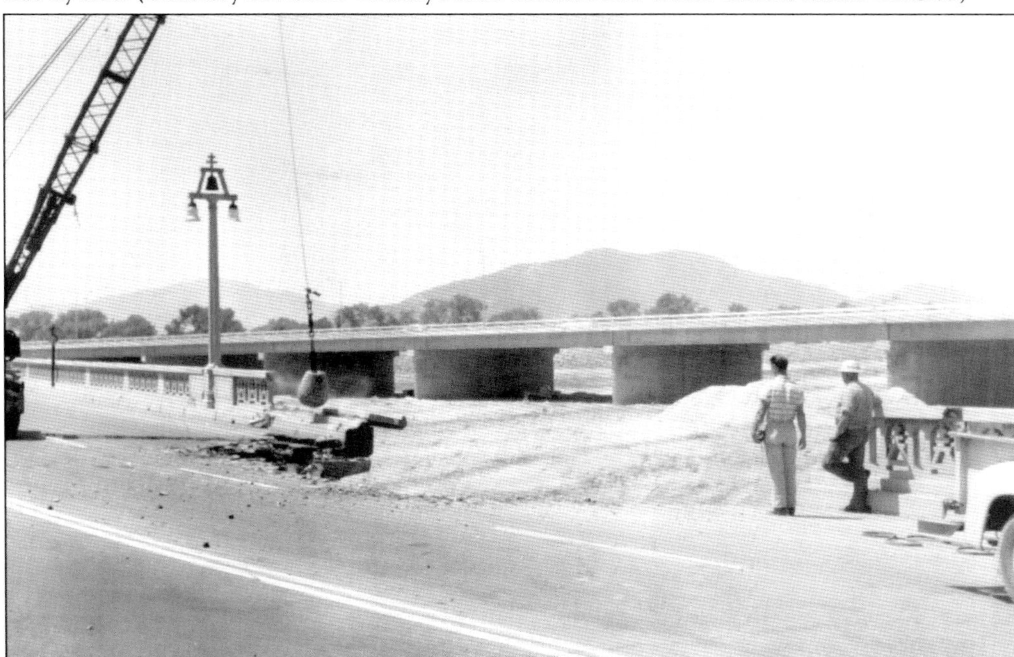

OLD BRIDGE REMOVED. After construction was completed on the new bridge in 1958, the old bridge was demolished. At the base of Mount Rubidoux, two of the bridge's towers still mark where it stood. (Courtesy Riverside County Flood Control and Water Conservation District.)

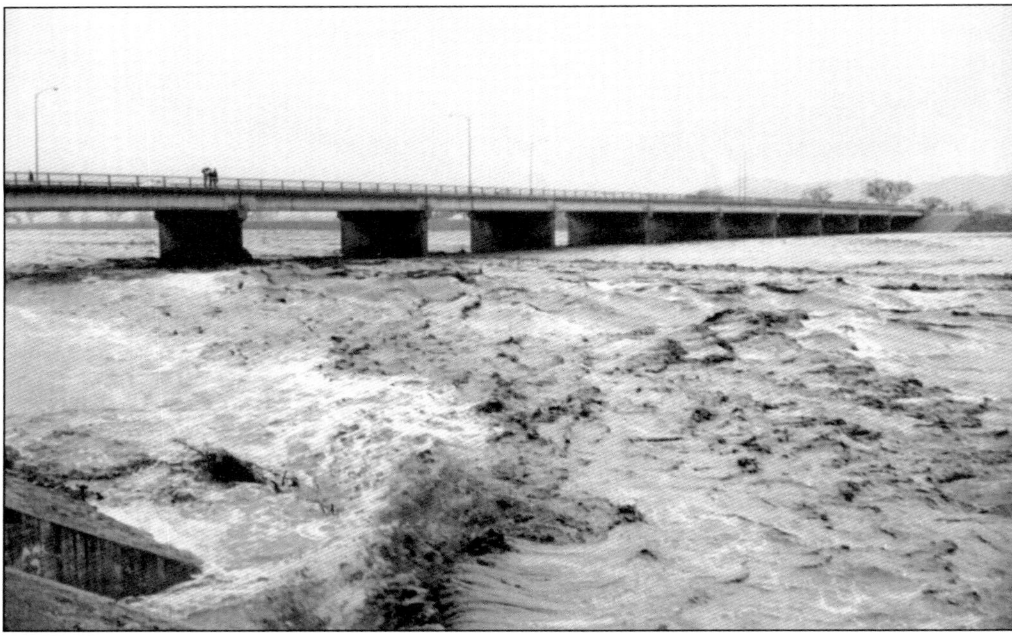

FLOODS, 1969. Floodwaters are seen coursing under the Mission Boulevard Bridge during the floods of 1969. January and February 1969 saw an incredible amount of rainfall along the Santa Ana River. Riverside saw nine inches of rainfall in January, with seven inches falling January 19–29. Almost six inches of rain fell February 24–26. (Courtesy Riverside County Flood Control and Water Conservation District.)

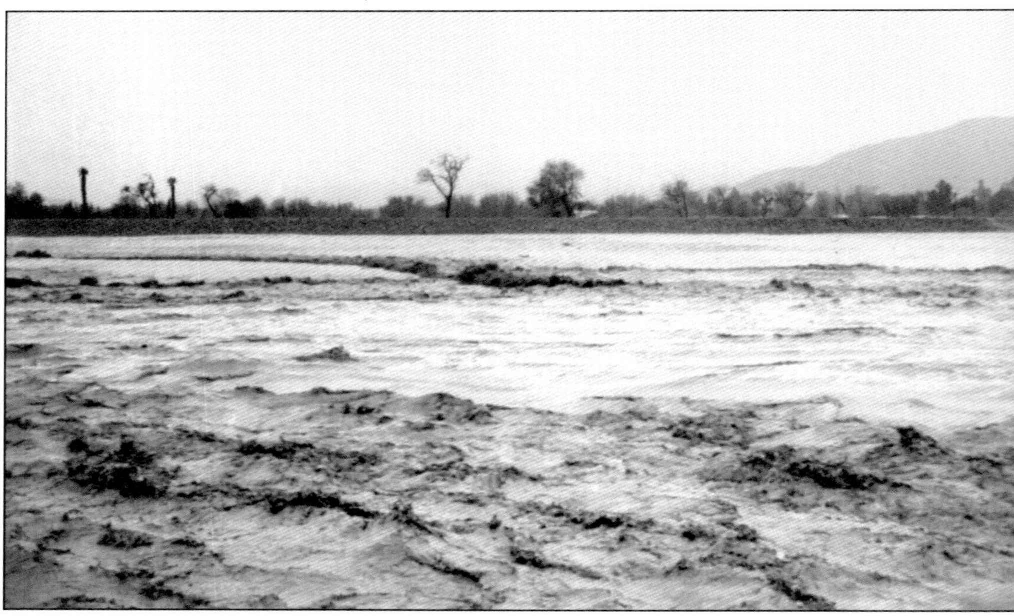

LEVEE SYSTEM PROTECTS RUBIDOUX. The levee system put into place in the 1950s protected Rubidoux in 1969 from the kind of significant flood damage it had sustained in previous floods. In this photograph, the levee can be seen on the Rubidoux side of the river. (Courtesy Riverside County Flood Control and Water Conservation District.)

Three

School Life

The story of school life in Rubidoux begins with the story of West Riverside School. It was the only school in Rubidoux until the 1950s. Set on seven acres, it had plenty of room to be the center of the community. Virtually every social event happened at the school. There were club meetings, dances, and reunions. Churches began at the school before they could build their own buildings. Festivals that included participation from all areas of Jurupa, not just Rubidoux, could occur because of the spacious grounds at West Riverside School. The 1950s and 1960s saw a building boom, which resulted in the addition of three more elementary schools, a junior high school, and a long-awaited high school in the Rubidoux area.

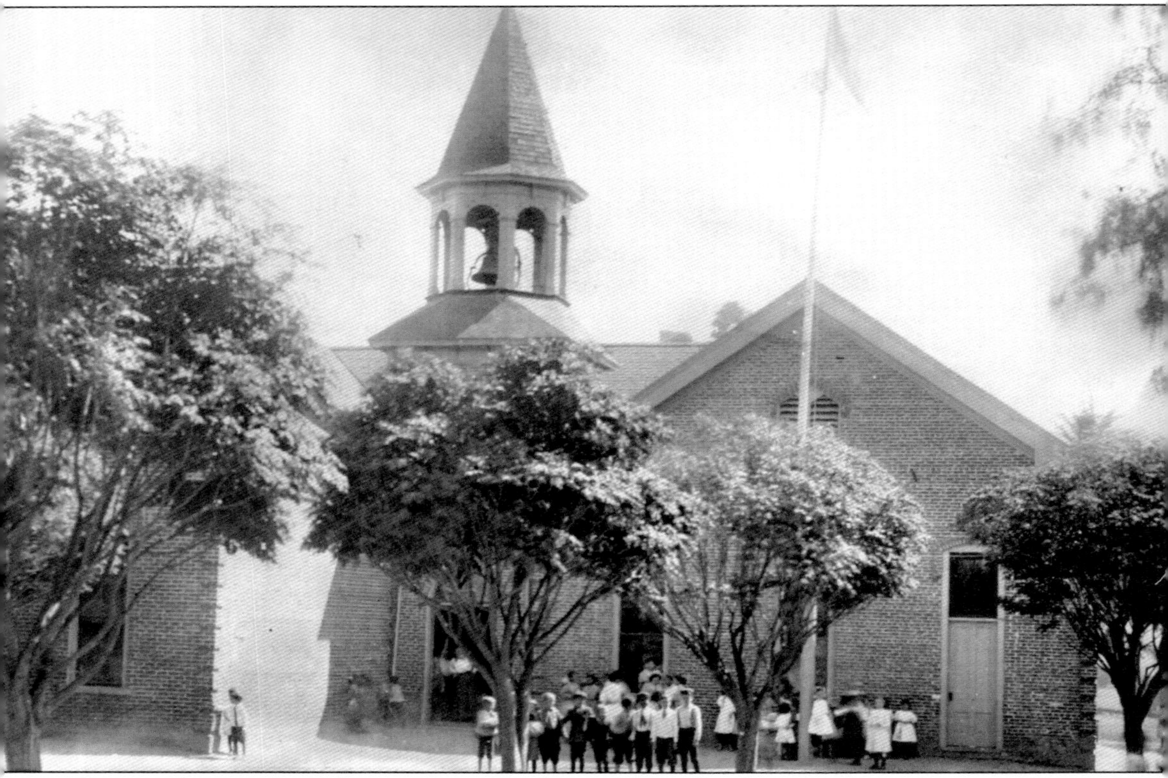

JURUPA SCHOOL. In 1868, seven acres was donated for a school on what is now Riverview Drive. The first school built on the site, known as the Jurupa School, was made from adobe and taught grades one through eight. In 1887, San Bernardino County allocated $110,846 for new school buildings in 11 school districts, including the Jurupa district. The new school was a two-room, brick building with a large hall, shown, that was built in 1888–1889. In 1915, the school and school district changed its name from Jurupa to West Riverside. The present West Riverside School is still located on this original school site. (Courtesy Riverside Metropolitan Museum.)

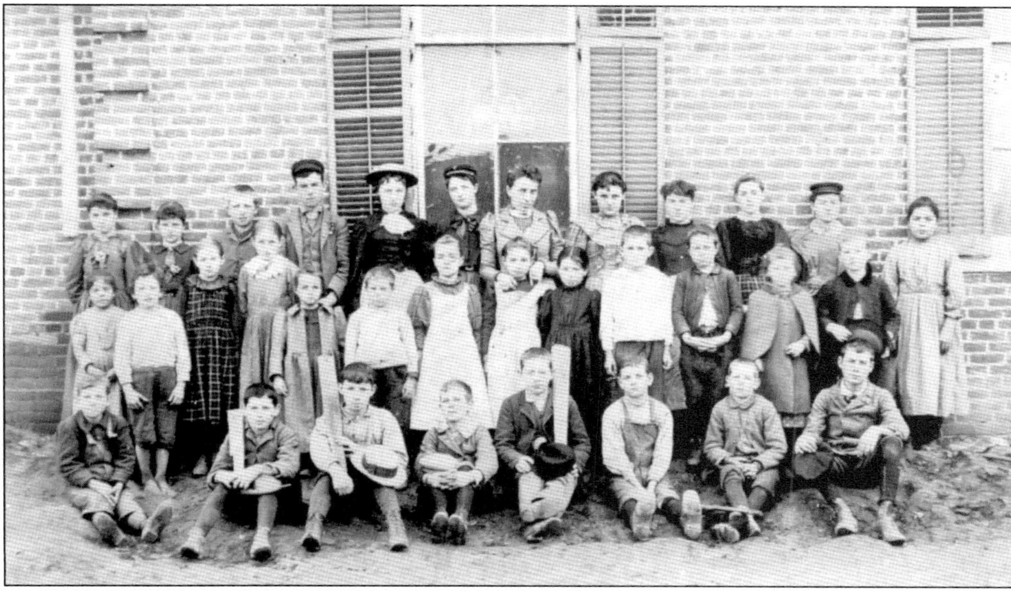

JURUPA SCHOOL STUDENTS. Students at the Jurupa School are shown in 1895 with the school building as a backdrop. (Courtesy Jensen family.)

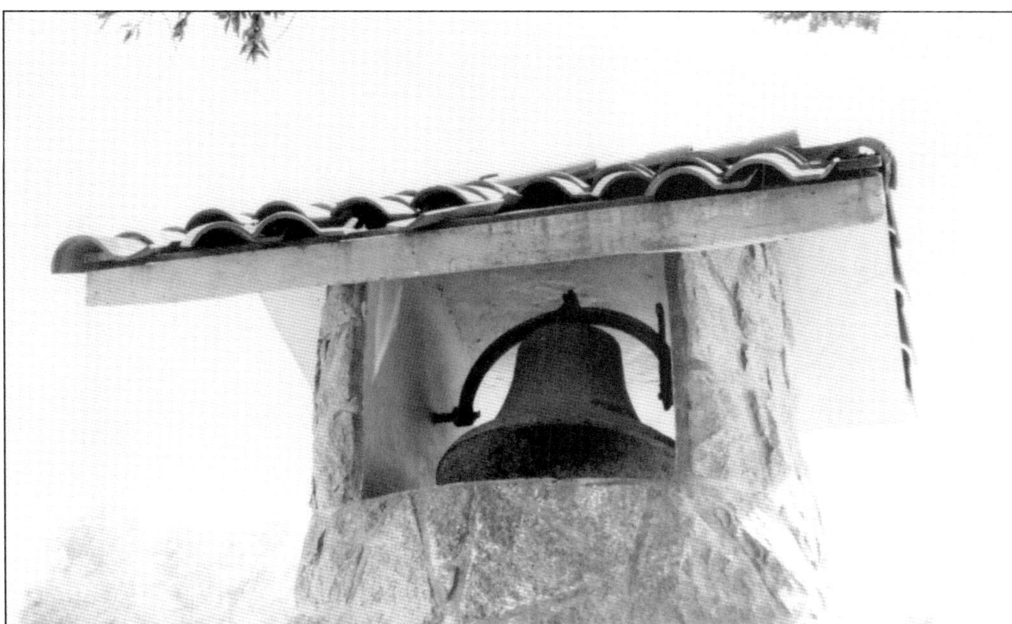

JURUPA SCHOOL BELL. This bell was purchased for the Jurupa School in 1889 at a cost of $87.50. When the Jurupa School was demolished in 1923, the bell was saved. In 1932, the Old Settlers group paid to have a gray, granite tower built on the grounds of the West Riverside School to hold the old bell. The bell and bell tower are still there today. (Courtesy Jurupa Unified School District.)

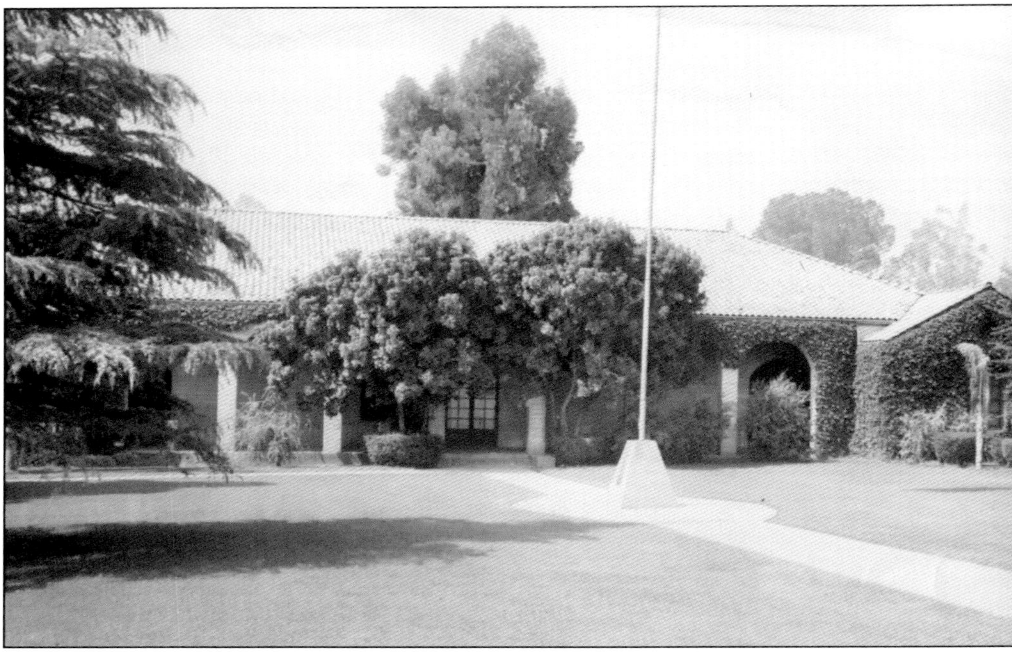

West Riverside School, 1920s. As the student population continued to grow, the brick West Riverside School was replaced in 1923–1924 with this Spanish-style school building, which cost the district $35,000. It was constructed of cement with a red-clay tile roof. Ivy was allowed to grow over the school walls, giving it a picturesque appearance. (Courtesy Riverside Metropolitan Museum.)

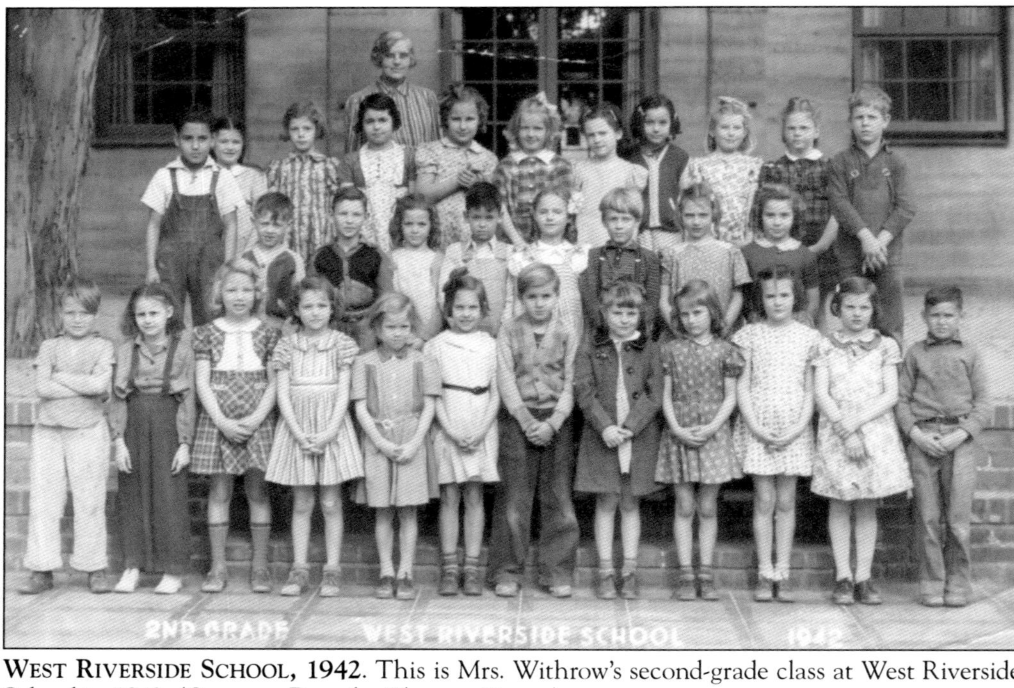

West Riverside School, 1942. This is Mrs. Withrow's second-grade class at West Riverside School in 1942. (Courtesy Dorothy Thorson Evans.)

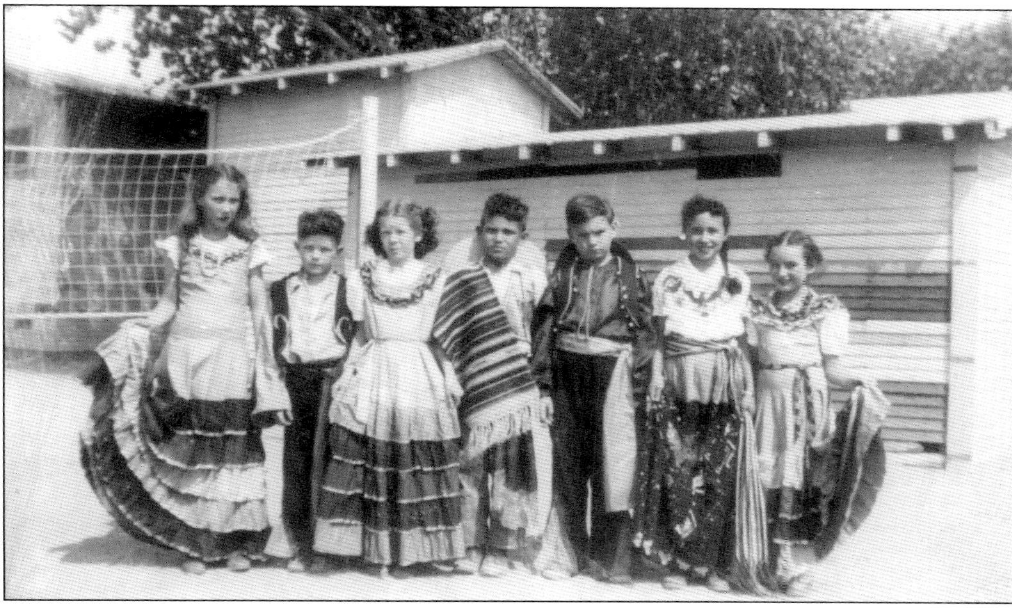

SPANISH HERITAGE DAY. During the 1940s, West Riverside School had a number of heritage days each year to explore different cultures. These students are dressed up for Spanish heritage day, c. 1945. Pictured from left to right are Margaret Fisk, unidentified, Marilyn Muir, Angel Aldama, unidentified, Marie Garcia, and unidentified. (Courtesy Byrd family.)

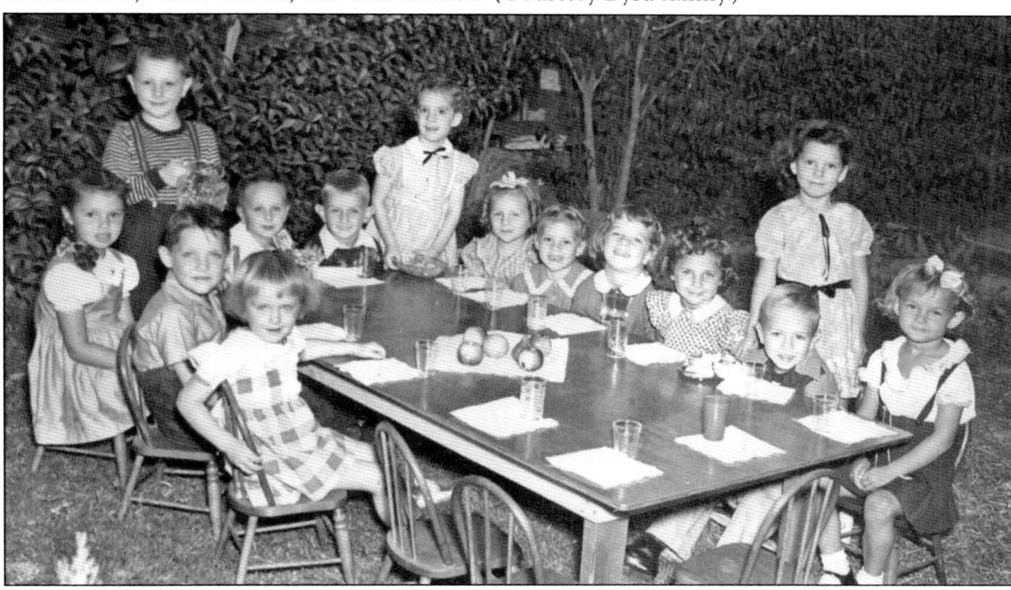

KINDERGARTEN CLASS. In 1947, West Riverside School did not have enough room to have a kindergarten, which was not mandatory at the time. Violet Curtis, who lived on Mennes Street, received permission from the school district to refurbish her living room and begin a kindergarten class. Pictured from left to right are (first row, seated) Laura Gallup, Ronnie Jones, Shirley Dudgeon, Alan Fish, Eddie McLaren, Sharon Graham, Arlene Bricker, Bonnie Chandler, Lonnie Lou Stevenson, Donnie McNeece, and Carol Shaffer; (second row, standing) Daune Darnell, Sharon Greek, and Leora Tracy. (Courtesy Laura Klure.)

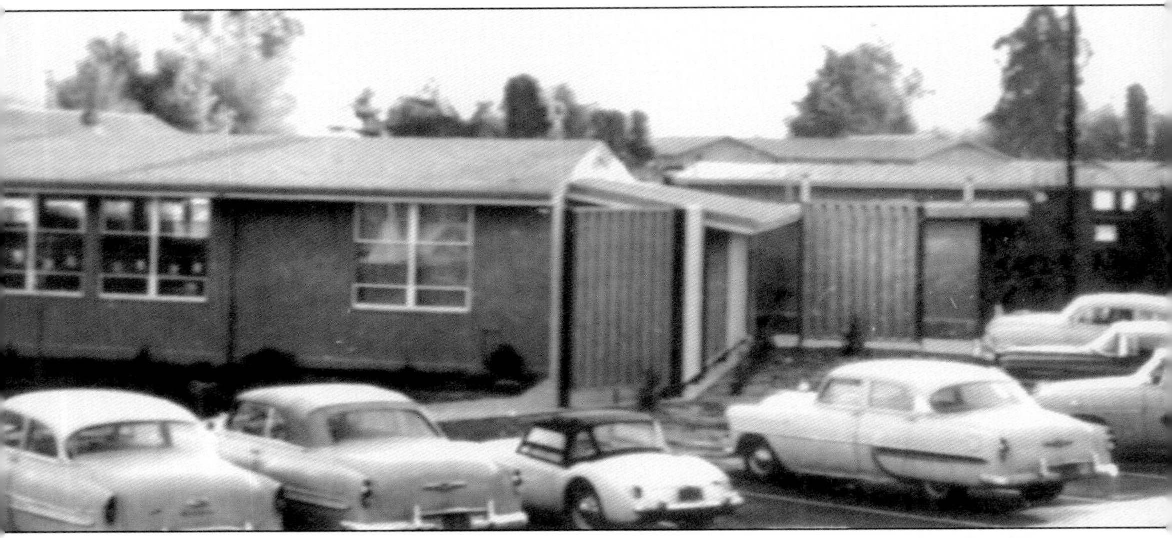

New West Riverside School. Continuing growth required the West Riverside School District to build a new school for the third time. The new school, built in 1949, is still there today. This photograph shows the school during the 1958–1959 school year. (Courtesy Chavez family.)

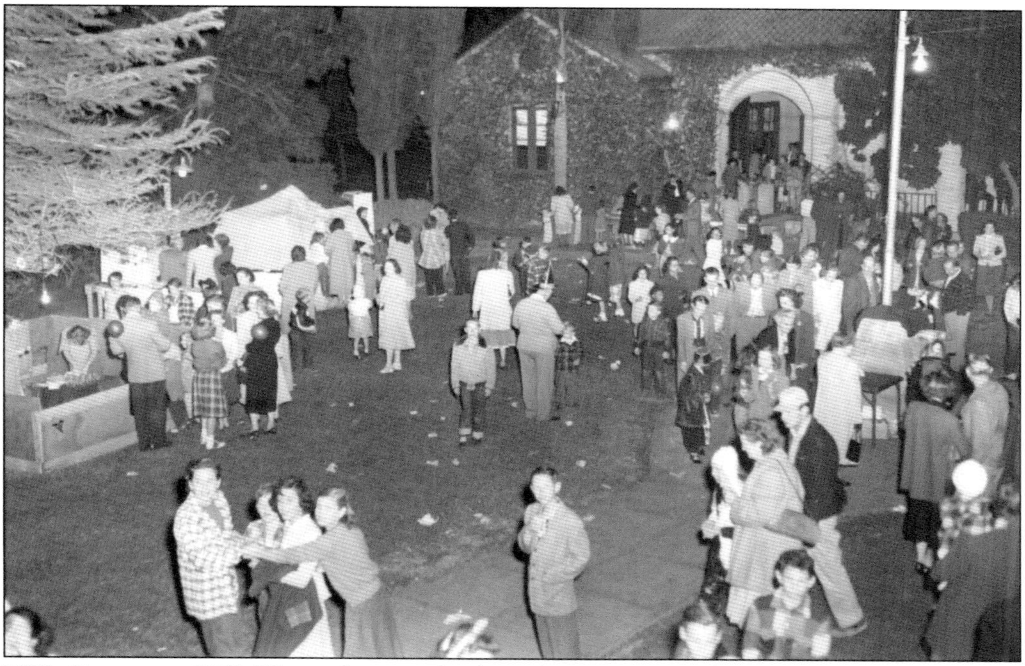

PTA CARNIVAL 1951. These photographs show the West Riverside School Fall PTA Carnival that was held in 1951. (Courtesy Jurupa Unified School District.)

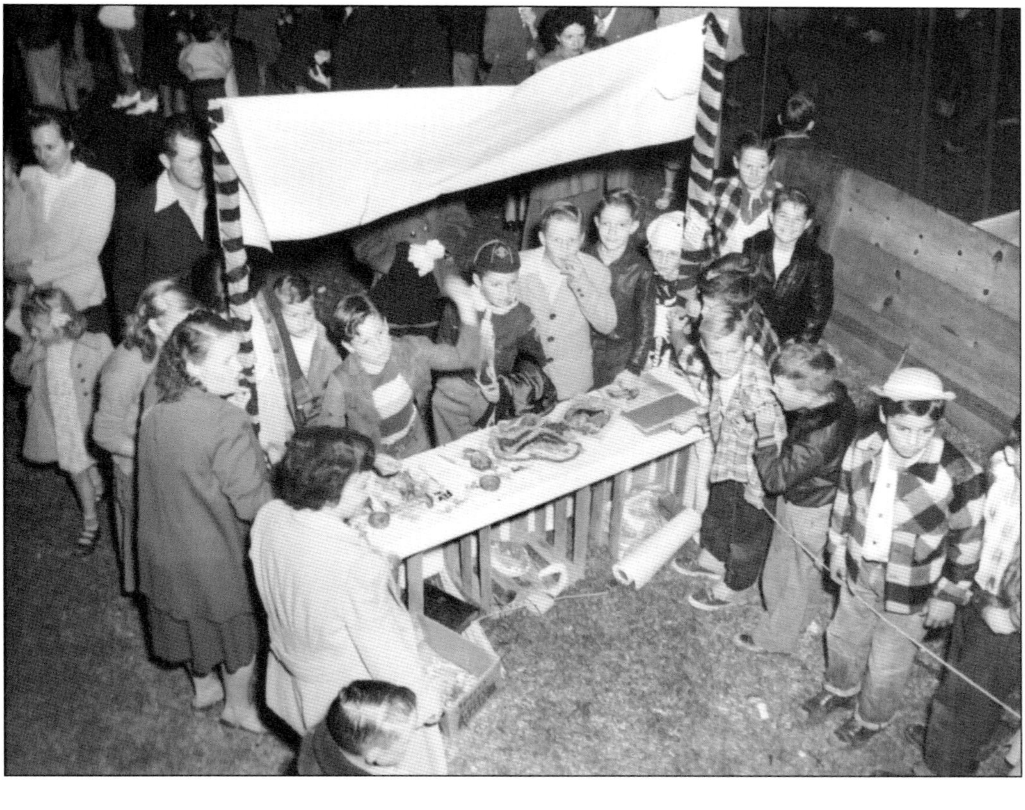

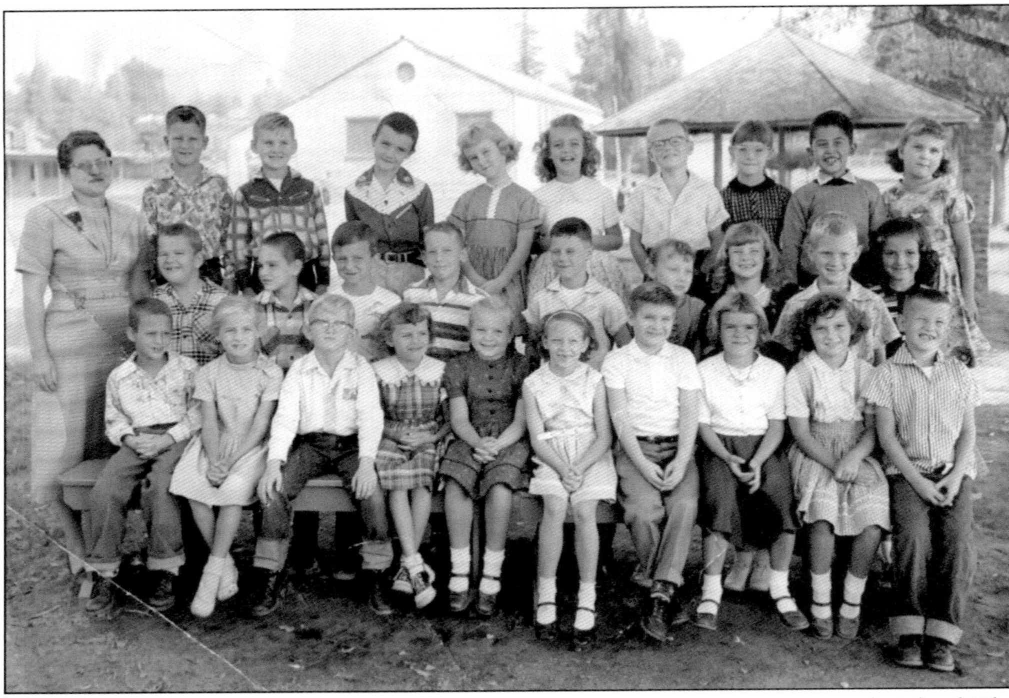

Class Photograph, c. 1956. This is Mrs. Watt's second-grade class at West Riverside School. This photograph was taken on the school playground. In the background to the left is the school building, and to the right is a shade shelter that was located on the playground. (Courtesy Taylor family.)

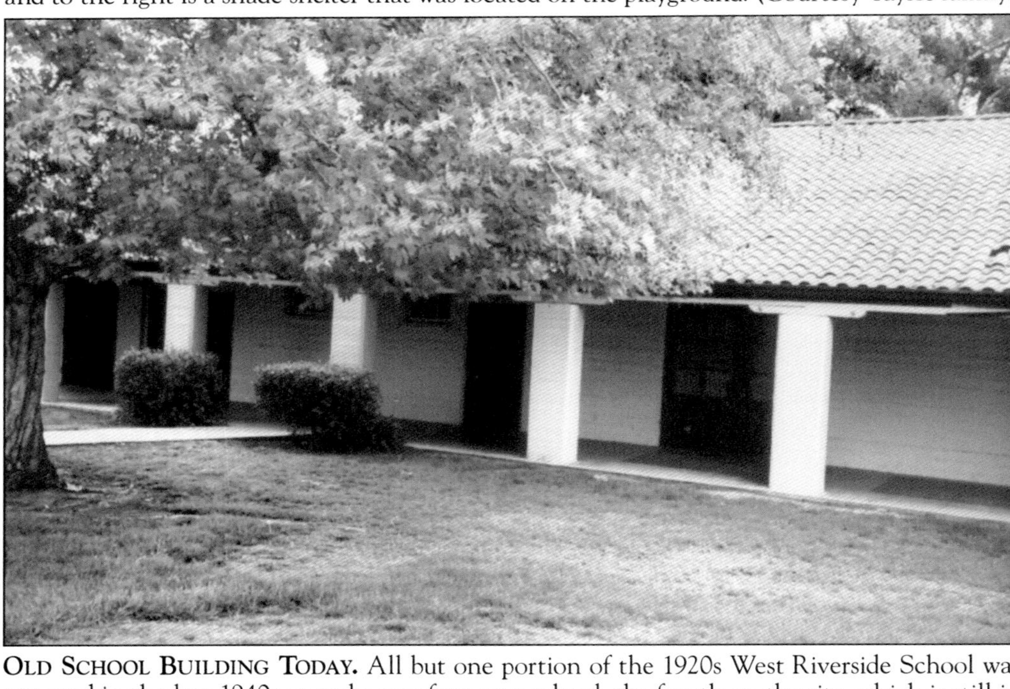

Old School Building Today. All but one portion of the 1920s West Riverside School was removed in the late 1940s to make way for a new school, the fourth on the site, which is still in use today. This building is used for storage at the school. (Courtesy author.)

INA ARBUCKLE SCHOOL GROUND BREAKING, 1955. Ina Arbuckle is shown breaking ground for the school that was named for this longtime teacher. State Senator Dillworth was also on hand for this ceremonial occasion. (Courtesy Ina Arbuckle School.)

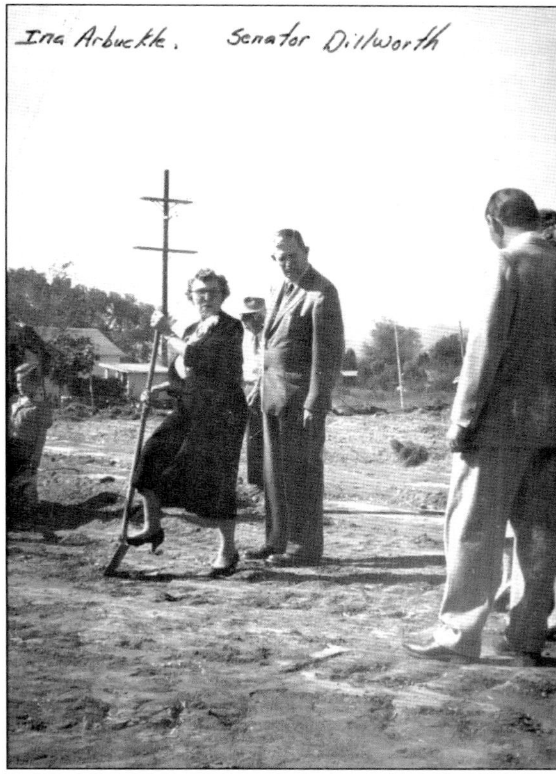

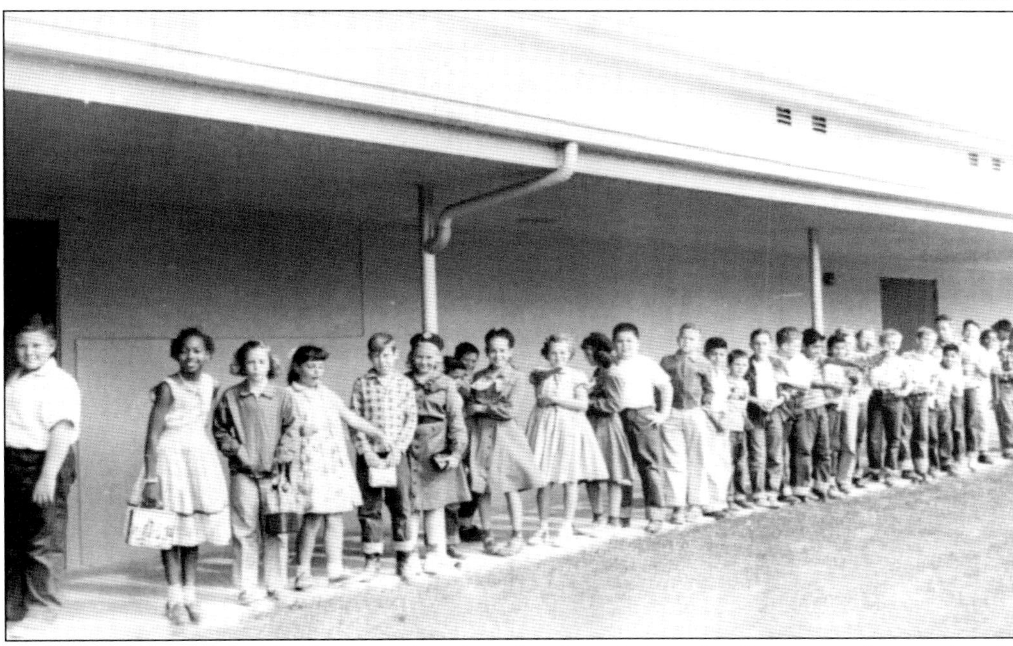

READY FOR SCHOOL. Children are lined up for class during the first year of operation for Ina Arbuckle School, 1956–1957. Note the girls in their Girl Scout uniforms. (Courtesy Ina Arbuckle School.)

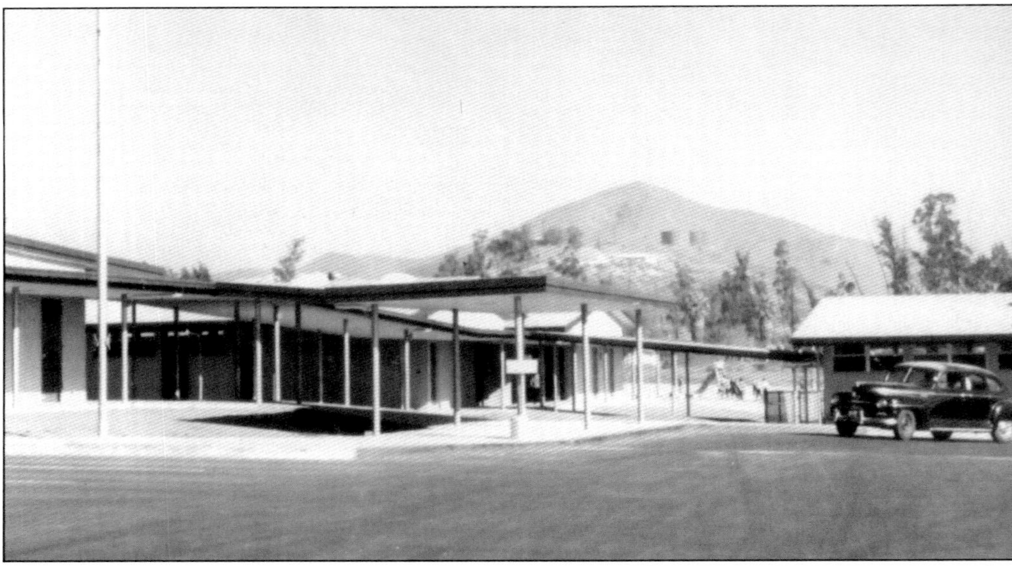

RUSTIC LANE SCHOOL. The school district continued to add more students. To accommodate the students from the new houses built in the area of Opal Street, Rustic Lane School was built at the end of Rustic Lane in 1958. This photograph of the school is from fall 1960. (Courtesy Rustic Lane School.)

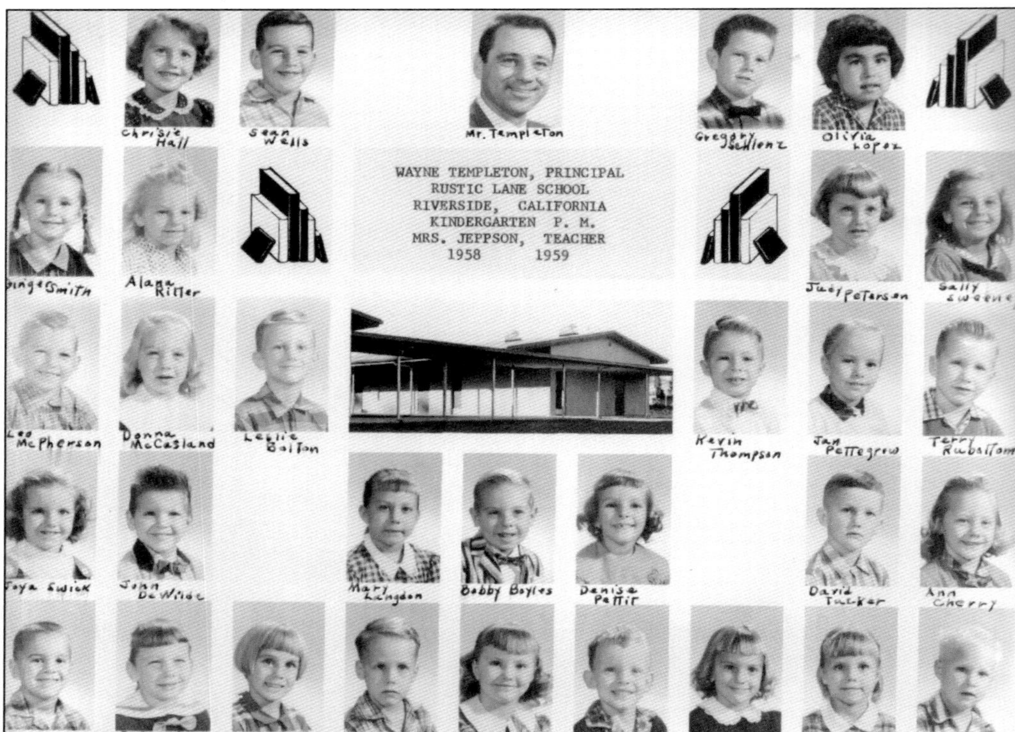

RUSTIC LANE KINDERGARTEN. This is Mrs. Jeppson's afternoon kindergarten class from Rustic Lane's first school year. Wayne Templeton was the principal. (Courtesy Rustic Lane School.)

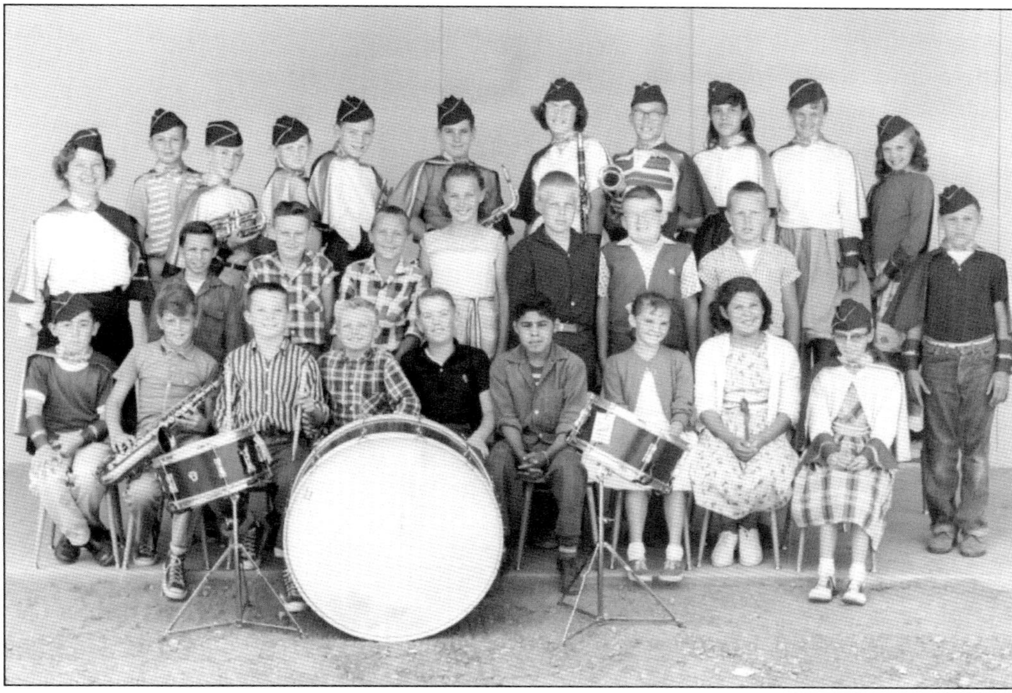

SCHOOL BAND. The Rustic Lane School band is shown here, *c.* 1960. Note the band hats and capes. (Courtesy Rustic Lane School.)

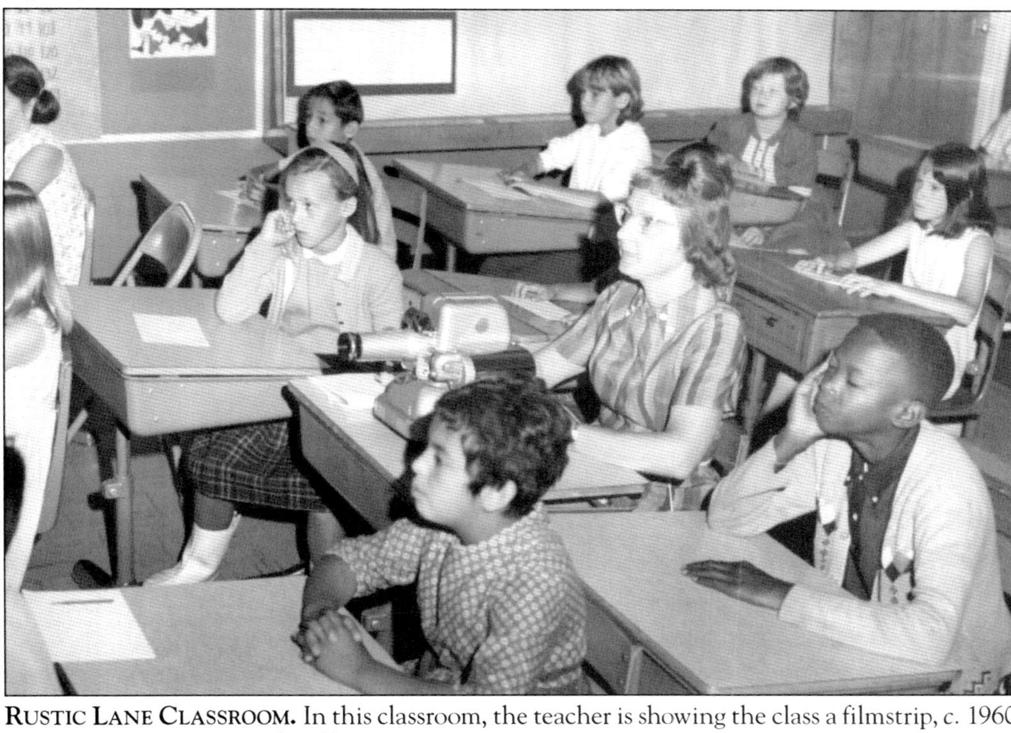

RUSTIC LANE CLASSROOM. In this classroom, the teacher is showing the class a filmstrip, *c.* 1960. (Courtesy Rustic Lane School.)

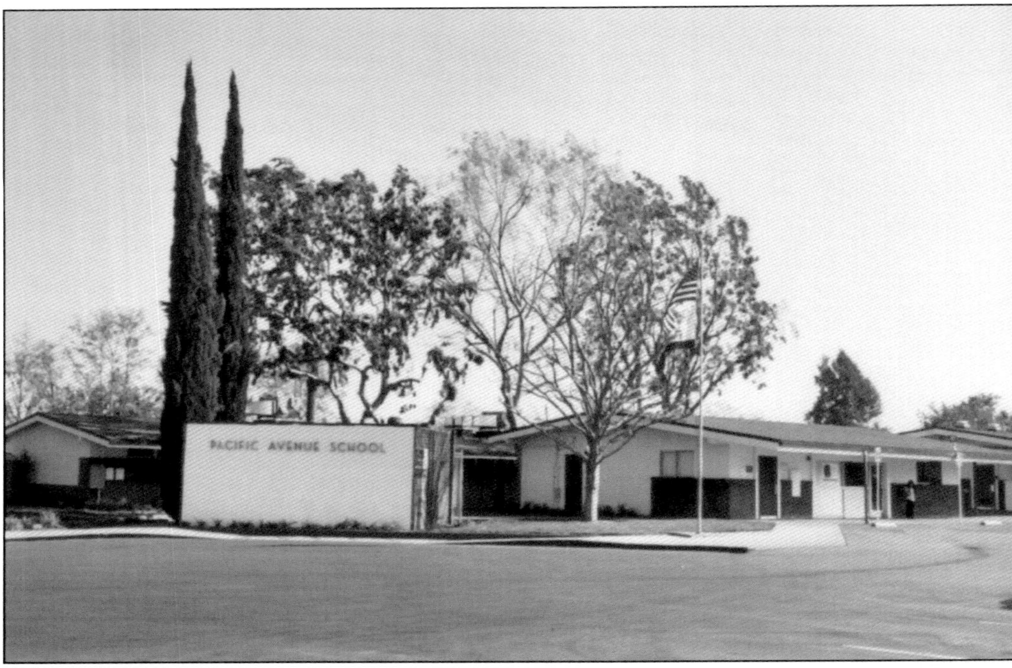

Pacific Avenue School. Still more classroom space was needed for the rapidly growing school district. Pacific Avenue School, at the corner of Pacific Avenue and Forty-fifth Street, was built in 1961. This photograph shows the front of the school. The school office is to the right of the image. (Courtesy author.)

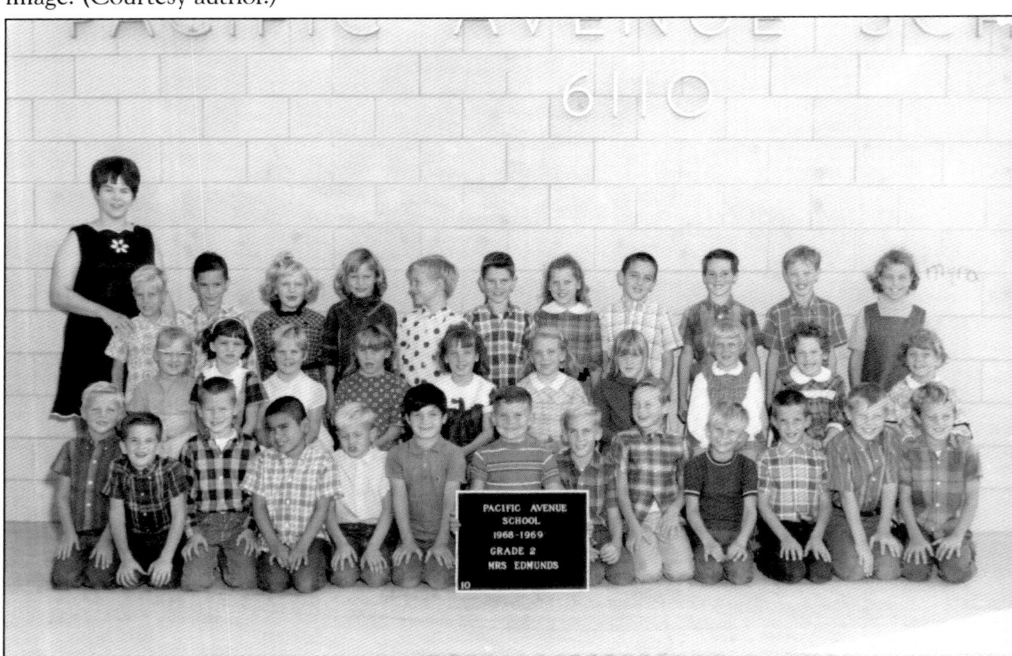

Second Grade. This is Mrs. Edmunds' second-grade class at Pacific Avenue School in 1968. The photograph was taken in front of the school. (Courtesy author.)

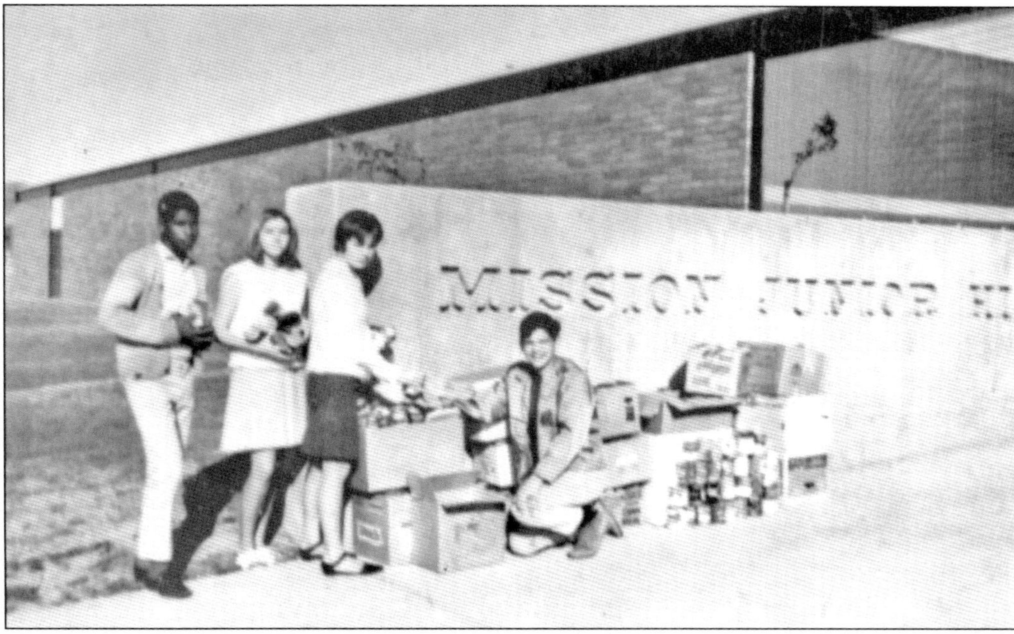

MISSION JUNIOR HIGH. The Jurupa area's second junior high (but the first to be built in the Rubidoux area) was opened in 1966 on property at the corner of Oso Lane and La Rue Street. Students are shown in 1966 in front of the school with items from a canned food drive. The school's name was later changed to Mission Middle School. (Courtesy Mission Middle School.)

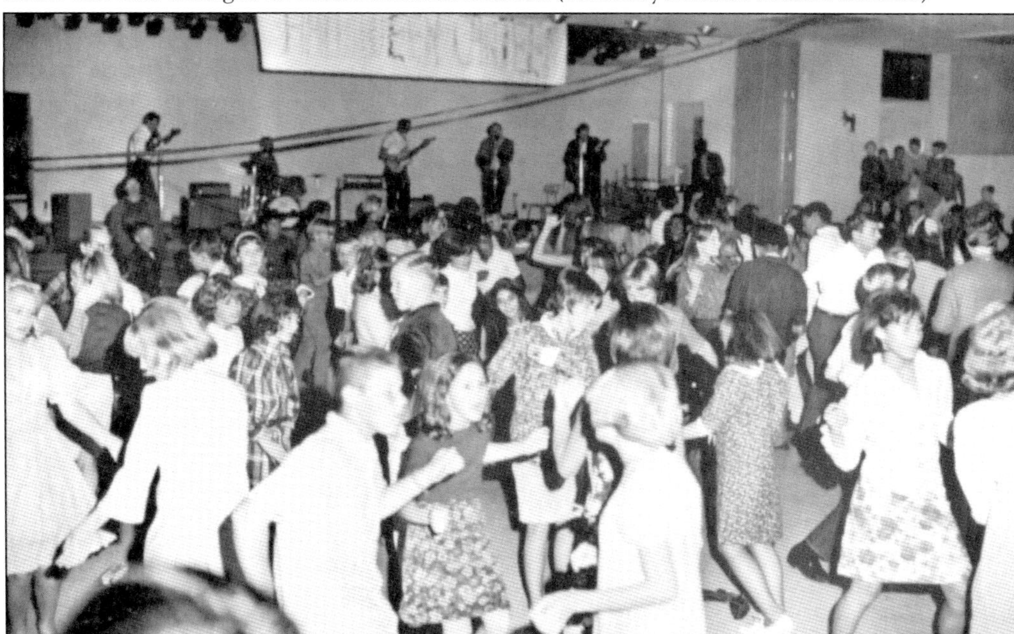

SCHOOL DANCE. This photograph was taken at the Halloween dance in 1966. The dance was held where school dances are still held today—in the school's cafeteria/auditorium. (Courtesy Mission Middle School.)

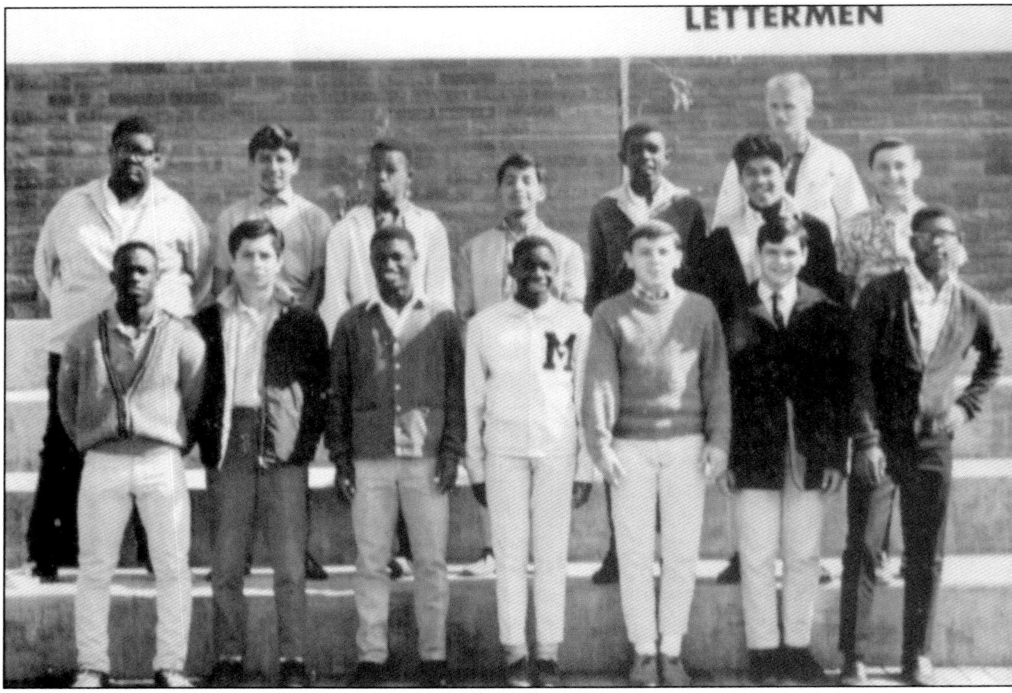

LETTERMAN'S CLUB. This photograph from the school's first yearbook shows the Mission Junior High Letterman's Club. (Courtesy Mission Middle School.)

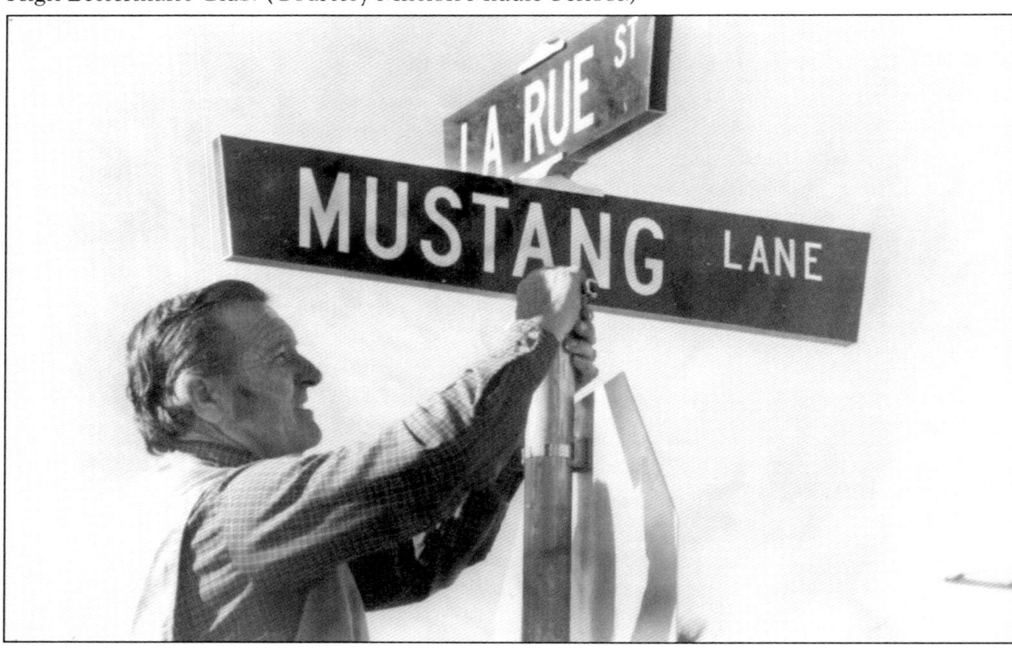

MUSTANG LANE. In 1985, the students at Mission petitioned the county board of supervisors to have the street in front of their school changed to Mustang Lane, in honor of the school's mascot. This photograph shows a school district employee changing the street sign. (Courtesy Mission Middle School.)

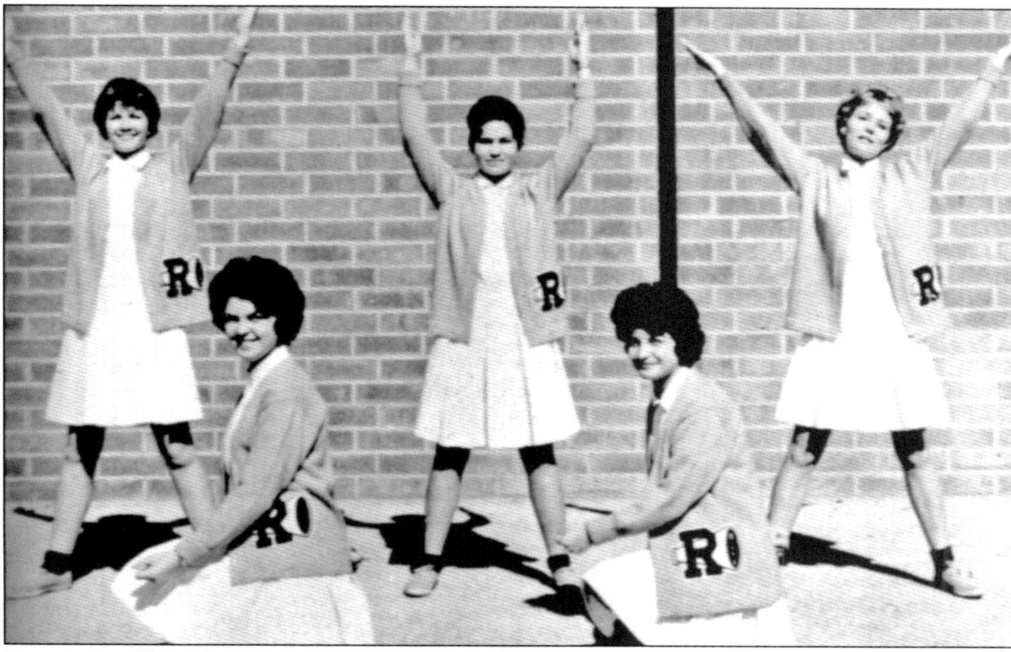

RUBIDOUX HIGH SCHOOL CHEERLEADERS. The construction of the area's first high school in 1959–1960 fulfilled the community's desire for a high school that dated back to the 1920s. Until Rubidoux High School was built, students had to go into Riverside to further their education past the eighth grade. Here are the cheerleaders from the 1961–1962 school year; from left to right are (first row) Nancy Fridel and Billie Nell Ruby; (second row) Sherry Medaris, Sandi Miller, and Pat McCooky. (Courtesy Norton family.)

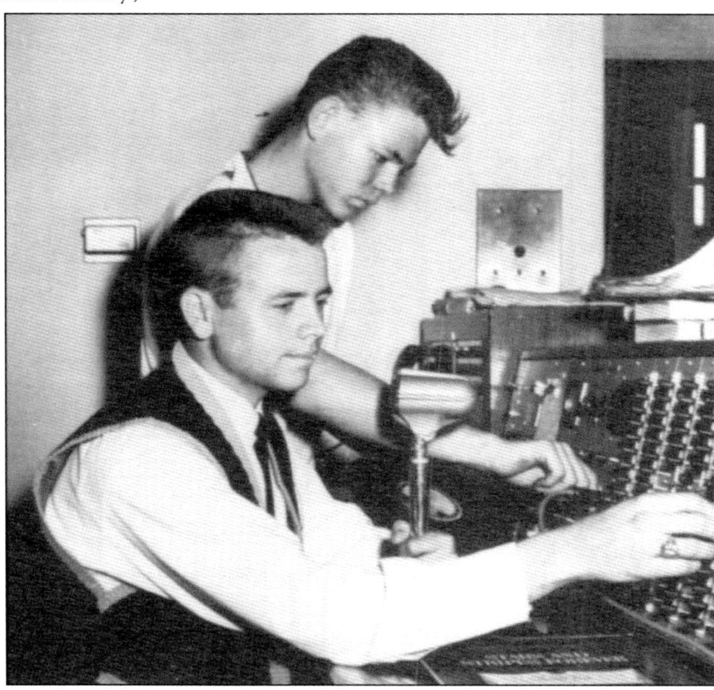

FALCON RECORD REVIEW. During its first years, Rubidoux High School had a sound system that allowed the students to play the latest records during lunch. The records came from Modern Music Mart, a record store located in downtown Rubidoux. According to the school yearbook, this was a "first" found only at Rubidoux. (Courtesy Norton family.)

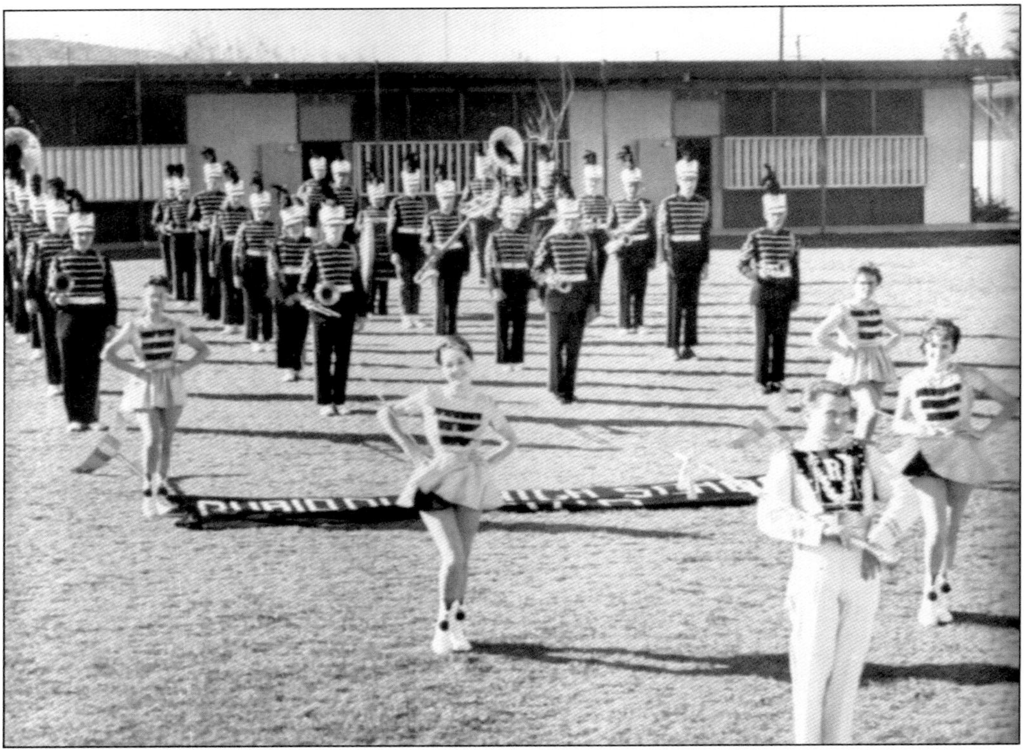

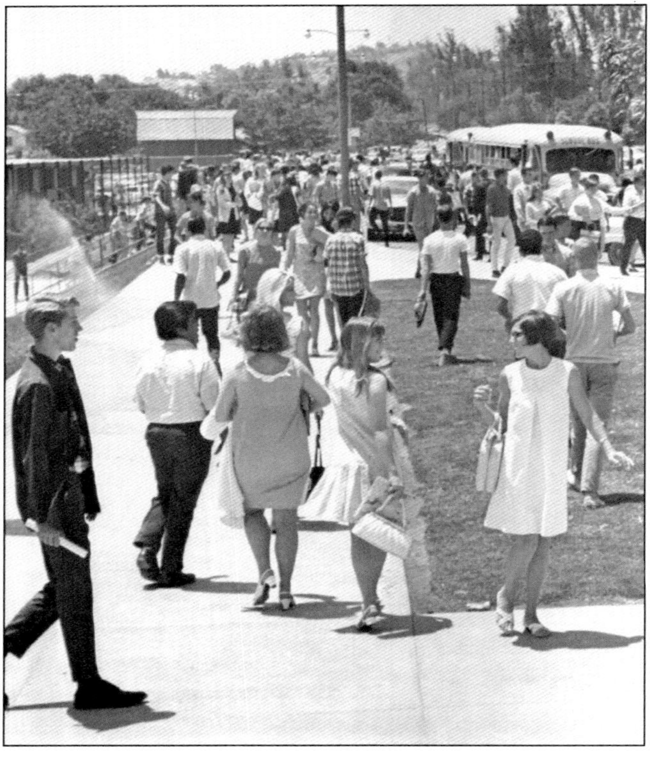

Rubidoux High School Band. The school band is shown in front of Rubidoux High School in 1961–1962. (Courtesy Norton family.)

School Campus. School had just let out, and the busses were waiting when this photograph was taken during the 1968–1969 school year. It was taken in front of Rubidoux High School on Opal Street. (Courtesy Norton family.)

Four

Community Life

The story of community life in Rubidoux was, for many years, the story of rural life. Most community organizations were started to bring more social life to area residents. Community life grew as Rubidoux grew, really taking off when the downtown area was subdivided into smaller residential lots in the 1920s, bringing more families to the area. This encouraged churches to form, often starting as Sunday schools that met at the local school. Bowling leagues formed at the local bowling alley. Organizations such as the Grange, the Lions Club, and the West Riverside Garden Club were formed. Community leaders emerged to help direct this new phase in Rubidoux's history.

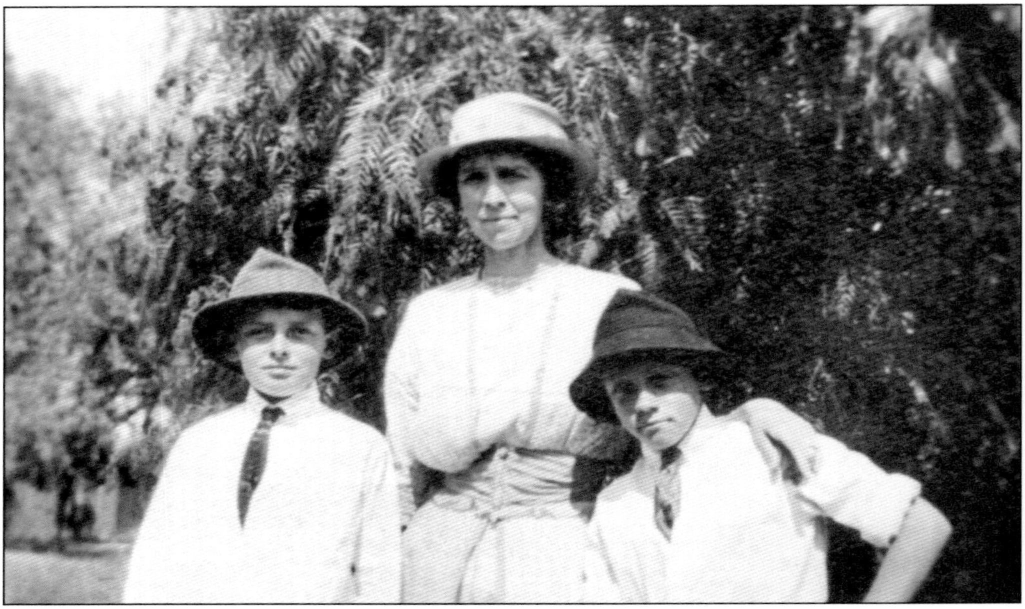

West Riverside Friendship Circle. This photograph shows the second president of the West Riverside Friendship Circle, Mrs. C. N. Sheldon, and her two sons, *c.* 1915. This women's group was founded in 1912 and continued until 1977. It was organized by a few women who felt the need for more social life in the community. (Courtesy Riverside County Regional Park and Open-Space District.)

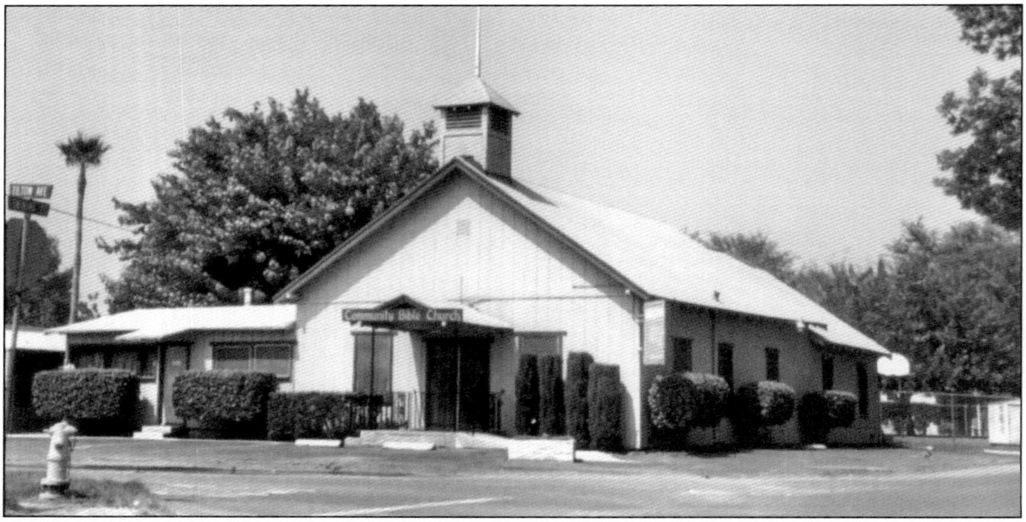

Fort Fremont Community Church. About 1900, a Sunday school was started that met in the Jurupa School. In 1925, it was moved to a new location in a commercial building on Mission Boulevard in West Riverside, closer to the families moving into the Fort Fremont subdivision. The Sunday school grew and in 1927 bought property at the corner of Tilton and Twining Streets. There a small building was constructed and called Fort Fremont Sunday School. Beginning in the early 1940s, ministers were brought in to preach on a regular basis. It formally organized as Fort Fremont Community Church in early 1945. It is now known as Community Bible Church. (Courtesy author.)

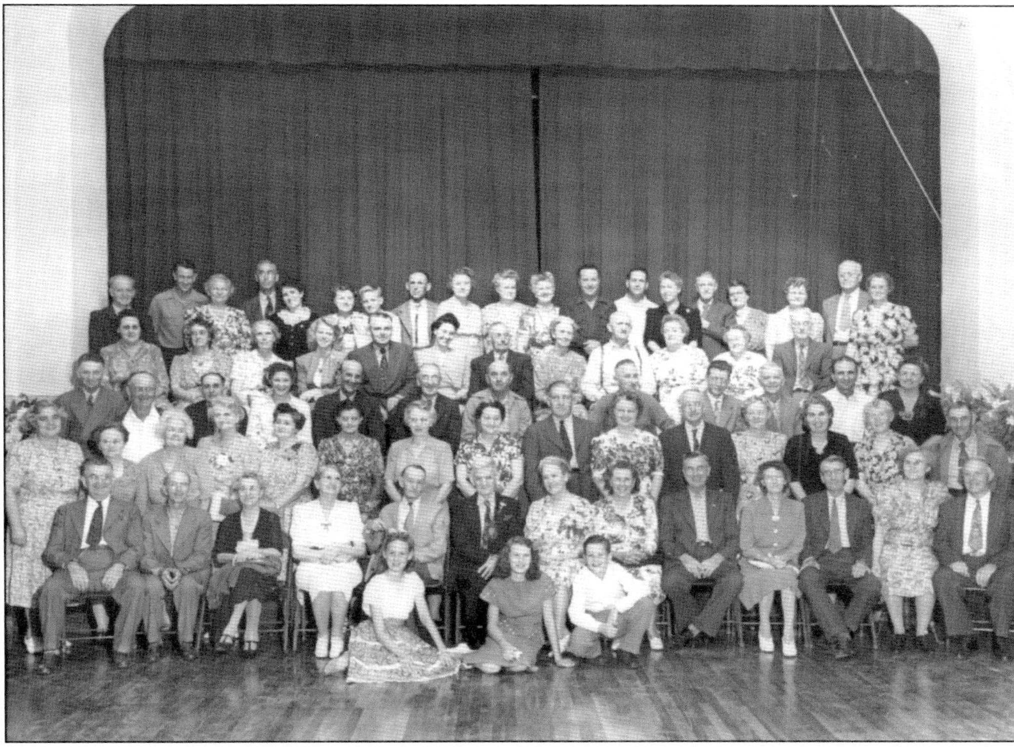

OLD SETTLERS REUNION. First held in 1924 at West Riverside School, this reunion of longtime and early residents of the area was such a success that it became a yearly event held until the 1980s. This is a group photograph of reunion attendees taken in the 1940s at the West Riverside School auditorium. (Courtesy Engelauf/Flowers families.)

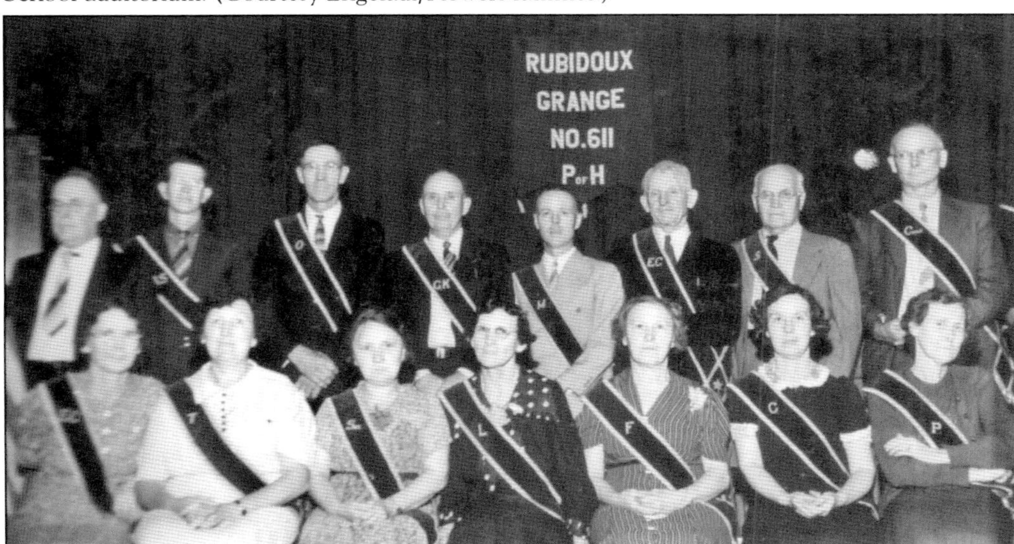

RUBIDOUX GRANGE. The Grange was a nationwide organization designed to provide information and social activities to farmers in rural areas. The Rubidoux Grange was organized in 1935. This 1939 photograph shows the Grange officers. (Courtesy Rubidoux Grange.)

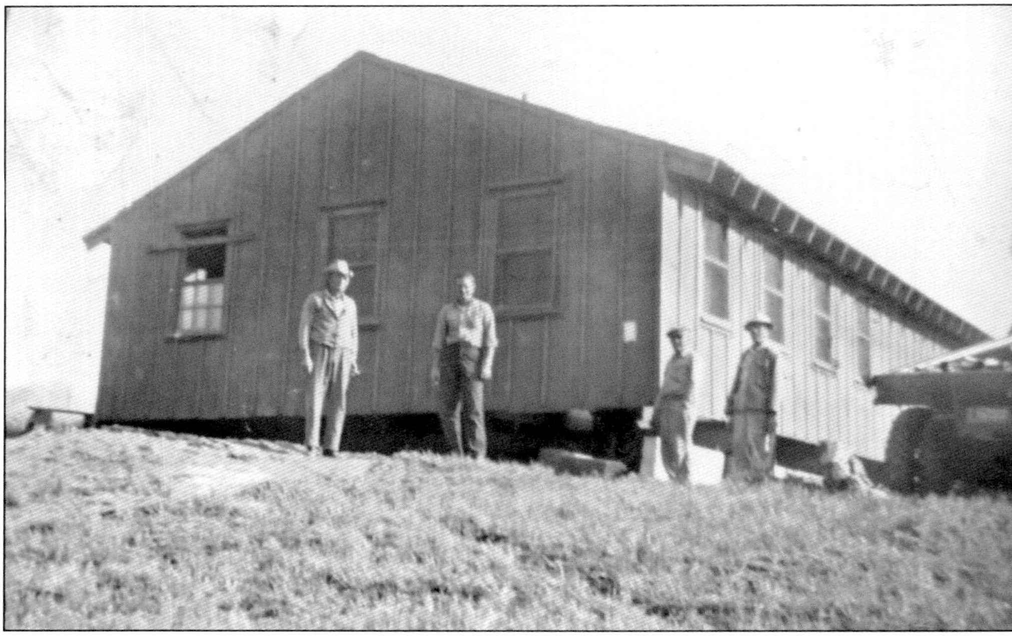

GRANGE HALL. In 1948, the Rubidoux Grange, which had been meeting at West Riverside School, acquired a war surplus building, shown, which it installed on donated property on Riverview Drive, across from West Riverside School. The hall was then covered with stucco and painted white. It is still located on Riverview Drive. (Courtesy Rubidoux Grange.)

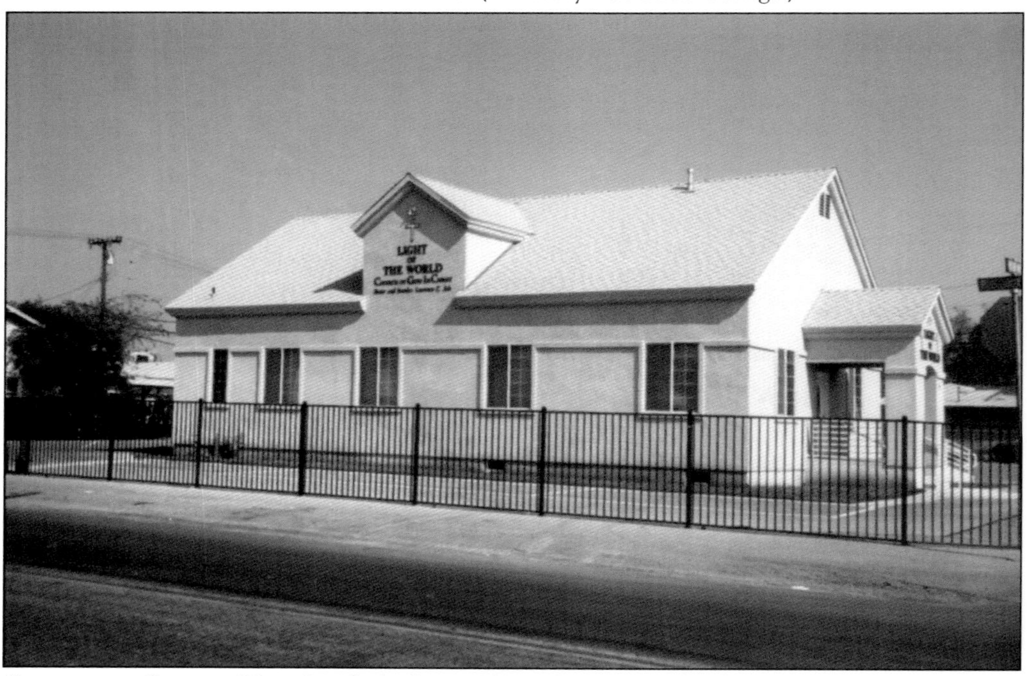

CHURCH OF CHRIST. This church, built in 1939 at the corner of Nakoma Street (now Rubidoux Boulevard) and Molino Way was originally a Church of Christ. Until it was recently remodeled, the building was covered in white clapboard siding. (Courtesy author.)

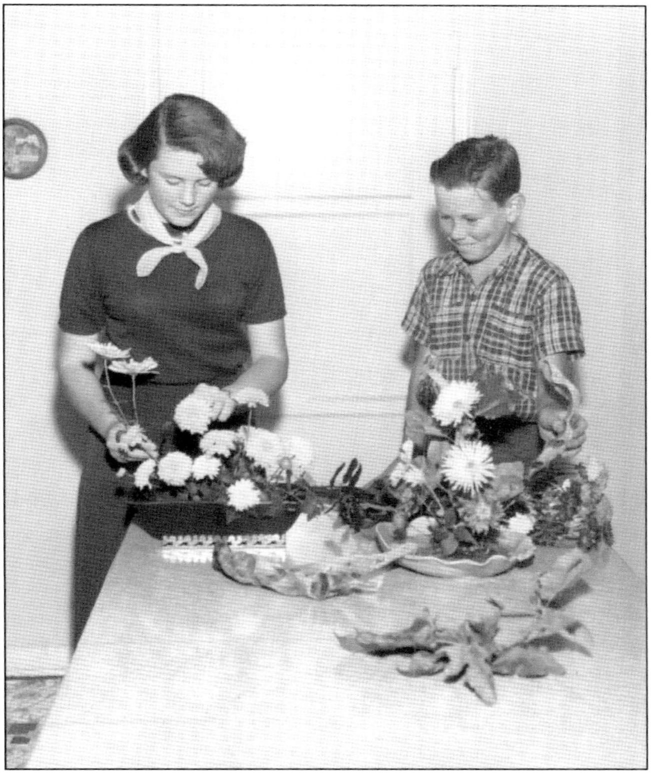

WEST RIVERSIDE GARDEN CLUB. The Garden Club was formed in 1948 and soon began holding flower shows. This photograph shows Judy and John Wimmer, ages 13 and 10 respectively, preparing for the flower show held at Memorial Hall in 1953. (Courtesy Jurupa Mountain's Cultural Center.)

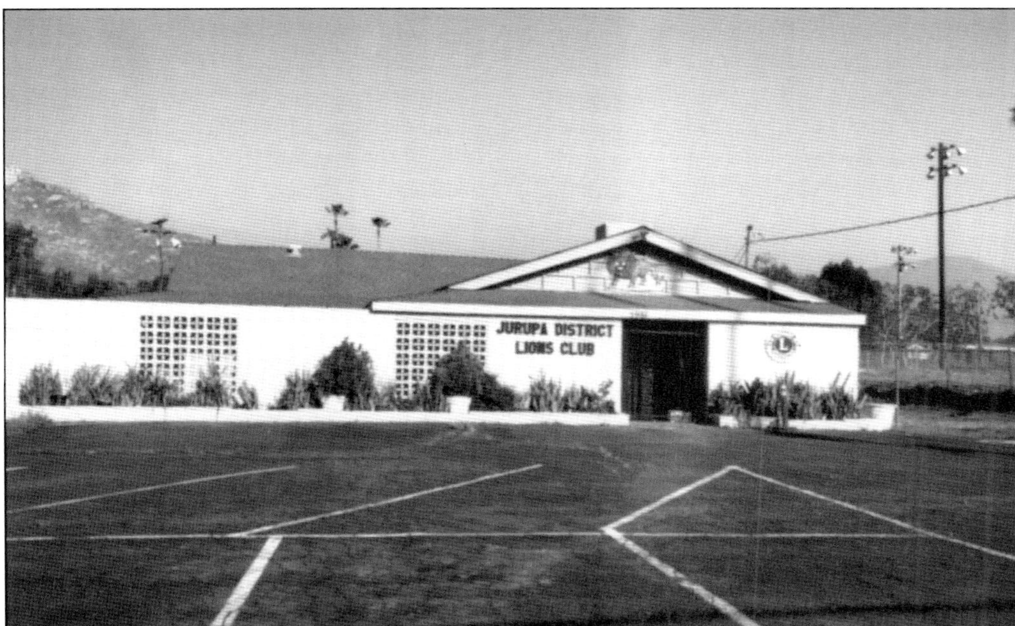

RUBIDOUX LIONS CLUB. This club was formed in 1949 with Carl Train as its first president. Their clubhouse on Limonite Avenue was built around 1952. The club later changed its name to Jurupa Lions Club. This is a current photograph of the club. (Courtesy author.)

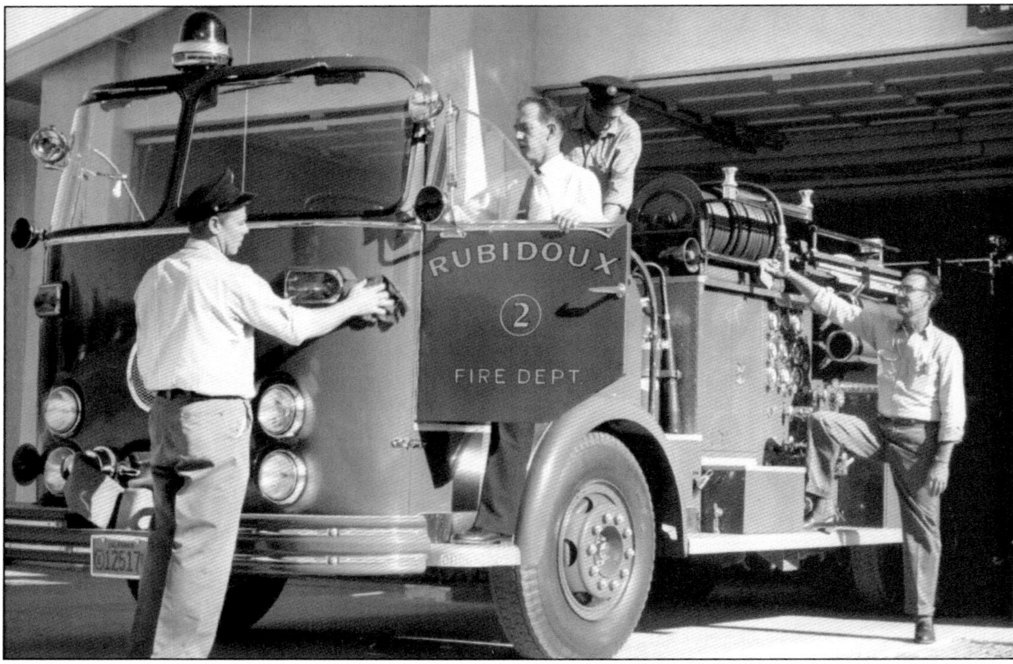

RUBIDOUX FIRE CHIEF. At a 1961 open house, Fire Chief Ed Weiss sits in the fire truck. The West Riverside Fire Protection District was formed in 1946. It was housed in an old Quonset hut located at Fort Freemont Street and Mennes Avenue. It merged with the Rubidoux Community Services District in 1955.

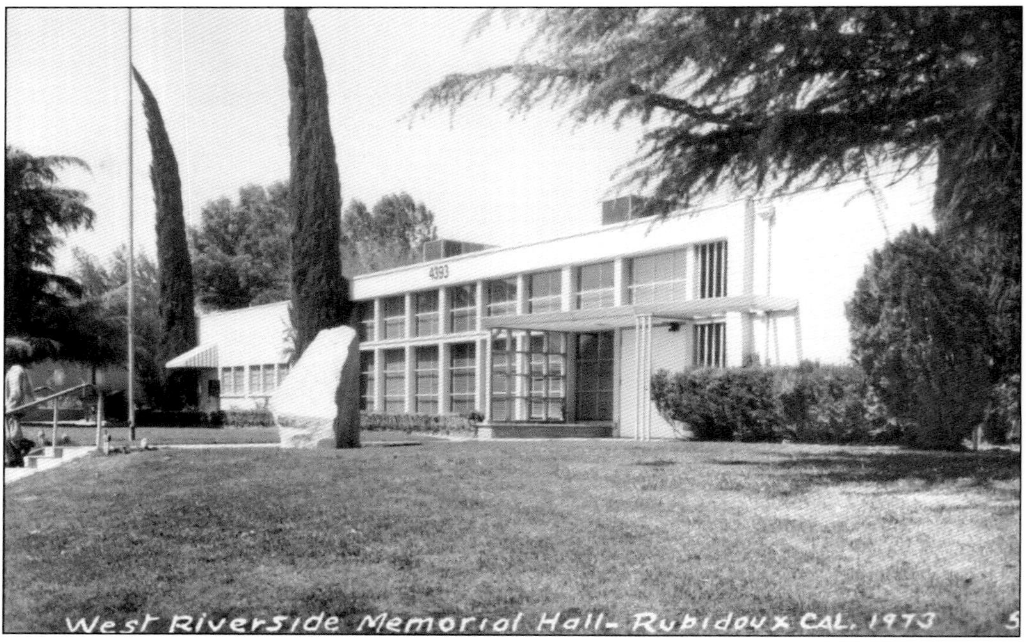

MEMORIAL HALL. This community center was built in the early 1950s. This photograph shows it as it looked in 1973. Remodeled in 2003, it still serves the Jurupa area today with youth programs as well as other events. (Courtesy Riverside County Library System, Louis Robidoux Library.)

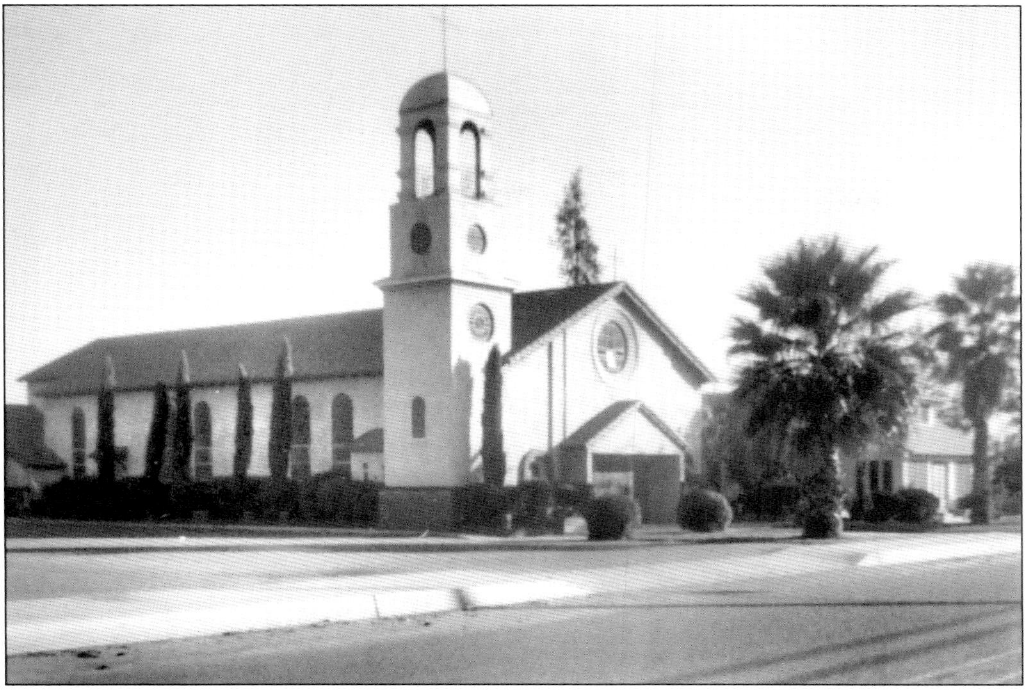

ST. JOHN THE APOSTLE CHURCH. This Catholic church was established in 1956. Property was purchased on Opal Street for the church, and ground was broken that same year. This photograph of the church was taken in 1967. (Courtesy Weaver family.)

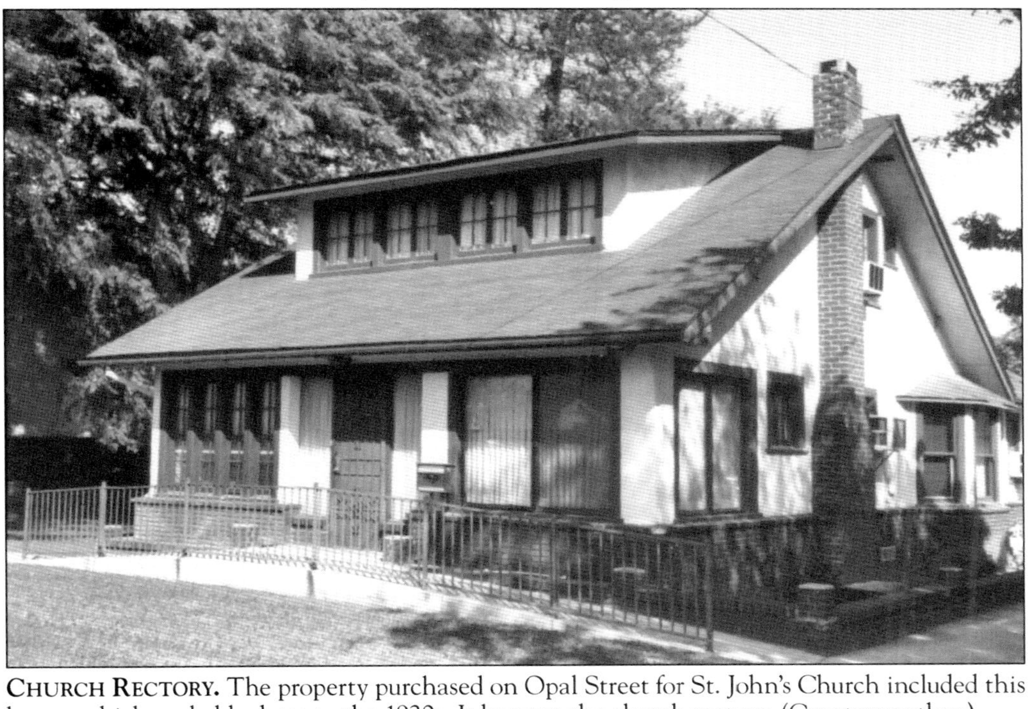

CHURCH RECTORY. The property purchased on Opal Street for St. John's Church included this house, which probably dates to the 1920s. It became the church rectory. (Courtesy author.)

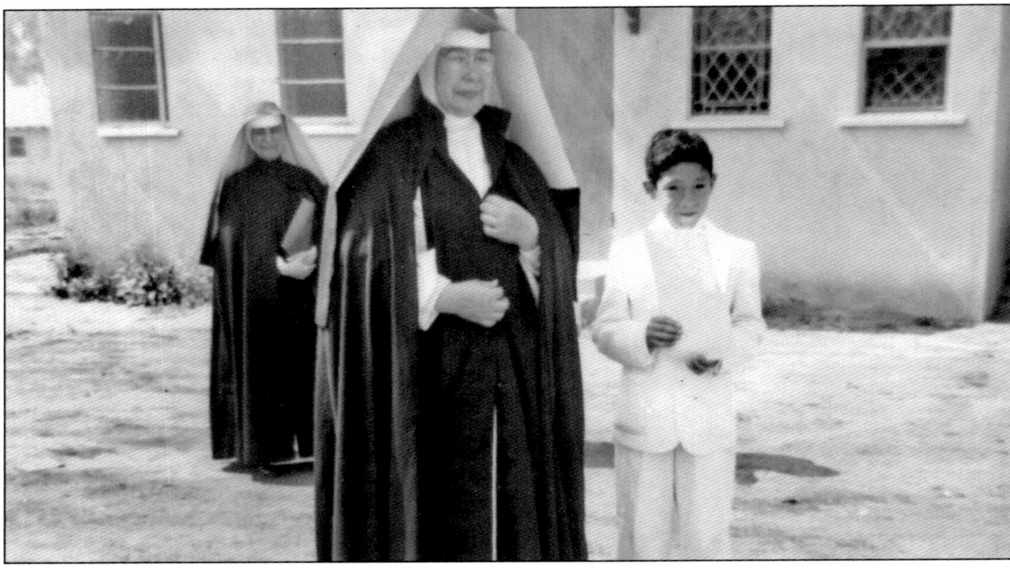

First Holy Communion. Rene Chavez is standing next to Sister Boniface after his first Holy Communion at St. John's Catholic Church on Opal Street, *c.* 1958. The sister came every Saturday from St. Francis De Sales Church in Riverside to teach catechism to the children at the church. (Courtesy Chavez family.)

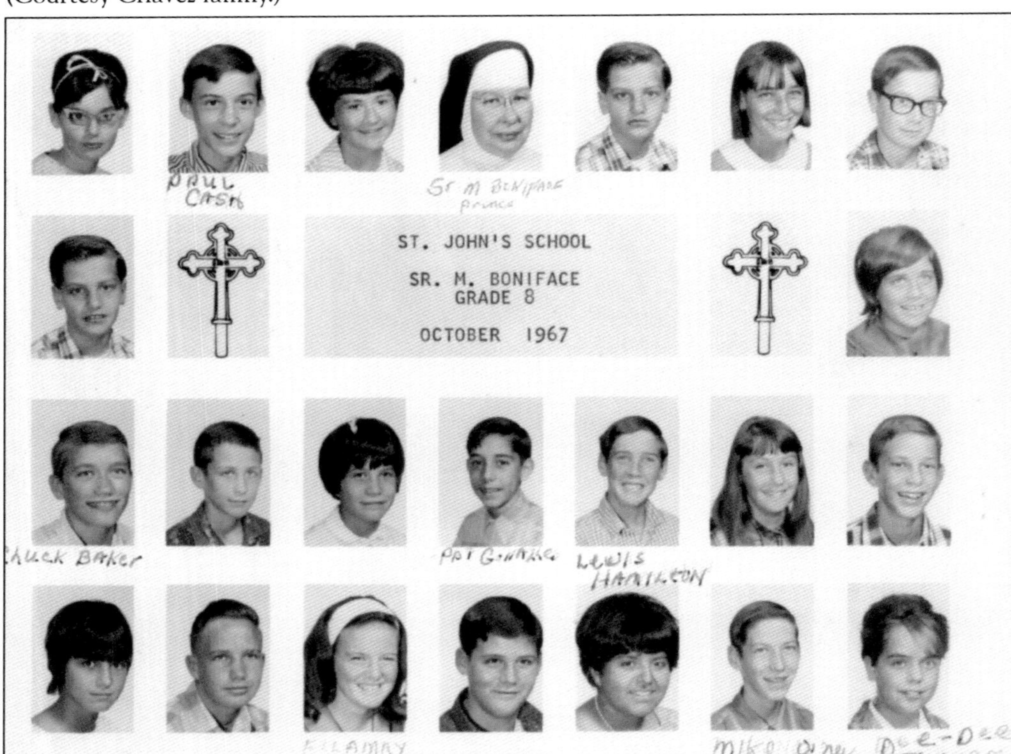

Church School. St. John's Church began a Catholic school in 1962. The school closed in the early 1970s. This is the eighth-grade class picture from 1967. (Courtesy St. John's Church.)

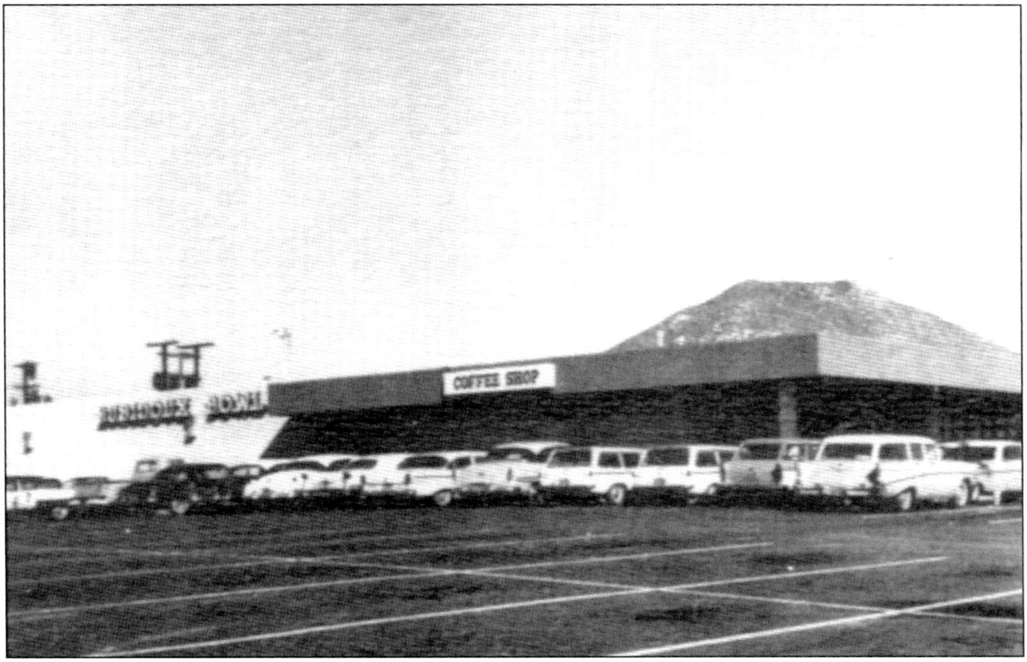

Rubidoux Bowling Alley. The local bowling alley was located at the corner of Pontiac Avenue and Mission Boulevard. This photograph was taken in 1960. (Courtesy Norton family.)

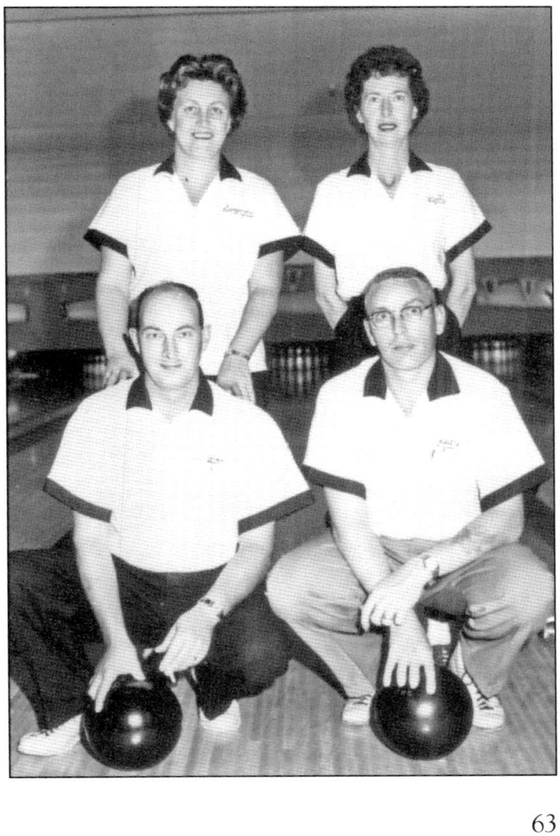

Bowling League. Many residents from all over Jurupa came to bowl at the Rubidoux Bowl. This foursome was in a bowling league, *c.* 1960. Pictured from left to right are (first row) Bob Harrison and Don Jarrell; (second row) Gwynneth Harrison and Nell Jarrell. (Courtesy author.)

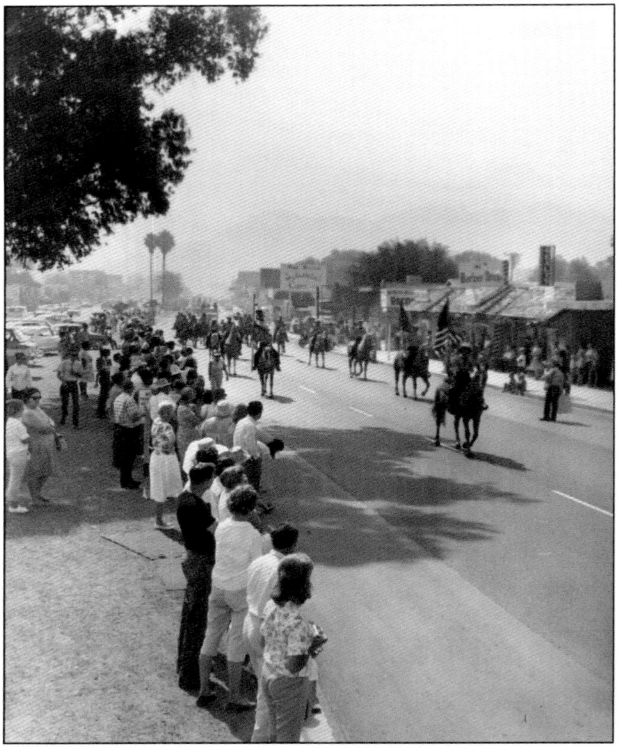

Western Days Parade, 1964. People lined Mission Boulevard to see the Western Days Parade. Western Days was a weeklong event that included a carnival, a queen contest, and a beard-growing contest for the men. A prominent man would be elected "mayor" for the duration of Western Days. (Courtesy Riverside Metropolitan Museum.)

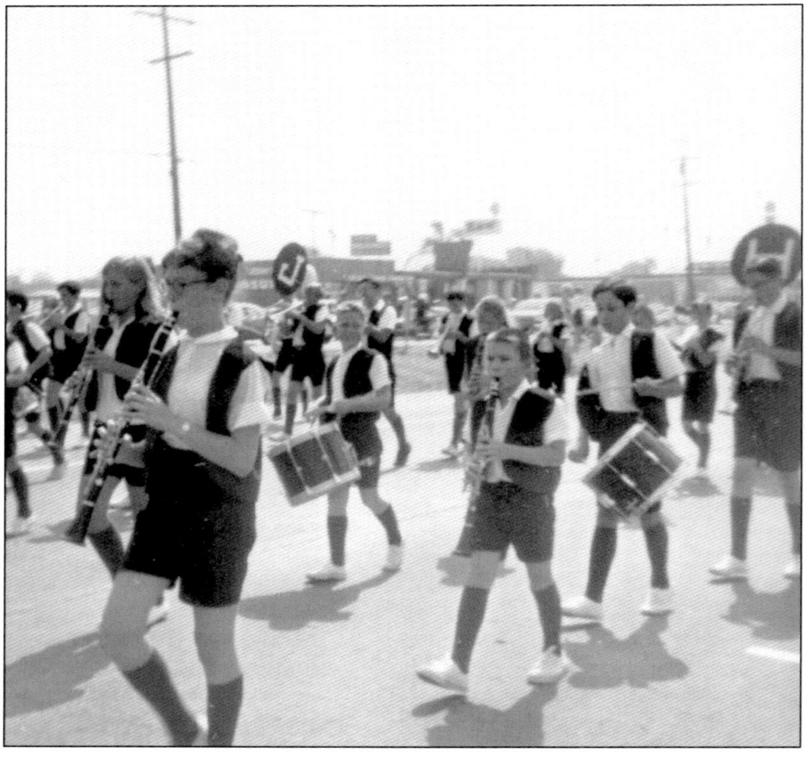

Mission Junior High School Band. The school band is shown marching in the Western Days Parade in March 1969. (Courtesy Engelauf/Flowers families.)

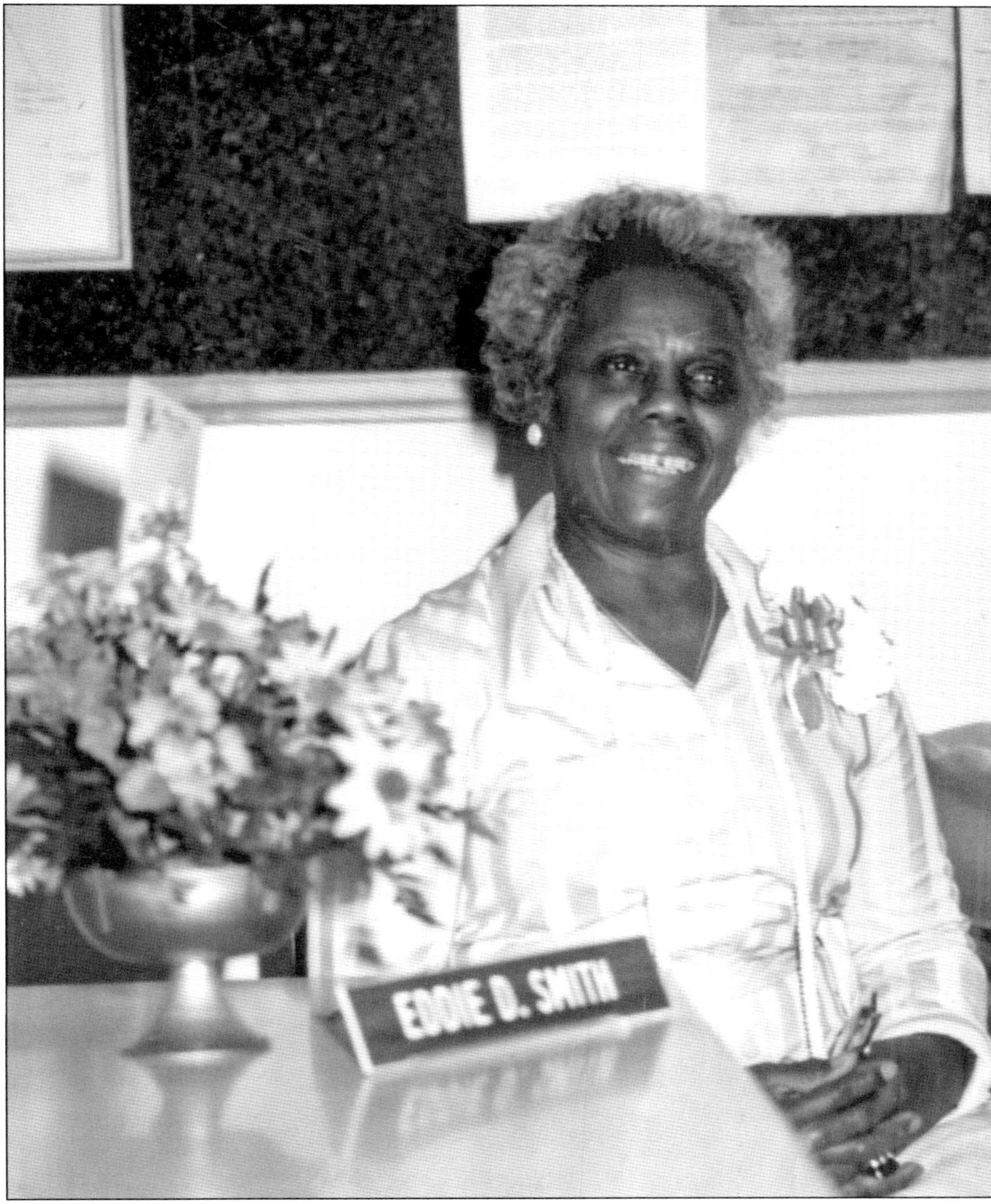

EDDIE DEE SMITH. Eddie Dee moved to the Jurupa area in 1938. She became an amazingly active community member, helping to found numerous organizations and even a church. Her work founding a local senior center led to it being named after her. (Courtesy Eddie Dee Smith Senior Center.)

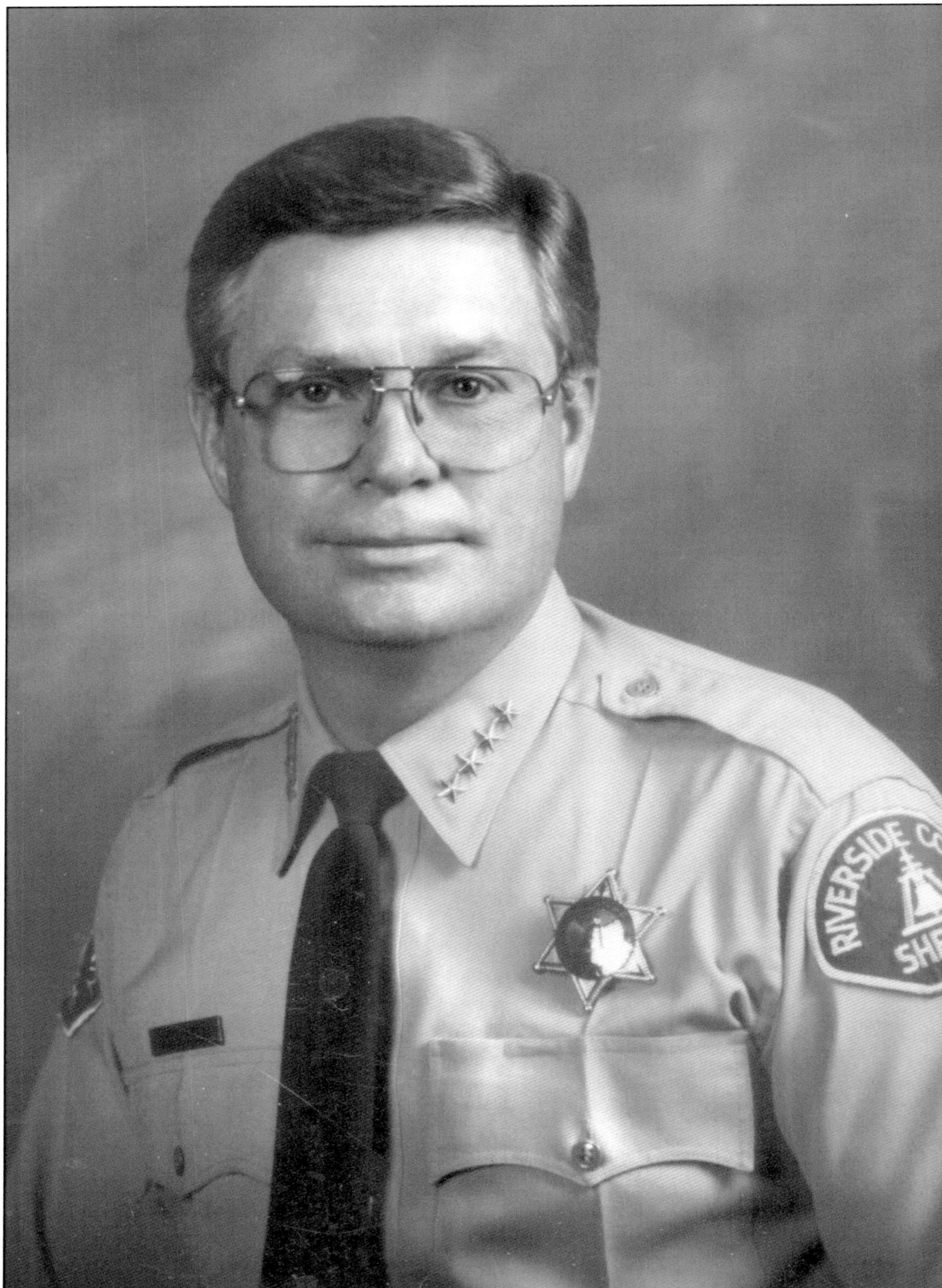

SHERIFF BYRD. Cois Byrd grew up in Rubidoux and attended West Riverside Elementary School. He was elected Riverside County sheriff in 1986 and served two terms. This photograph shows Sheriff Byrd in 1988. (Courtesy Byrd family.)

Five

BUSINESS LIFE

The story of Rubidoux's business life is centered on Mission Boulevard, an important state highway. In the years before freeways, it was a gateway between Los Angeles and the world beyond: Palm Springs, San Diego, Riverside International Raceway, and more. There were businesses along Mission Boulevard that catered to local folks like grocery markets, hardware stores, and five-and-dimes. There were also businesses such as restaurants, gas stations, and motor inns that provided services to the drivers who were passing through Rubidoux. Because of its close proximity to downtown Riverside, Rubidoux never had department stores, but it had plenty of small and medium-sized businesses of all types.

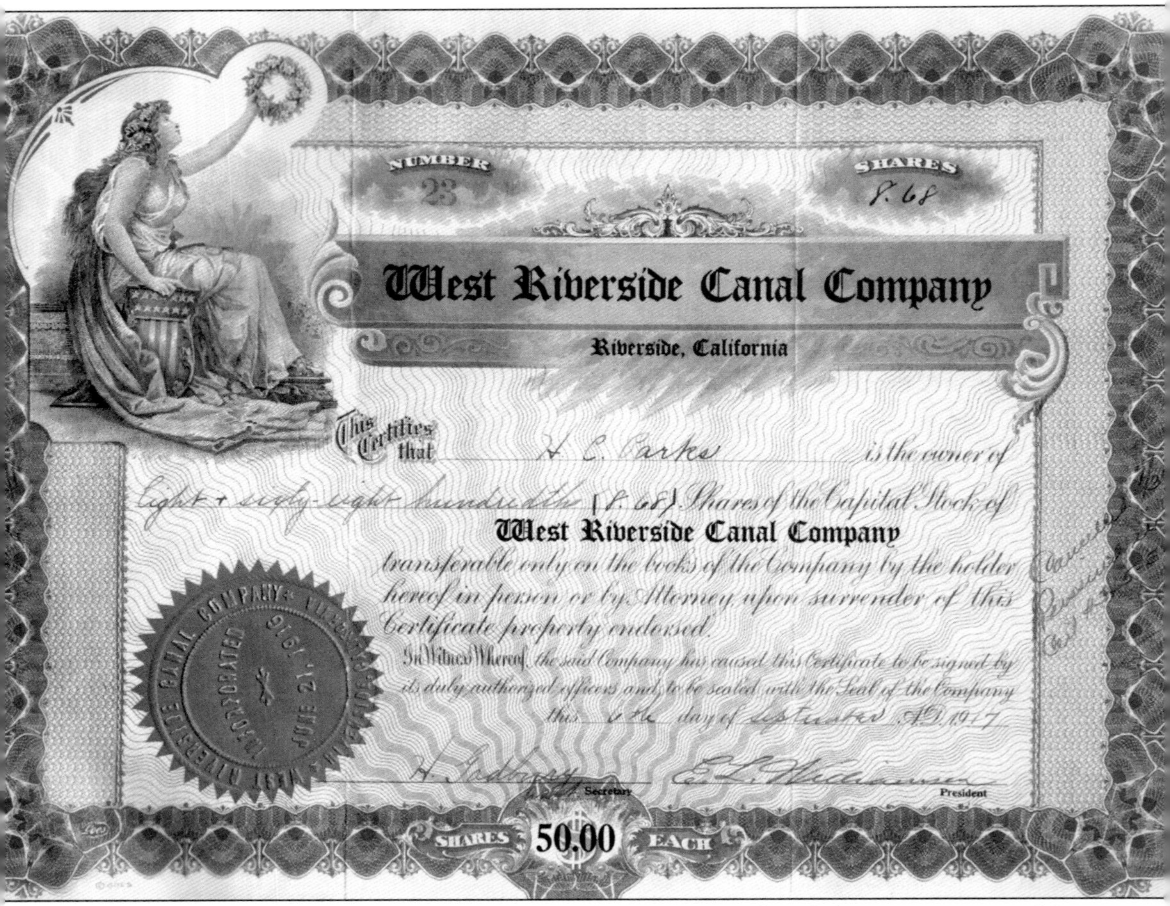

NUMBER 23 SHARES 8.68

West Riverside Canal Company

Riverside, California

This Certifies that H. C. Parks is the owner of eight + sixty-eight hundredths (8.68) Shares of the Capital Stock of

West Riverside Canal Company

transferable only on the books of the Company by the holder hereof in person or by Attorney upon surrender of this Certificate properly endorsed.

In Witness Whereof, the said Company has caused this Certificate to be signed by its duly authorized officers and to be sealed with the Seal of the Company this 6th day of September A.D. 1917

Secretary President

West Riverside Canal Company Incorporated June 21, 1916

SHARES 50.00 EACH

West Riverside Canal Company. This canal company was founded June 21, 1916, to deliver water to shareholders along its 18-mile length. This shareholder certificate was issued to early pioneer Heber Parks. Today the canal can still be seen along Golden West Drive and Canal Street. (Courtesy Chuck Cox.)

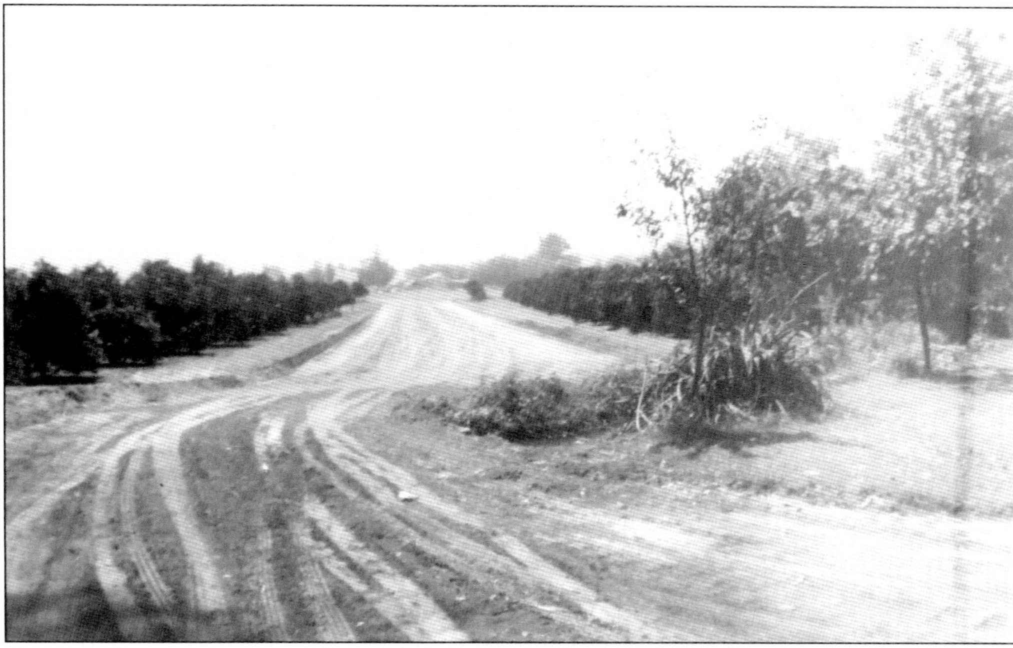

ORANGE GROVE, C. 1920S. This road, shown going through the Arch Parks family orange grove, is now Pioneer Drive, right in the heart of downtown Rubidoux. (Courtesy Richard Nyman.)

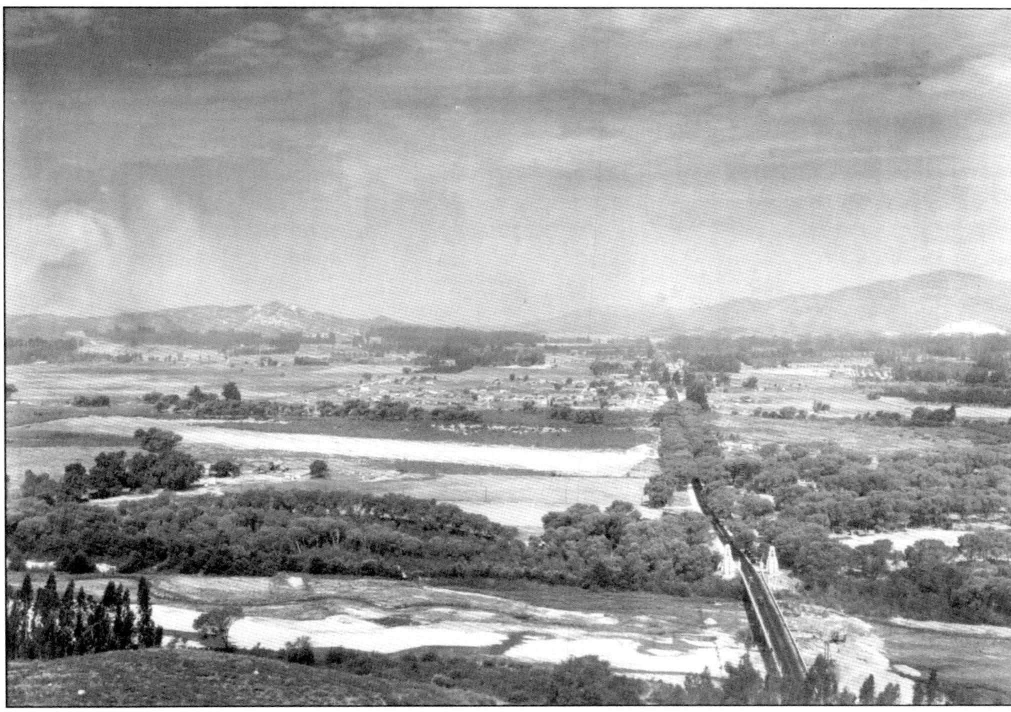

VIEW OF WEST RIVERSIDE FROM MOUNT RUBIDOUX. The Santa Ana River and West Riverside are seen in this photograph, taken from Mount Rubidoux, around the mid- to late 1920s. (Courtesy Riverside Metropolitan Museum.)

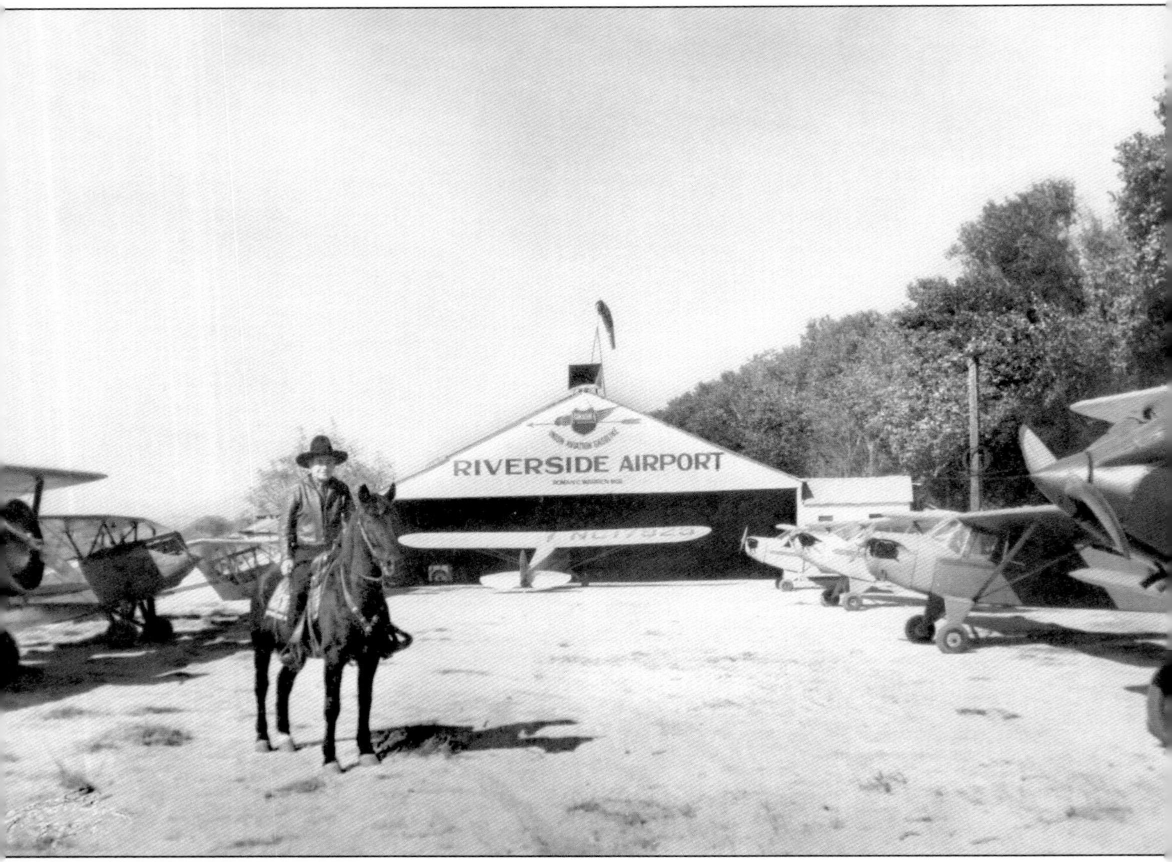

ROMAN WARREN AND THE RIVERSIDE AIRPORT. Roman Warren, founder of Riverside's first airport, which was actually located in Rubidoux, is shown on his horse in front an airplane hanger. Warren, an aviation pioneer, founded the airport in the 1920s. It was located on the south side of Mission Boulevard near the site of today's Flabob Airport. It closed after the 1938 flood, when most of the landing area was washed away. (Courtesy Madariaga family.)

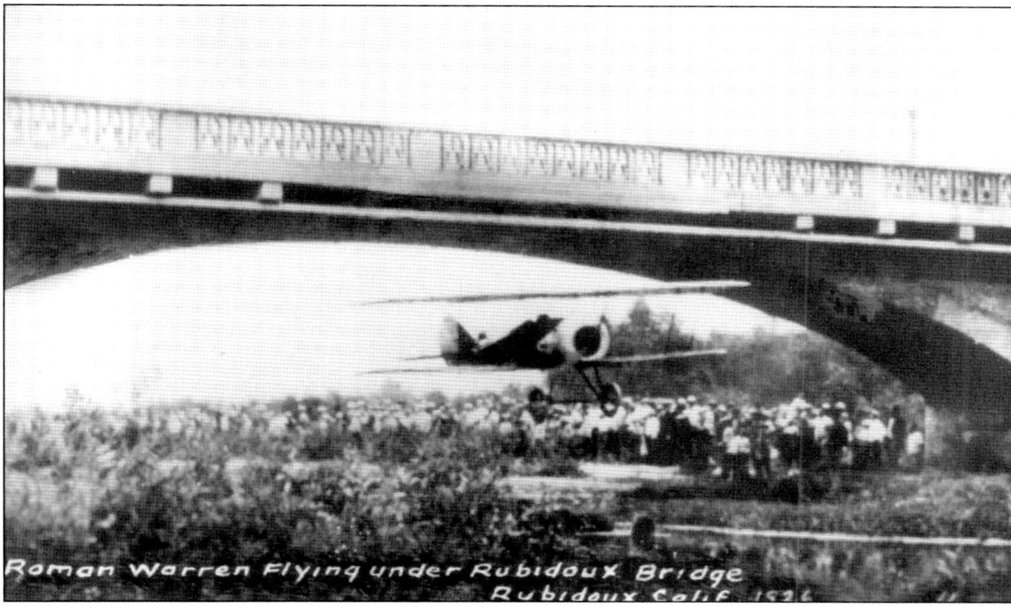

FLIGHT UNDER THE SANTA ANA RIVER BRIDGE. Roman Warren was known as the "Cowboy Aviator," and on June 13, 1926, he accomplished his most famous feat, flying his plane under the 16-foot-tall center arch of the West Riverside Bridge. He was trying to drum up publicity for his business of giving rides and flying lessons. Thousands watched the flight from both sides of the river and from Mount Rubidoux. The headline in the *Riverside Enterprise* on June 15 read, "Cowboy Aviator Bets Life and Wins." Film footage of that flight amazes people still. Unfortunately, Warren did not get much new business from his stunt. (Courtesy Steve Lech.)

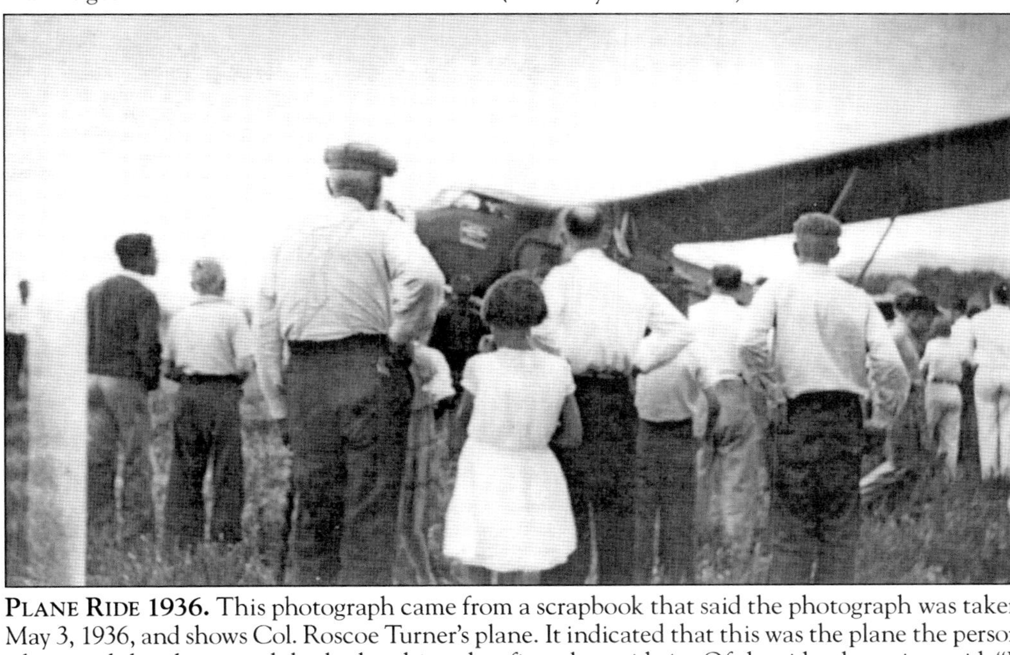

PLANE RIDE 1936. This photograph came from a scrapbook that said the photograph was taken May 3, 1936, and shows Col. Roscoe Turner's plane. It indicated that this was the plane the person who saved the photograph had taken his or her first plane ride in. Of the ride, the writer said, "It was keen." (Courtesy Flabob Airport.)

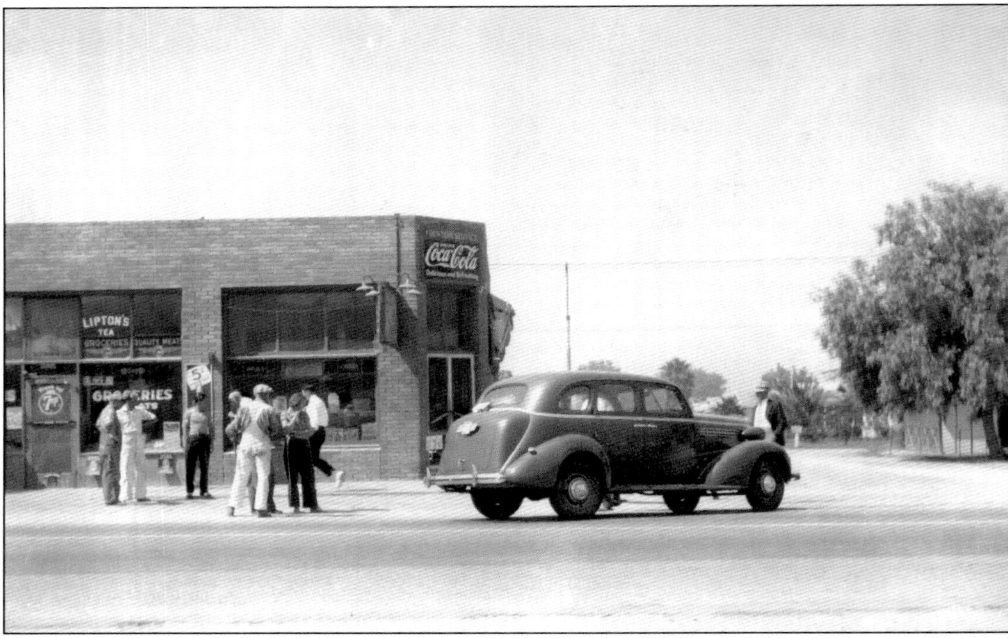

EARLY MARKET. This building at the corner of Mission Boulevard and Mennes Avenue was originally Phillian's Market. The building probably dates to the late 1920s or early 1930s, making it one of the oldest commercial buildings still in existence in Rubidoux. (Courtesy Jurupa Mountains Cultural Center.)

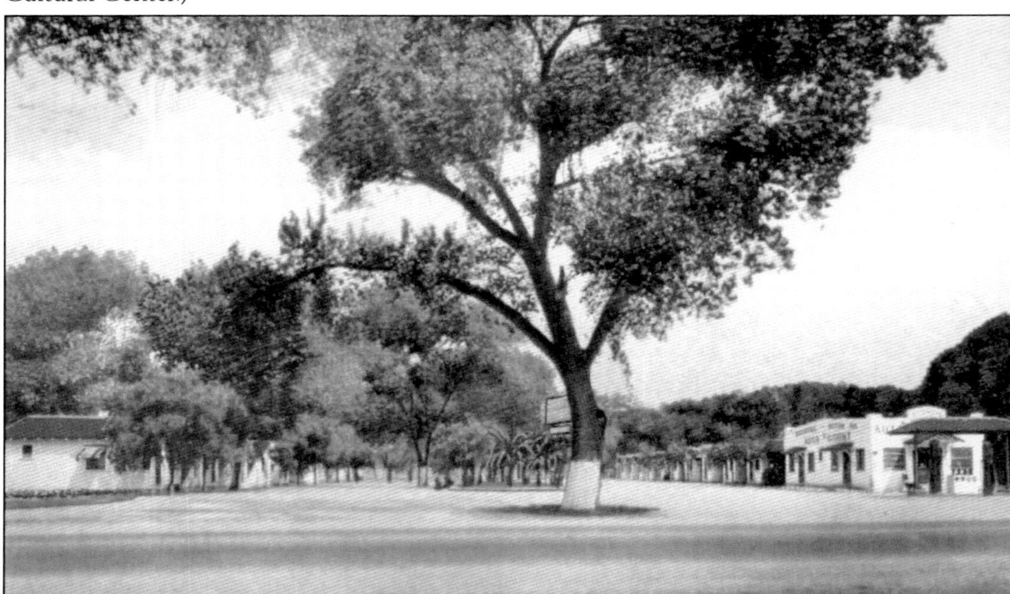

RIVERSIDE MOTOR INN. Mission Boulevard through Rubidoux was also the main road from Los Angeles to San Diego and the desert. Many motor inns, such as this one, sprang up to serve the motoring public. This postcard, postmarked 1932, advertises that the Riverside Motor Inn has strictly modern cabins with a gas station, too, all at the foot of "Famous Mt. Rubidoux." (Courtesy Steve Lech.)

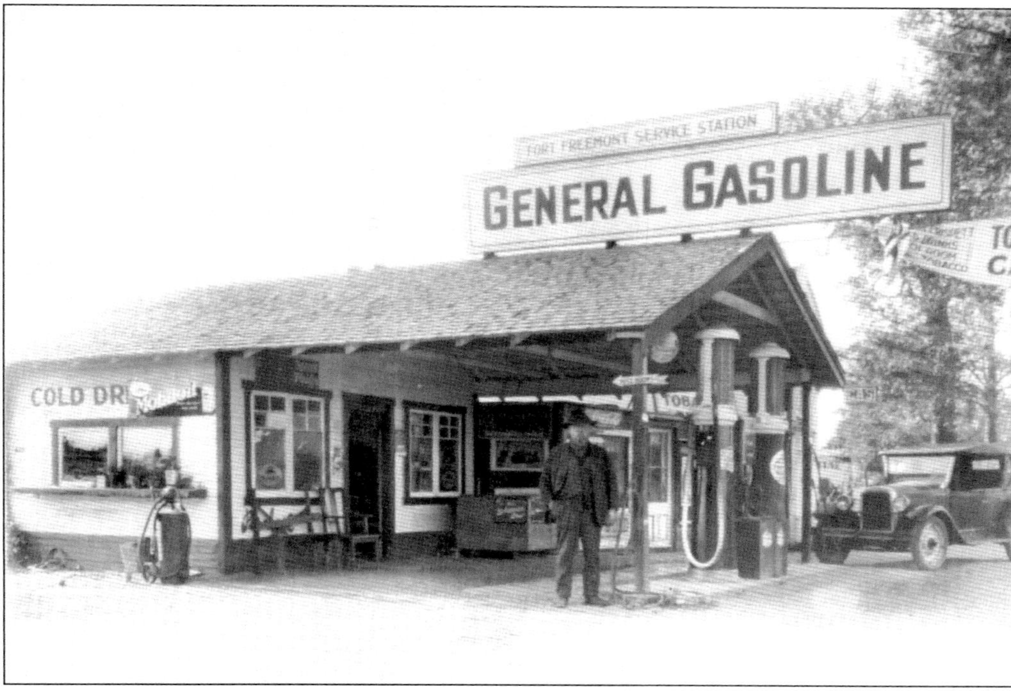

GAS STATION. This is Columbus L. "Lon" Berry and his gas station, *c.* 1930. The station was located at the corner of Mission Boulevard and Wallace Street. (Courtesy Marjorie Paige.)

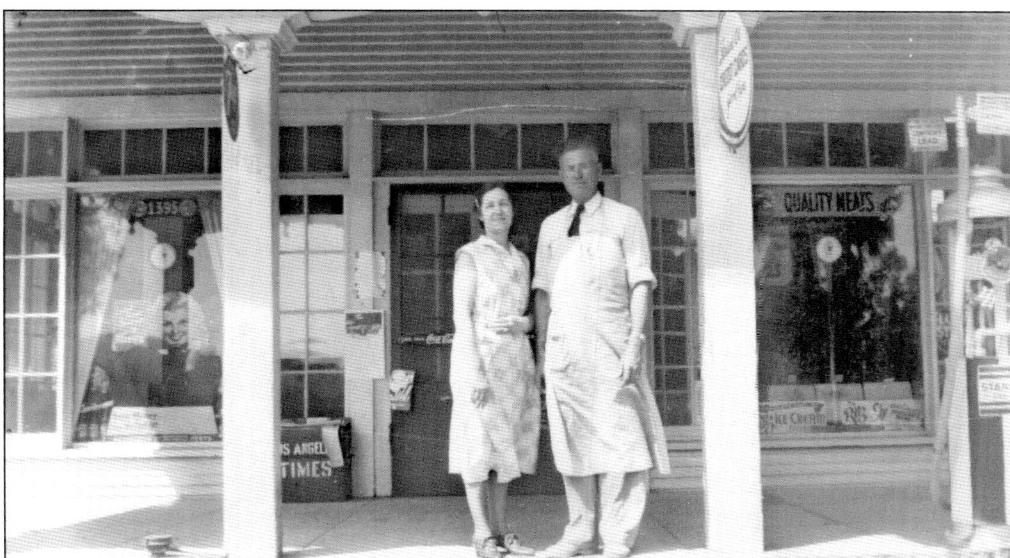

MOREY'S MARKET. Grace and Walter Morey are shown standing in front of their market at Mission Boulevard and Pacific Avenue in the late 1930s. They also opened a two-story furniture store next door after World War II. Later both buildings were connected and became the Rubidoux Mortuary. Morey Street behind the mortuary is named after this couple. (Courtesy Don Peck.)

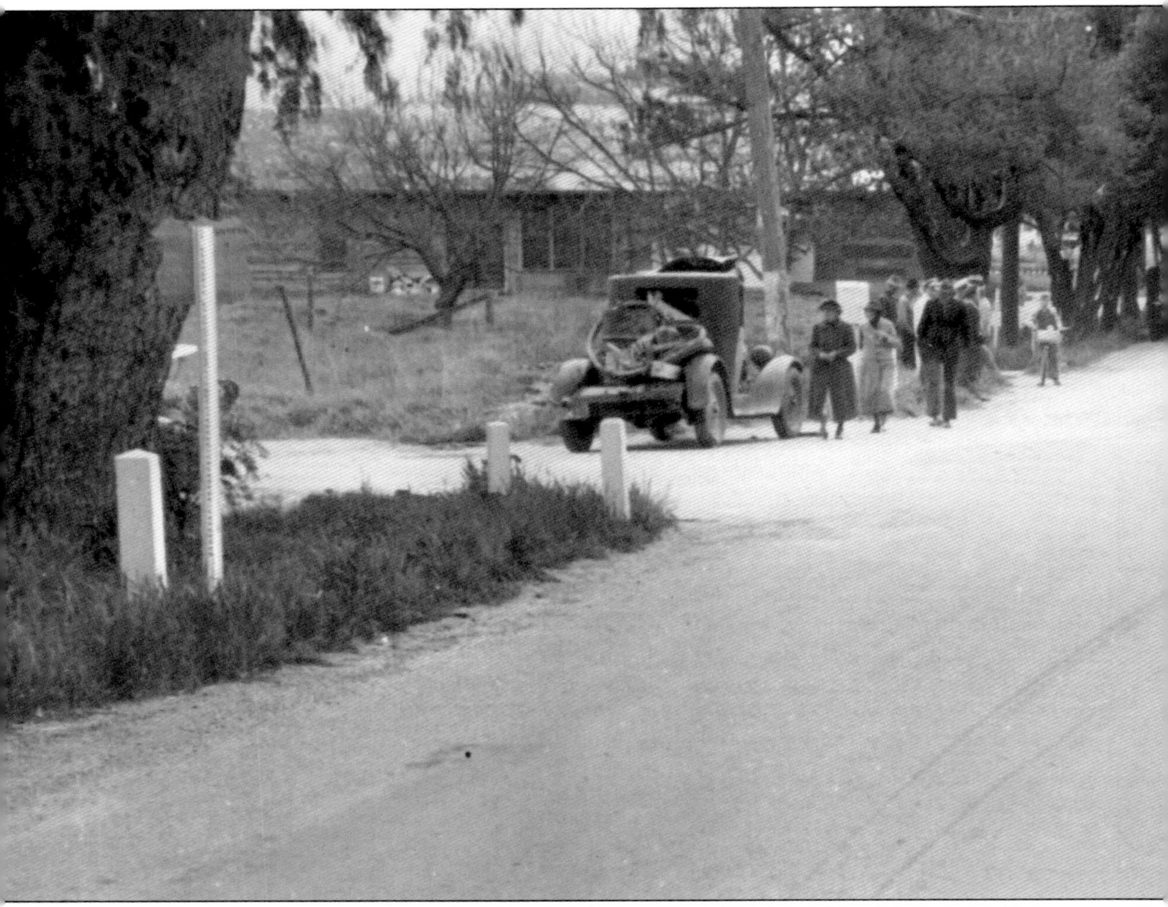

Auto Accident. This auto accident occurred at Mission Boulevard and Riverview Drive-in

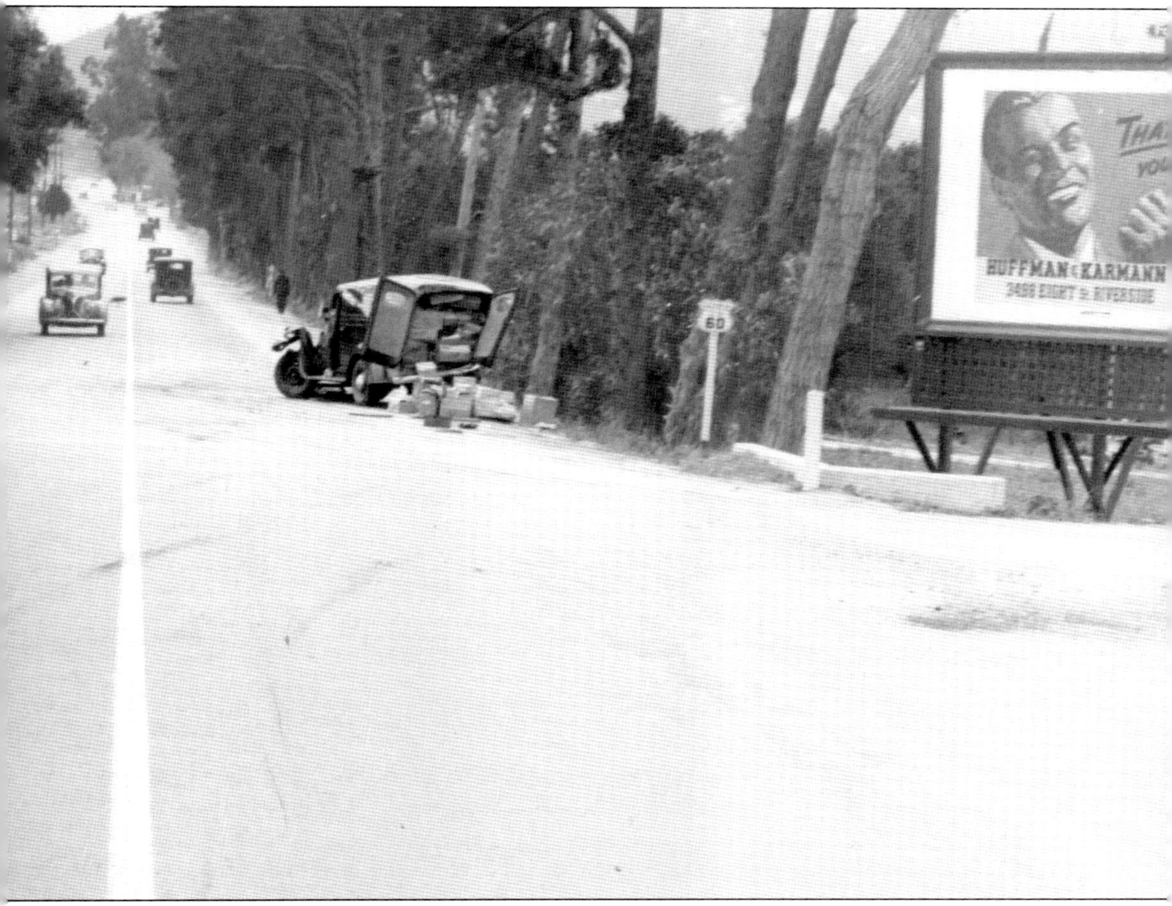

1938. (Courtesy Jurupa Mountains Cultural Center.)

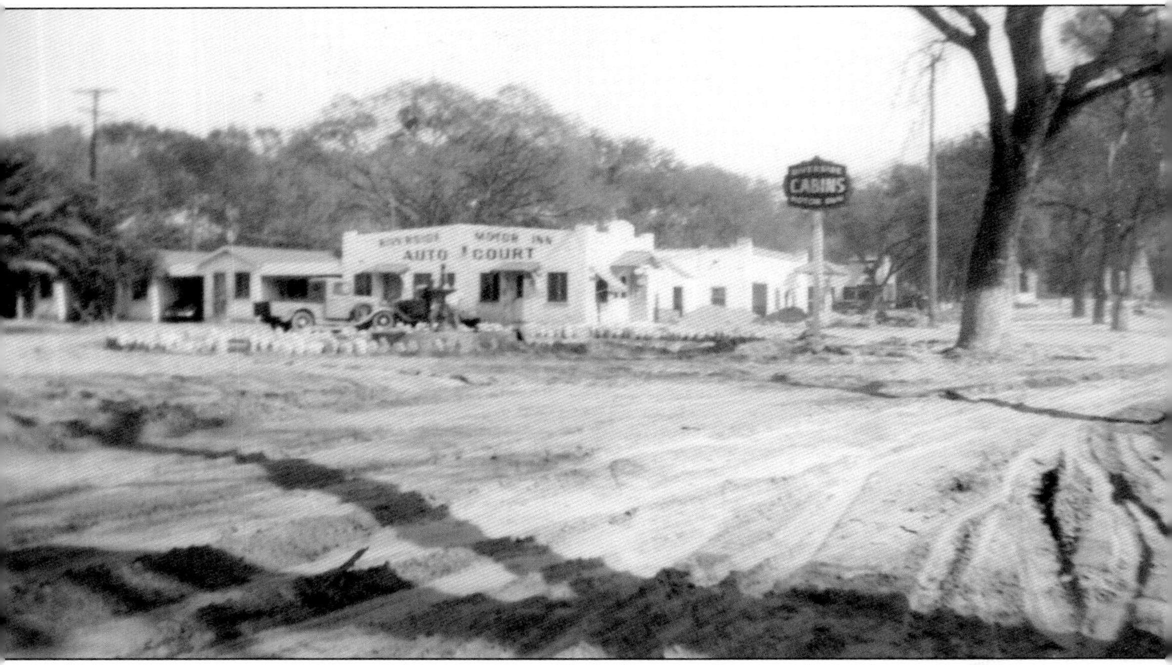

Businesses along Mission Boulevard. This photograph was taken March 21, 1938, almost three weeks after the devastating flood of that year. It shows the kind of businesses that were located along Mission Boulevard that catered to the motoring public. (Courtesy Riverside County Flood Control and Water Conservation District.)

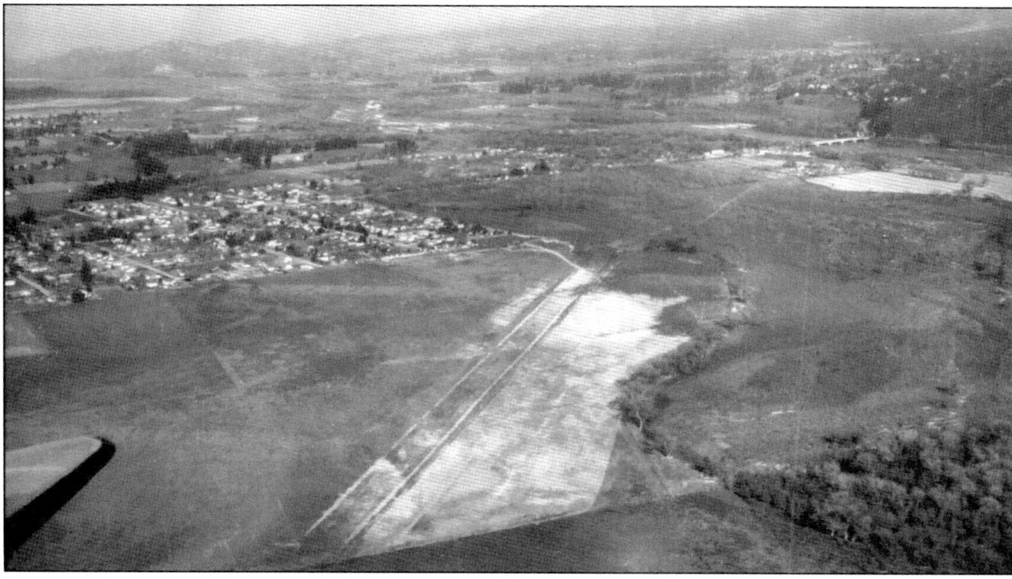

FLABOB AIRPORT. This aerial photograph shows Flabob Airport in 1945. The one runway can be seen running diagonally through the center of the image. Flabob was a small, civil air patrol airport when Flavio Madariaga and Bob Bogan purchased it in 1943. Known then as "Riverside Airport," the new owners later changed the airport's name to avoid confusion with another airport in Riverside's Arlington area. They combined the first three letters of Flavio with Bob to give the small, dirt airstrip its new name. (Courtesy Madariaga family.)

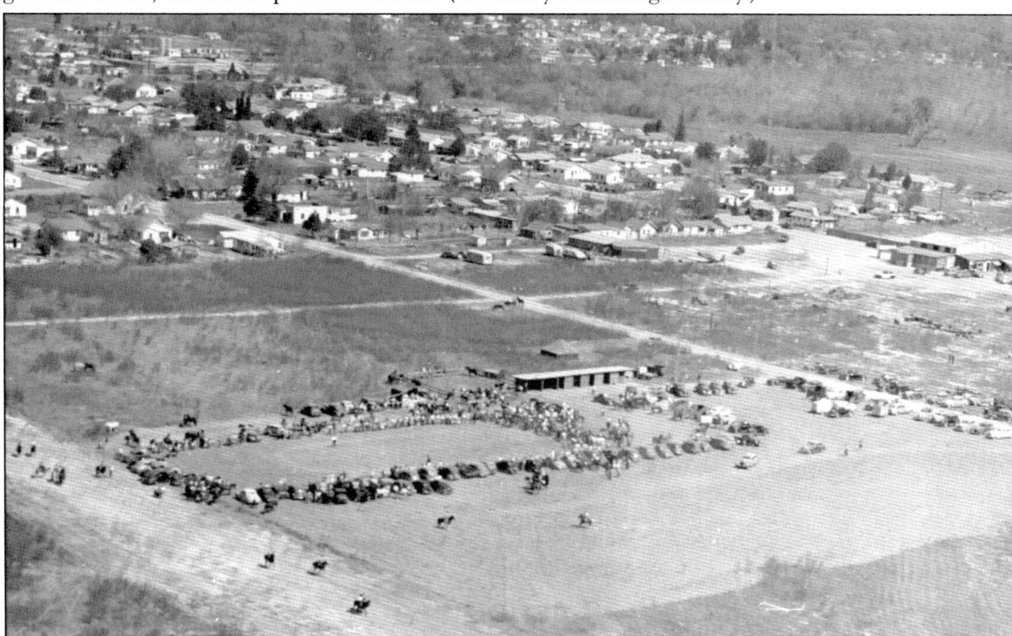

RODEO, 1946. Flavio Madariaga's brother-in-law, Lou Krug, operated a horse stable on the Flabob Airport property. He would occasionally have rodeos in association with the stable business. This aerial photograph shows a rodeo in 1946. (Courtesy Madariaga family.)

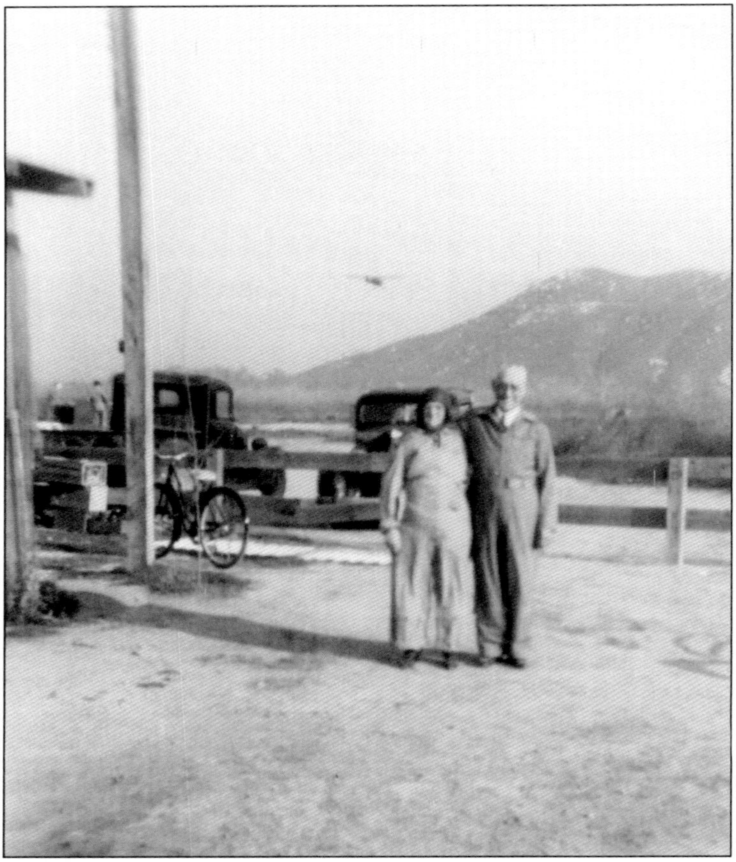

Pancho Barnes at Flabob. Florence "Pancho" Barnes, a pioneer in woman's aviation, visited Flabob Airport in 1947. She is shown with an unidentified man. (Courtesy Madariaga family.)

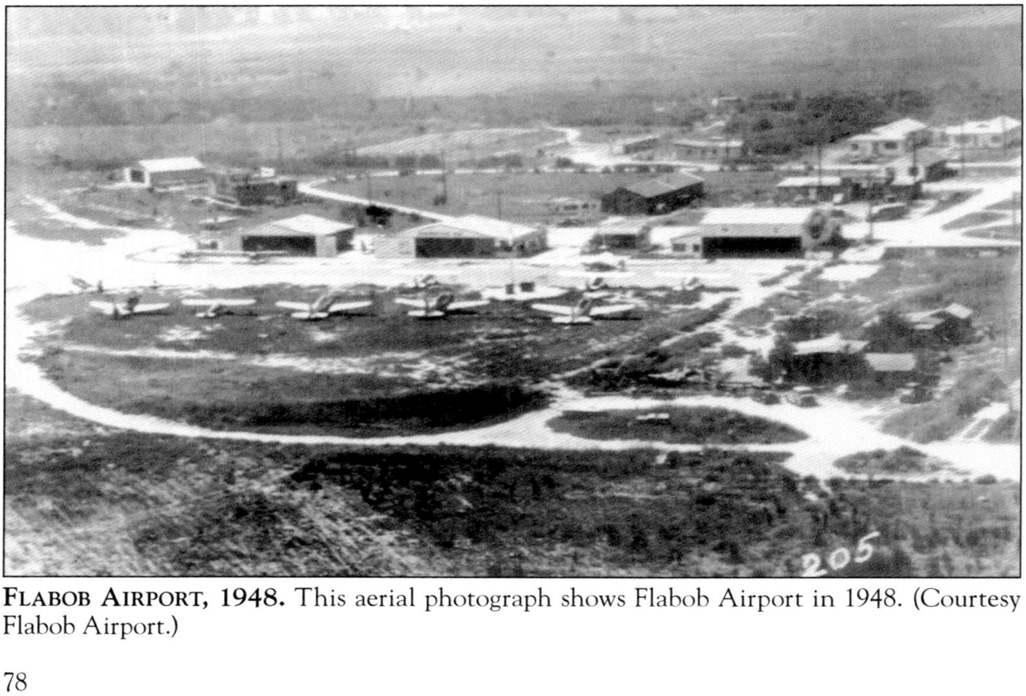

Flabob Airport, 1948. This aerial photograph shows Flabob Airport in 1948. (Courtesy Flabob Airport.)

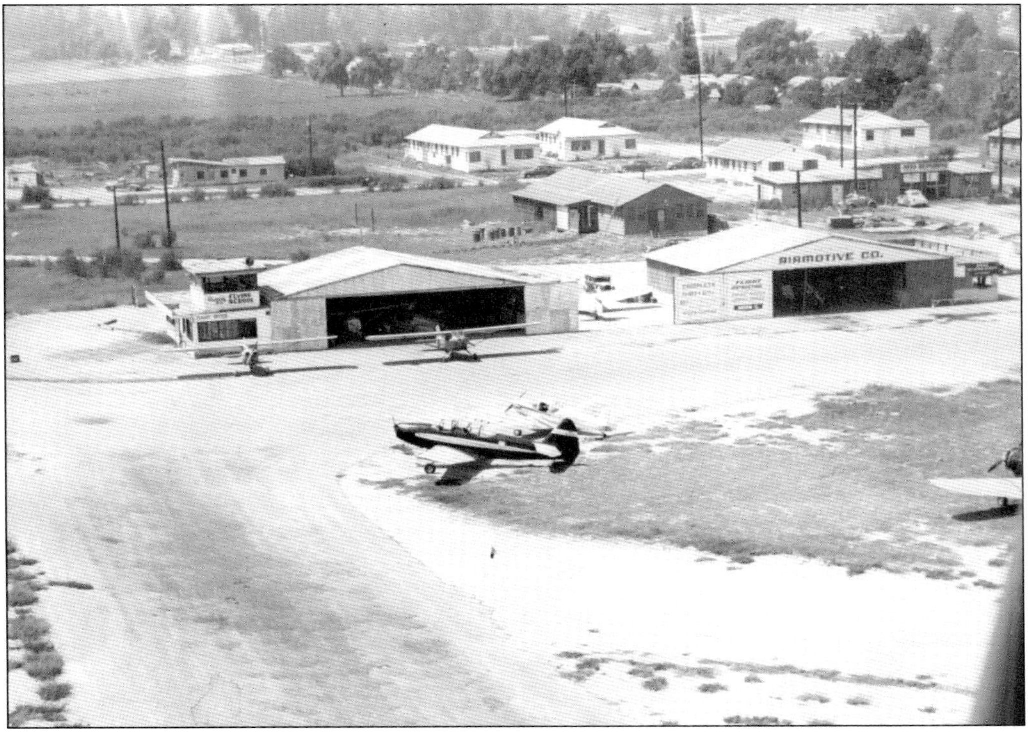

Automotive Company and Flying School. Flavio Madariaga ran a family operation at Flabob Airport. Several family members ran their own businesses on the airport property. This photograph is of Flavio's brother's Nugg's businesses. Nugg had both a flying school and an automotive business. This image was taken in 1948. (Courtesy Madariaga family.)

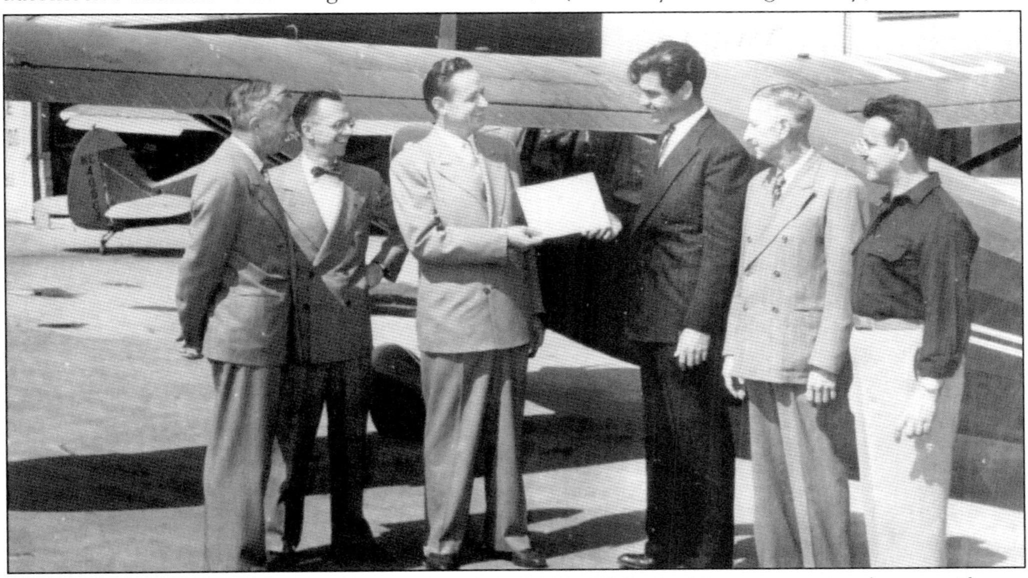

Airport Dedication. On September 30, 1949, Flabob Airport received a certificate naming it a "Skyway Airport." Cofounder Flavio Madariaga is third from the right. (Courtesy Flabob Airport.)

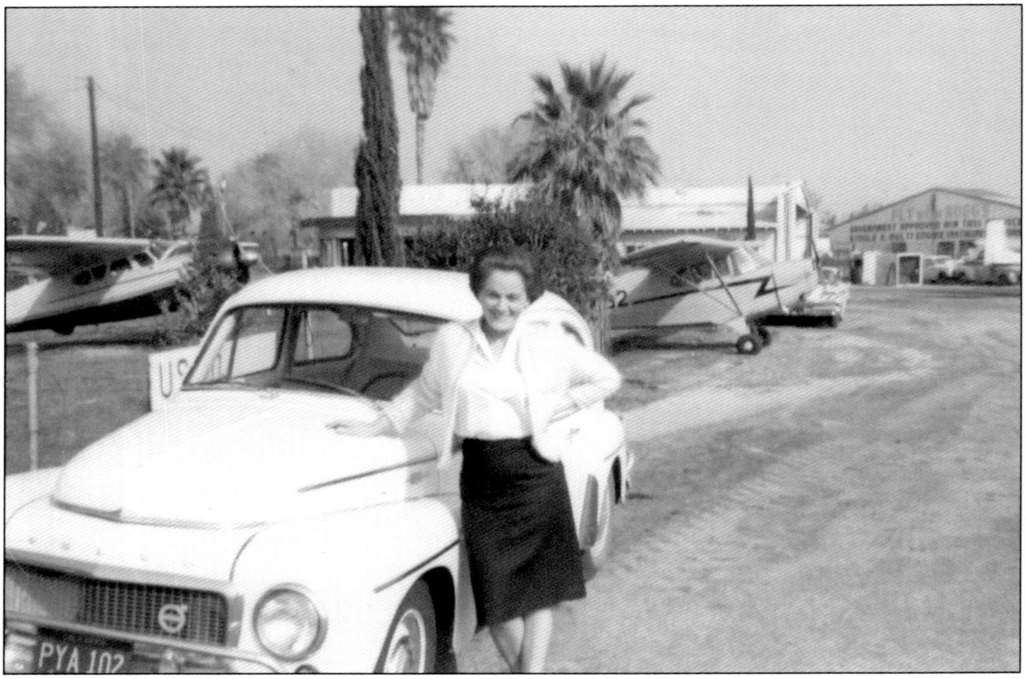

BERT MADARIAGA. Flavio's wife, who went by the nickname "Bert," is shown here at the airport in 1965. (Courtesy Madariaga family.)

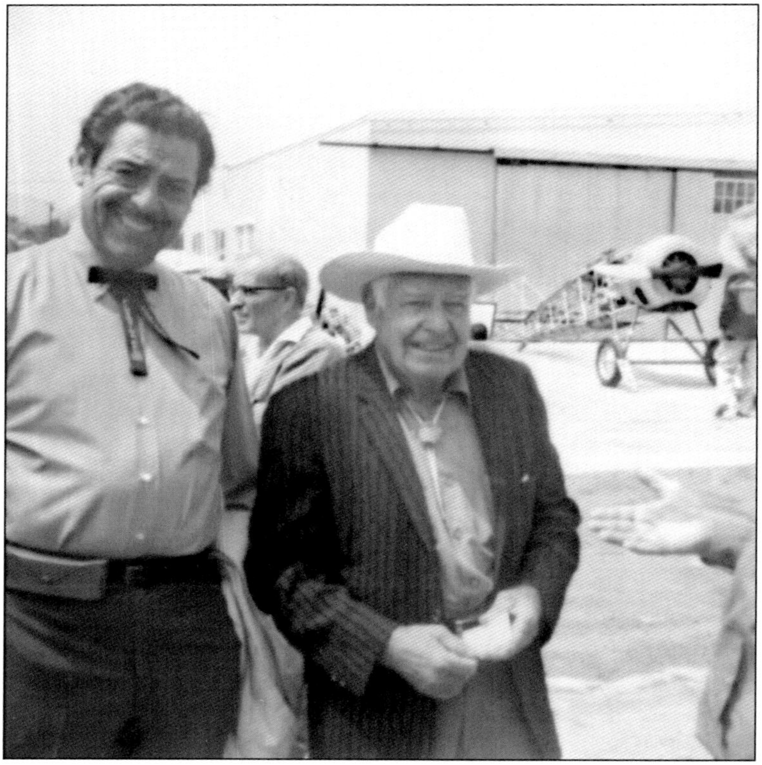

ROMAN WARREN DAY. Flavio Madariaga (left) and Roman Warren are pictured at Flabob Airport in the 1970s. Flavio had special days when he honored aviation pioneer Roman Warren. (Courtesy Madariaga family.)

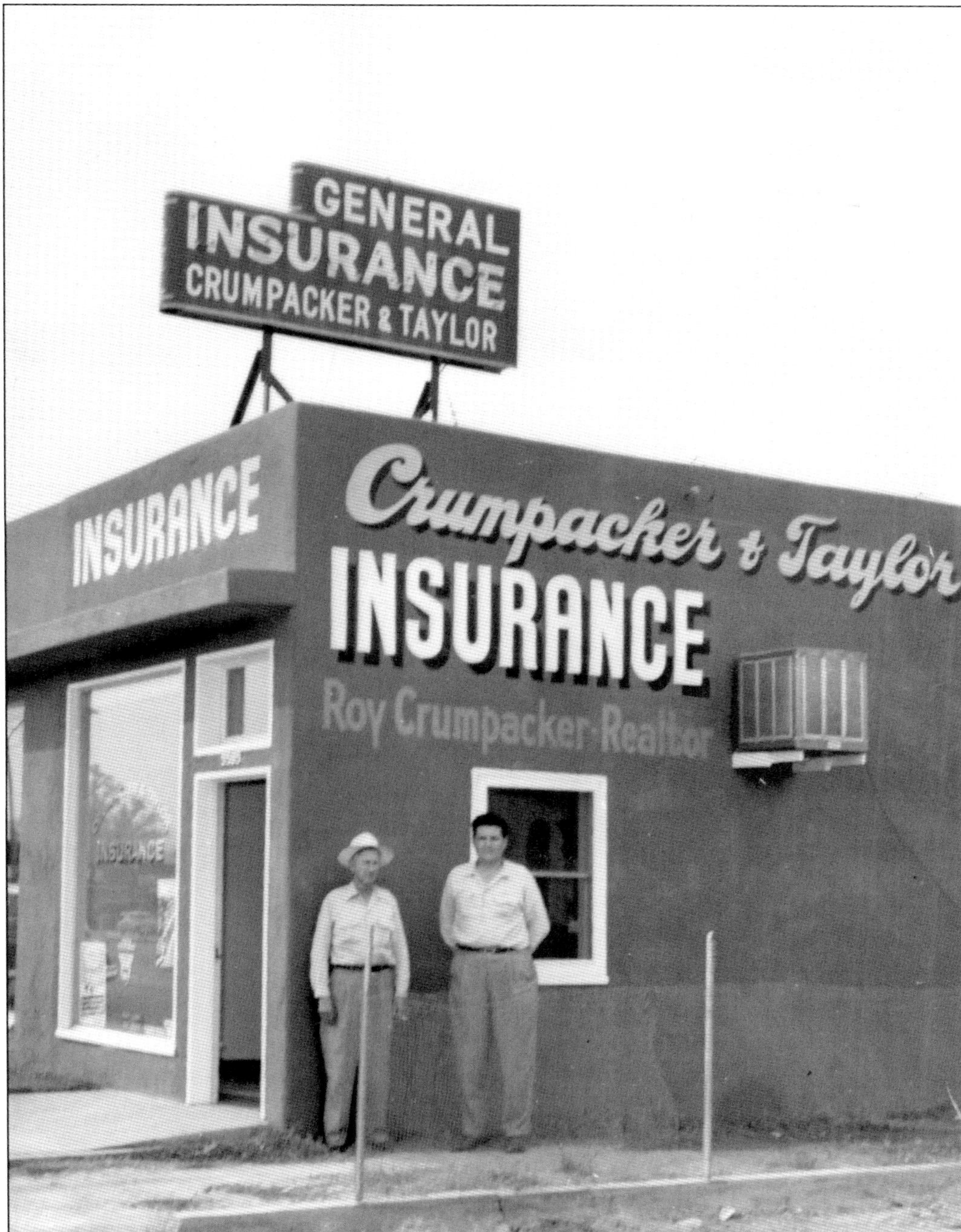

CRUMPACKER AND TAYLOR. Roy Crumpacker and his son-in-law Josh Taylor stand in front of their insurance and real estate office on Mission Boulevard *c.* 1947. The office was located where the parking lot of Stater Brothers Market is now found. (Courtesy Taylor family.)

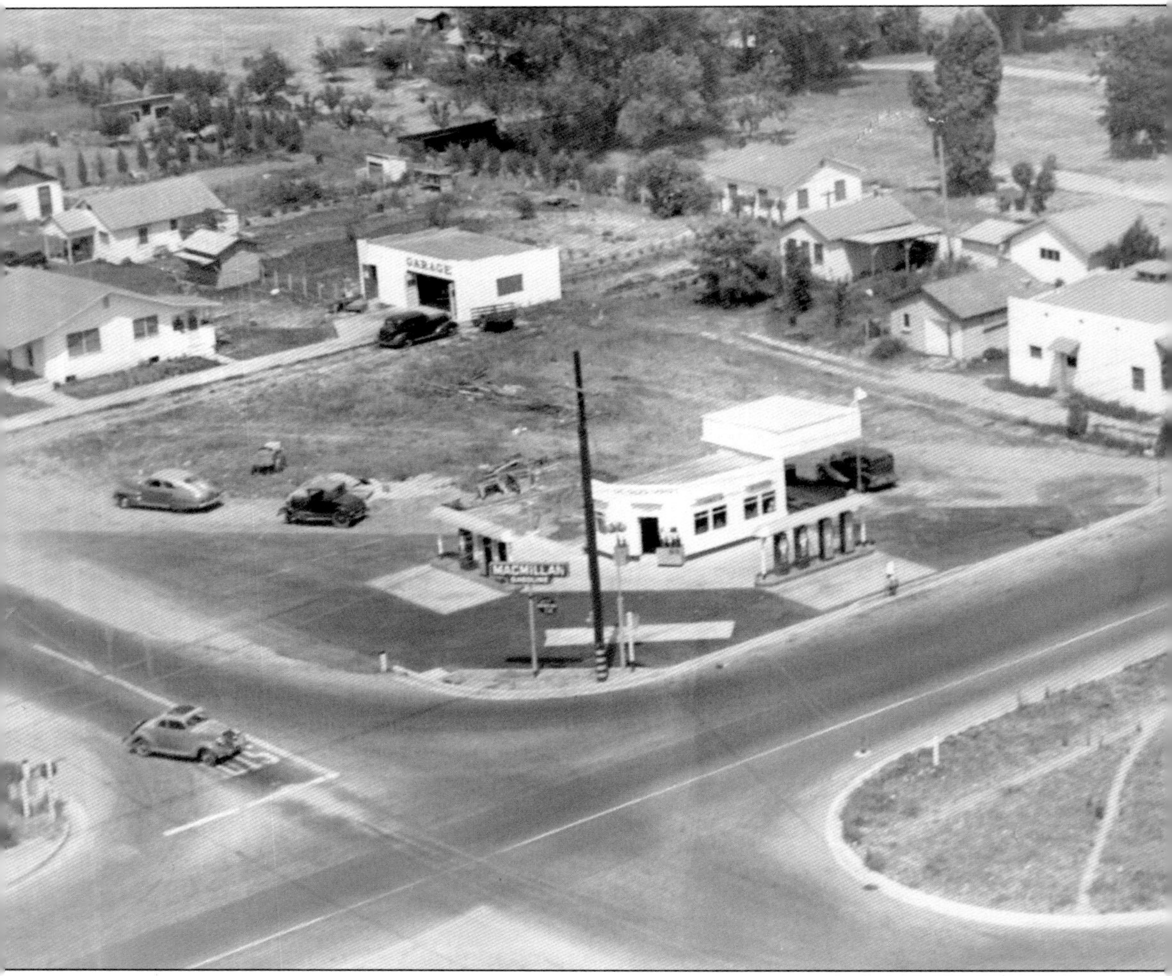

CORNER OF MISSION AND RUBIDOUX. This aerial photograph of the northeast corner of the intersection of Rubidoux Boulevard and Mission Boulevard is from 1945 or 1946. Mission is running along the bottom of the photograph. At the center of the image is the Lybarger Garage, purchased by the Lybarger family during World War II. The garage is still there today and is still run by the Lybarger family. In the center right of the photograph is El Rancho Cleaners, the white building facing Mission Boulevard. At the top center of the photograph, in the grove of trees, are the remnants of the Louis Rubidoux home and ranch buildings. (Courtesy Lybarger family.)

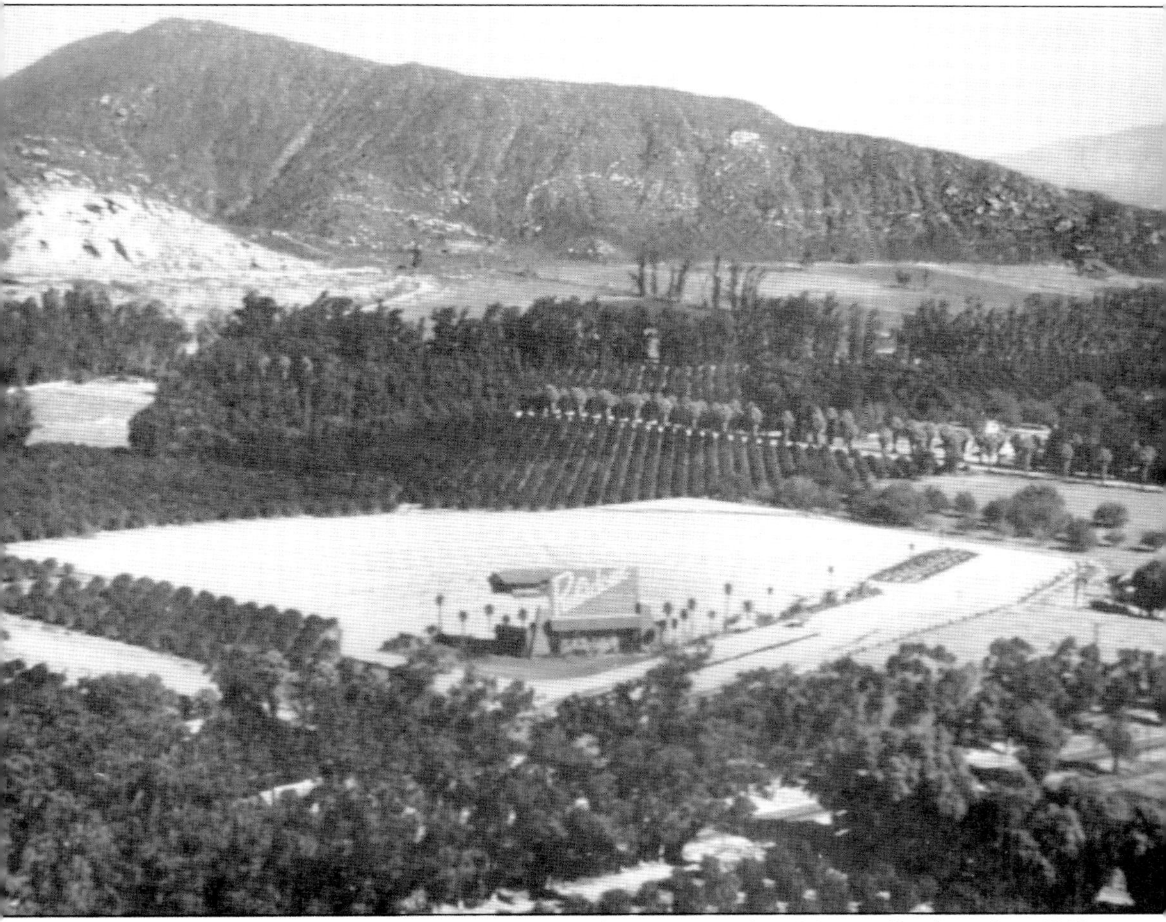

Rubidoux Drive-In. The Rubidoux Drive-In Theatre opened on Mission Boulevard in 1948 as the first drive-in in Riverside County. This aerial photograph, *c.* 1950, shows the drive-in surrounded by groves of fruit trees. Mission Boulevard, in the lower portion of the image, is still a two-lane road. The 60 Freeway had not been built yet. This first drive-in is now also one of the last in Riverside County. (Courtesy Mark Johnson.)

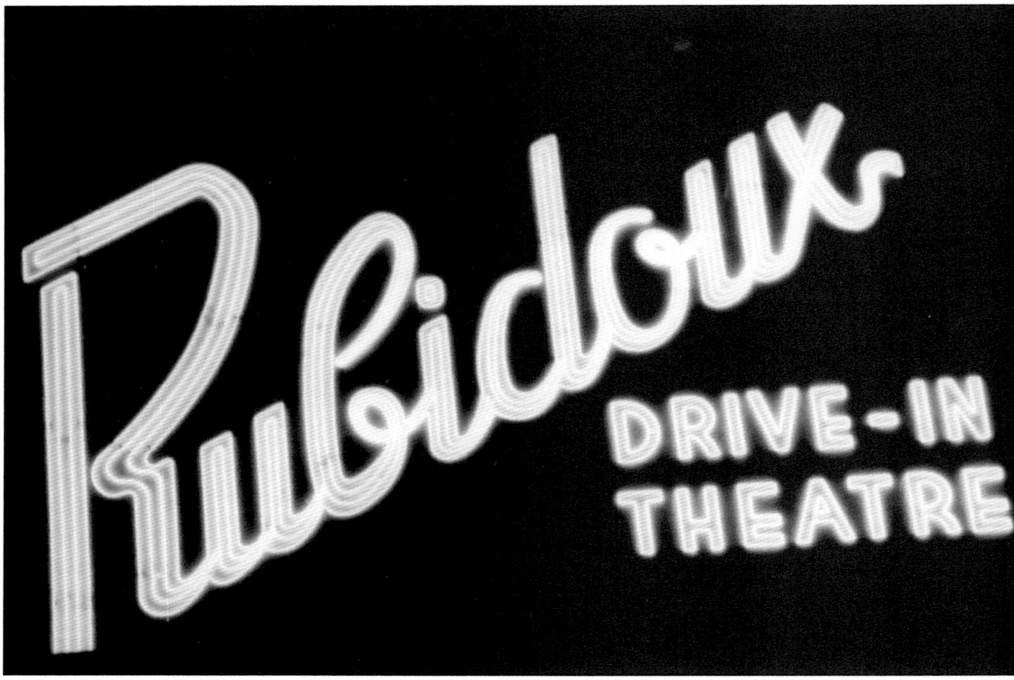

DRIVE-IN SIGN. Here the drive-in's name is spelled out in neon on the back of the large movie screen. (Courtesy Alice Brumgardt.)

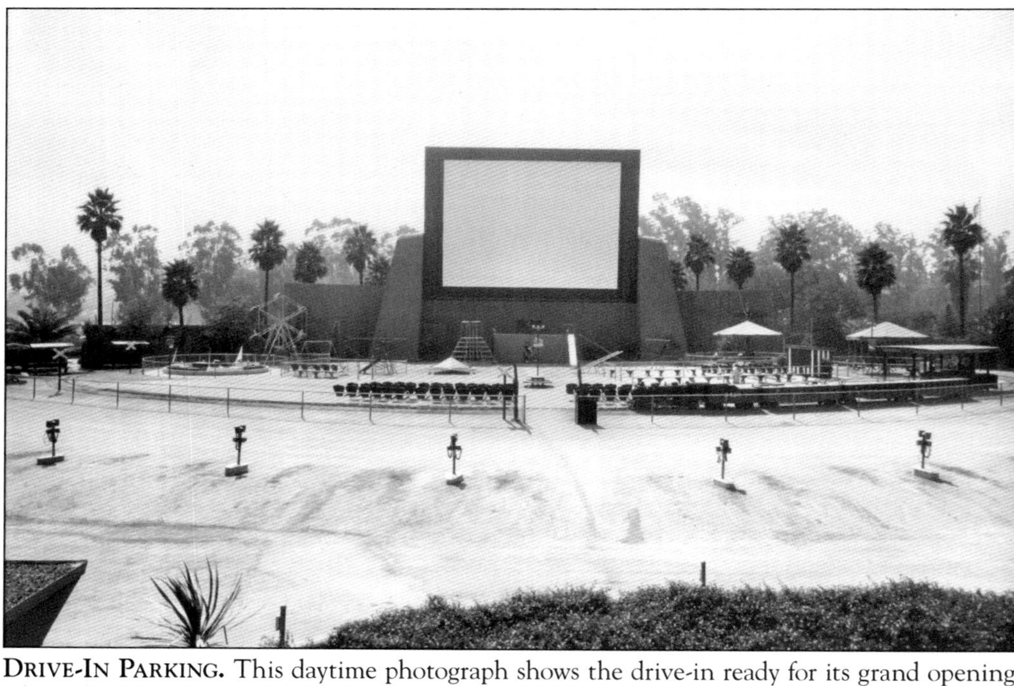

DRIVE-IN PARKING. This daytime photograph shows the drive-in ready for its grand opening. The poles in the lower portion of the image held the speakers for each car. Wings were later added to the original movie screen, shown here, in 1954 to accommodate cinemascope films (Courtesy Alice Brumgardt.)

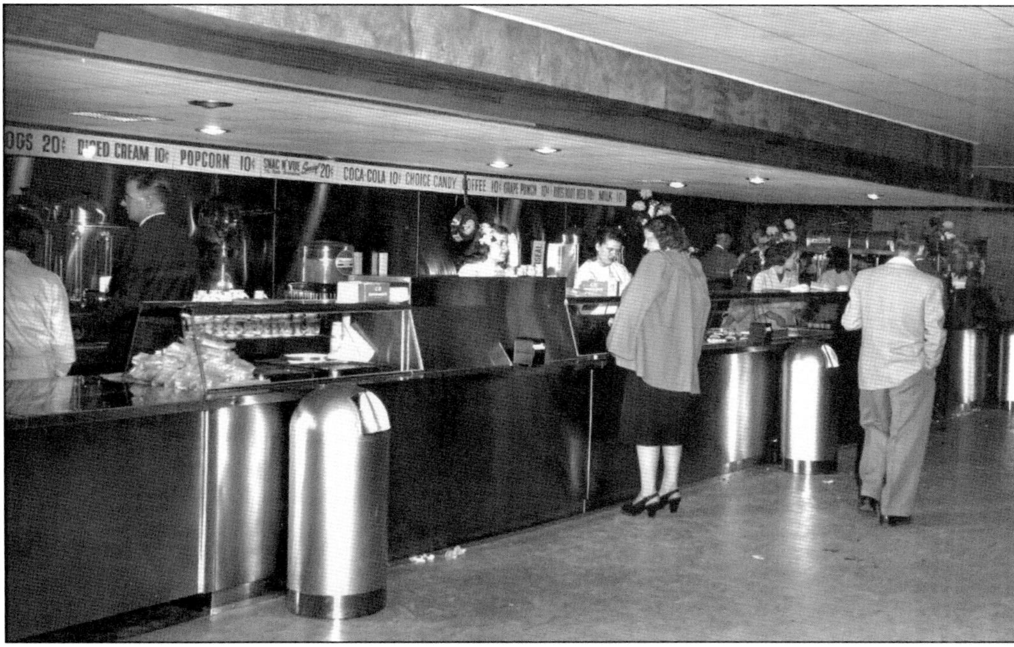

Snack Bar. The refreshment area included what a grand opening advertisement called a "new innovation for Drive-In Theaters," the Snac 'n' Vue Room that allowed you to continue to watch the movie while keeping the popcorn, drinks, and hot dogs out of your car (and off your upholstery). (Courtesy Alice Brumgardt.)

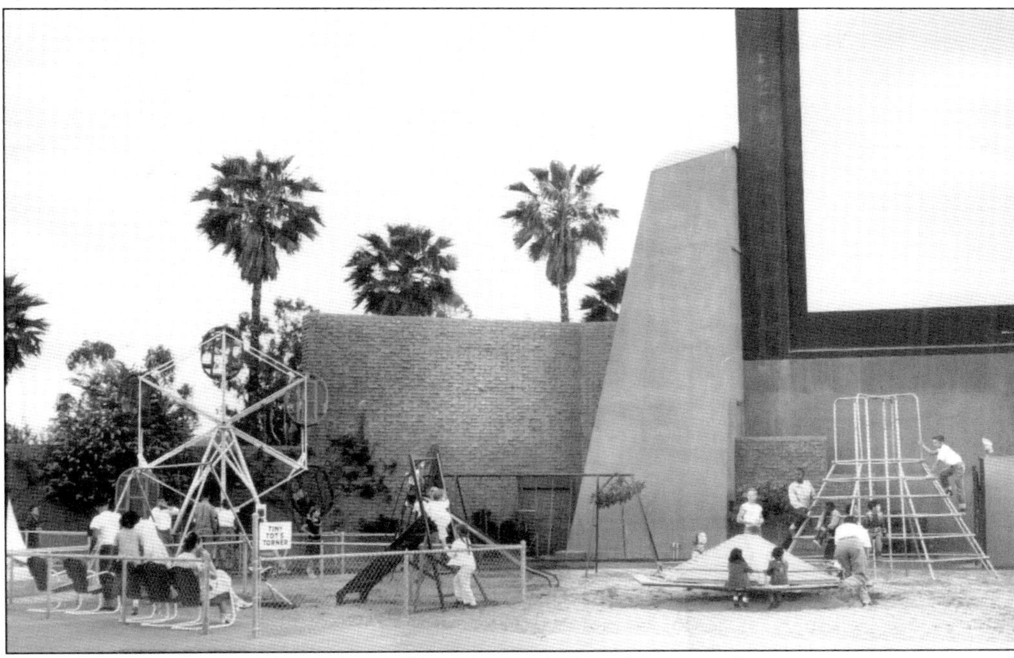

Amusement Area. To keep the children happy before the movie began, an amusement area with rides and attractions was installed at the base of the large movie screen, visible in the upper right corner of the photograph. (Courtesy Alice Brumgardt.)

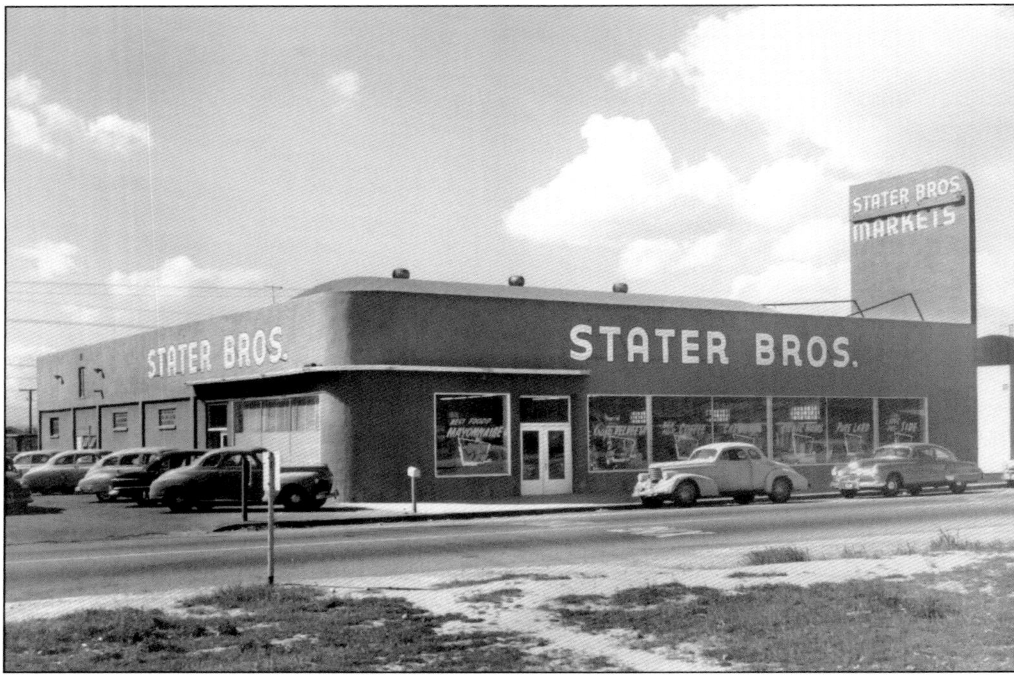

STATER BROTHERS MARKET. Stater Brothers opened their first "super" market, the sixth market in their chain, at the corner of Mission Boulevard and Pontiac Street in Rubidoux in April 1948. It was "super" because it had 12,500 square feet, fluorescent lighting, air-cooling, and an intercom system that played music. It was the only store to include an apartment above the market where part of the Stater family lived. (Courtesy Stater Brothers.)

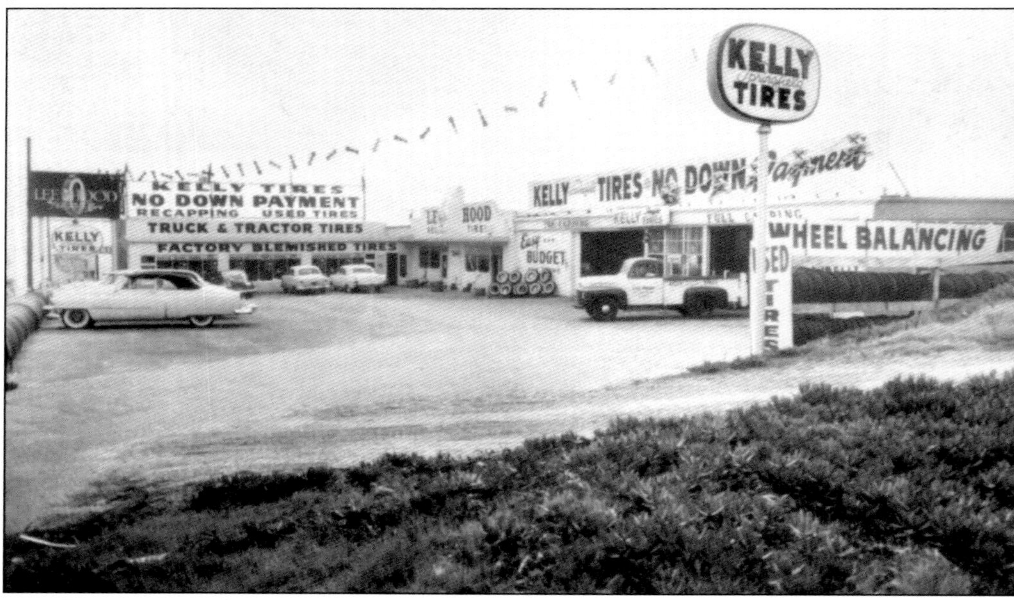

LEE HOOD TIRES. This tire sales and tire recapping business was located on Mission Boulevard near Riverview Drive from 1948 to 1965. This photograph was taken *c.* 1952. (Courtesy Hood family.)

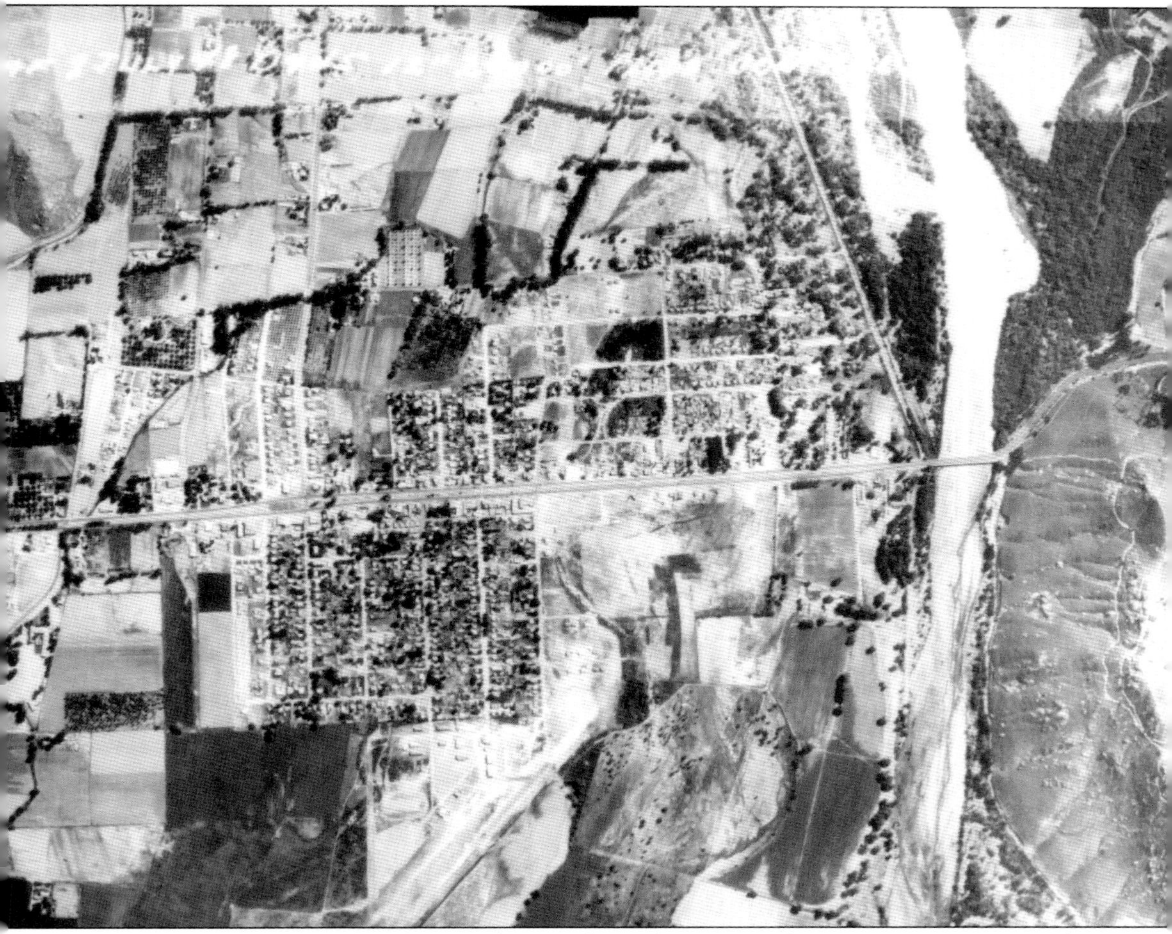

AERIAL PHOTOGRAPH. This photograph was taken July 8, 1948. The Santa Ana River is at the right of the image and Mount Rubidoux is in the lower-right corner. Mission Boulevard runs through the middle of the image. At that time, development came much closer to the river on the north side of Mission Boulevard than on the south side. (Courtesy Riverside County Flood Control and Water Conservation District.)

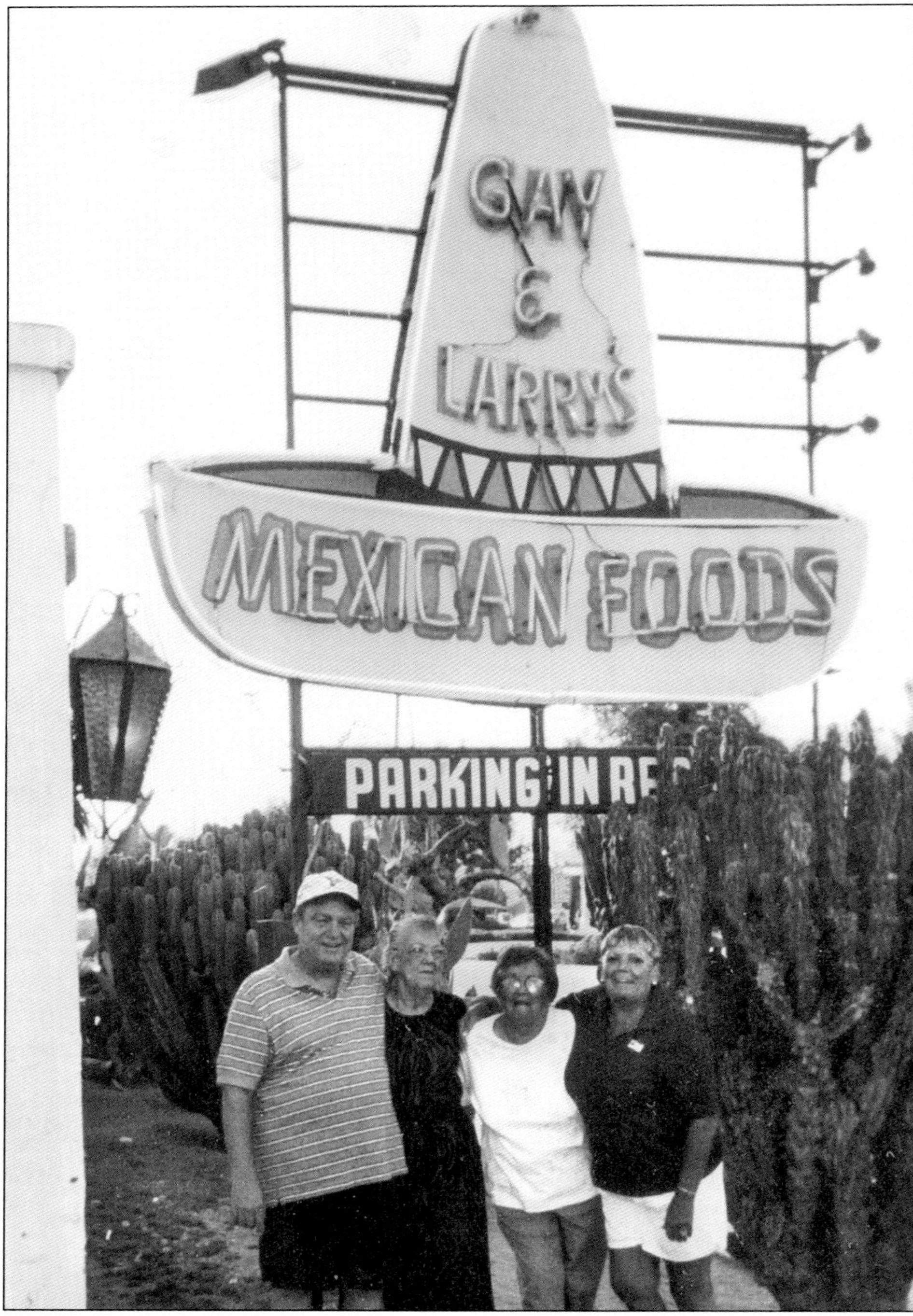

GAY AND LARRY'S. Opened in 1943 in Riverside, this well-known Rubidoux eating-place moved to Mission Boulevard in 1950 at the corner of Mission Boulevard and Fort Street. Its neon sombrero sign was a distinctive landmark in Rubidoux for many years. This image shows, from left to right, unidentified, owner Trudy Moller, longtime waitress Bea Leivas, and unidentified. (Courtesy Tiny Monfils.)

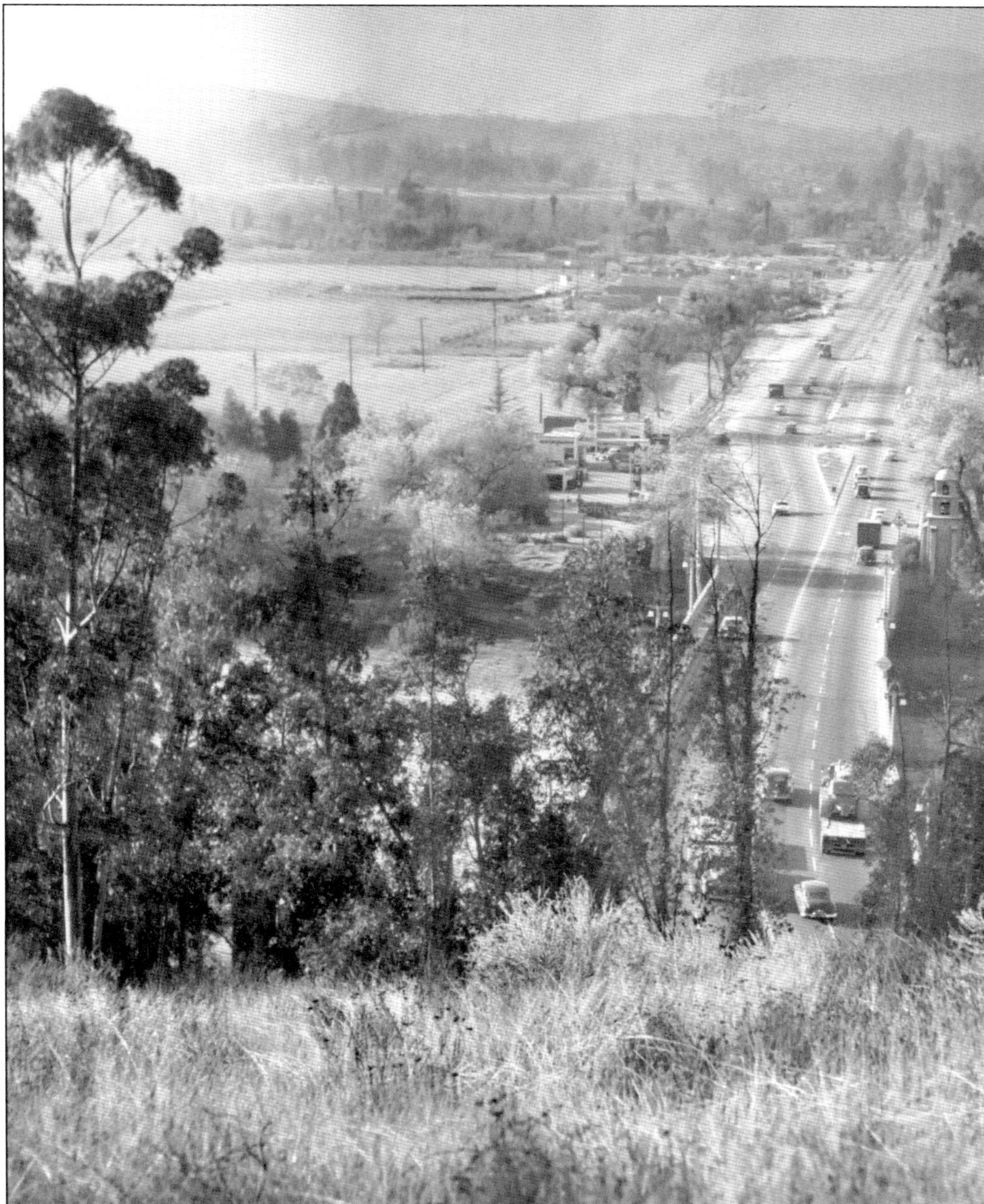

WEST RIVERSIDE. This view, *c.* 1950, shows West Riverside from Mount Rubidoux. As the highest point in the area and easily accessible because of a road carved up to its summit, Mount Rubidoux was the site of many pictures taken of West Riverside/Rubidoux. (Courtesy Jurupa Mountains Cultural Center.)

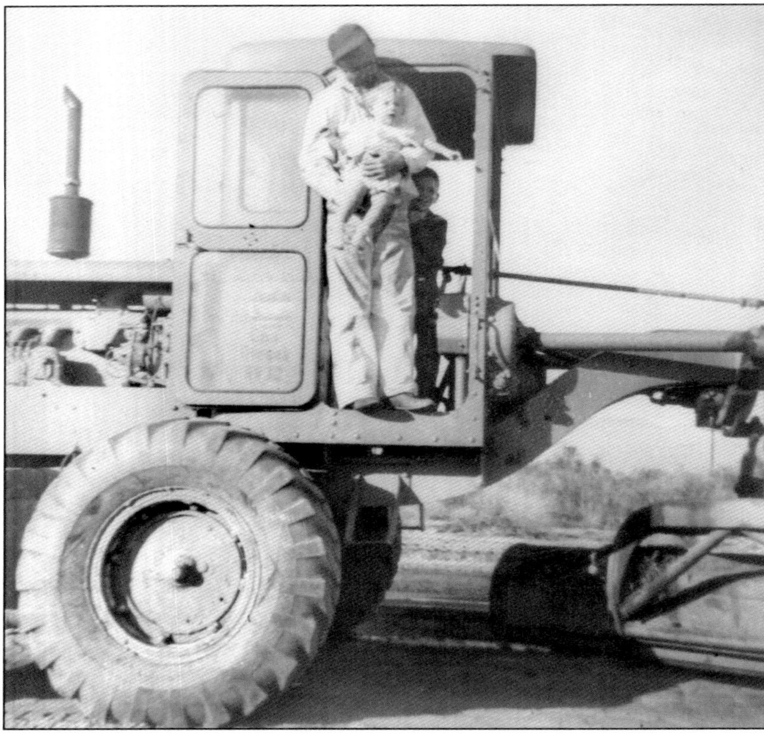

COUNTY ROAD GRADER. Claud "Shorty" Byrd is shown in 1952 with his daughter Claudia on a motor grader. Shorty worked for the County Road Department for many years and was involved with the improvement of many of Rubidoux's roads. (Courtesy Byrd family.)

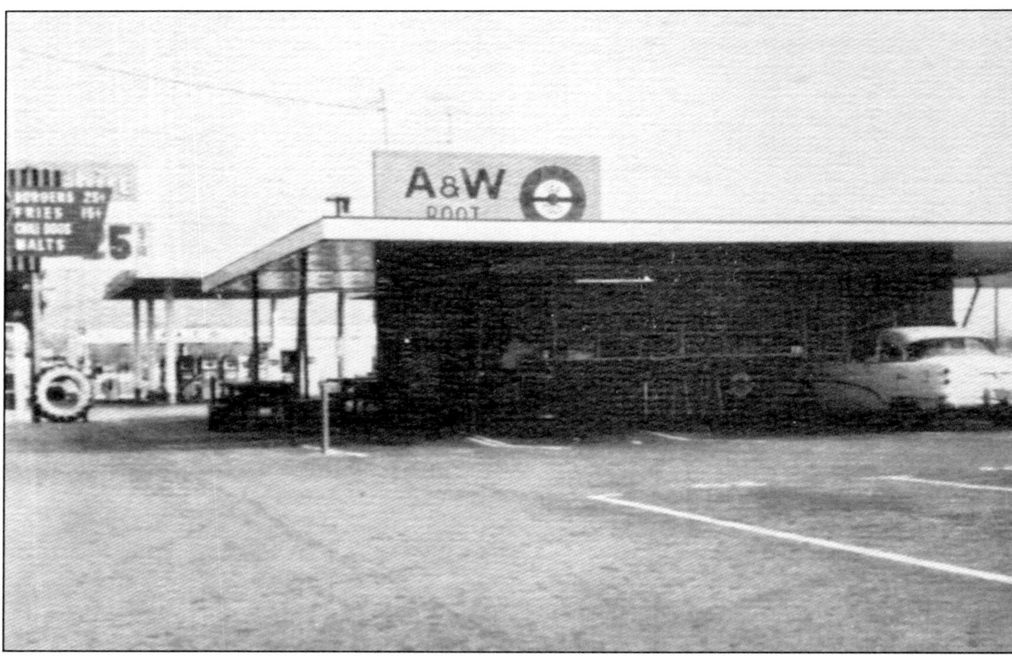

A&W ROOT BEER DRIVE-IN. Located on Mission Boulevard near the corner of Opal Street, this drive-in was a popular hangout. Note the prices on the sign—hamburgers were 25¢ and fries were 15¢. Behind the drive-in was a Texaco gas station. Its sign says gas could be purchased for 25.9¢ a gallon. This photograph of the drive-in was taken in 1960. (Courtesy Norton family.)

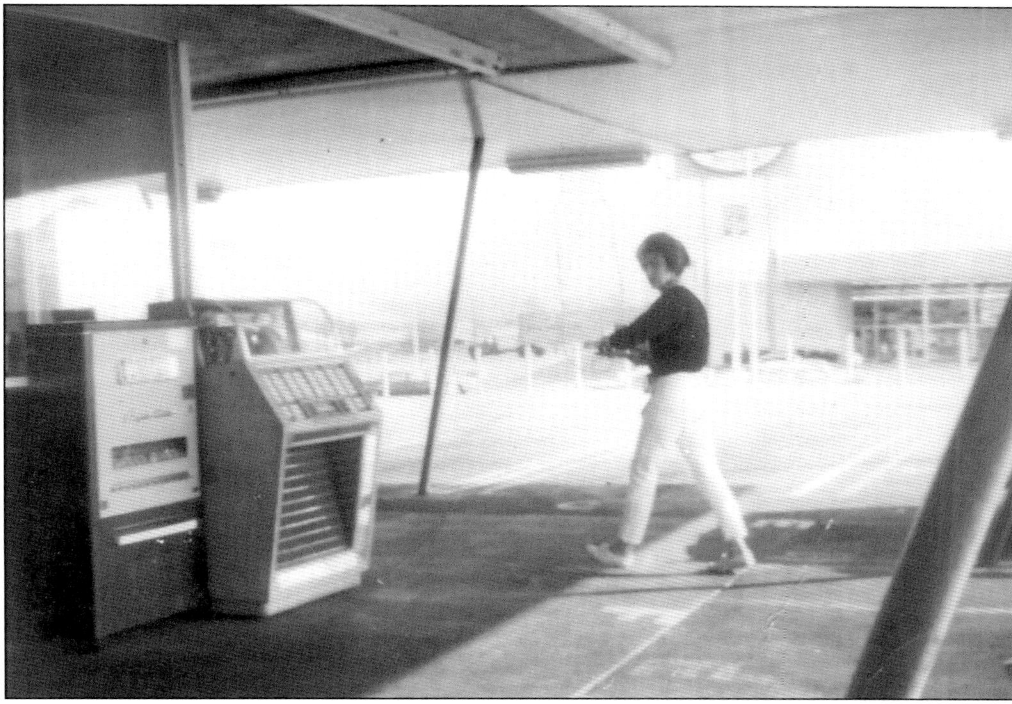

Drive-In. This image shows the A&W Drive-In in 1967. Note the jukebox and cigarette machine. In the rear of the photograph is the Alpha Beta grocery store. (Courtesy Tiny Monfils.)

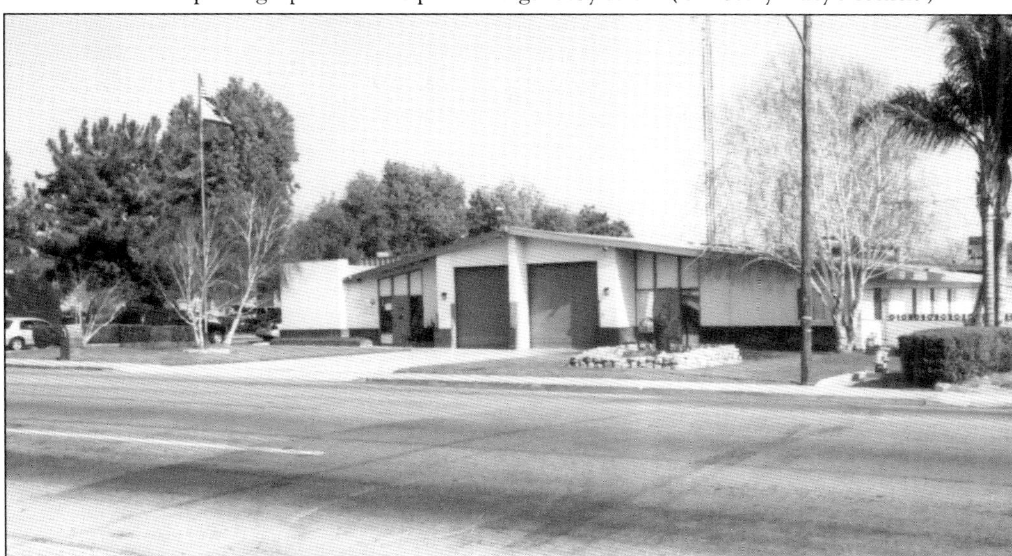

Rubidoux Community Services District. Established in 1952, Rubidoux Community Services District became the first services district in the state. It provides water, sewer, and fire protection services to a customer base that has grown from 4,000 to over 26,000. The district headquarters, shown, was built on Rubidoux Boulevard around the late 1950s. Until 2006, it housed both the district offices and the fire department. The fire department moved to a new building on Mission Boulevard at that time. (Courtesy author.)

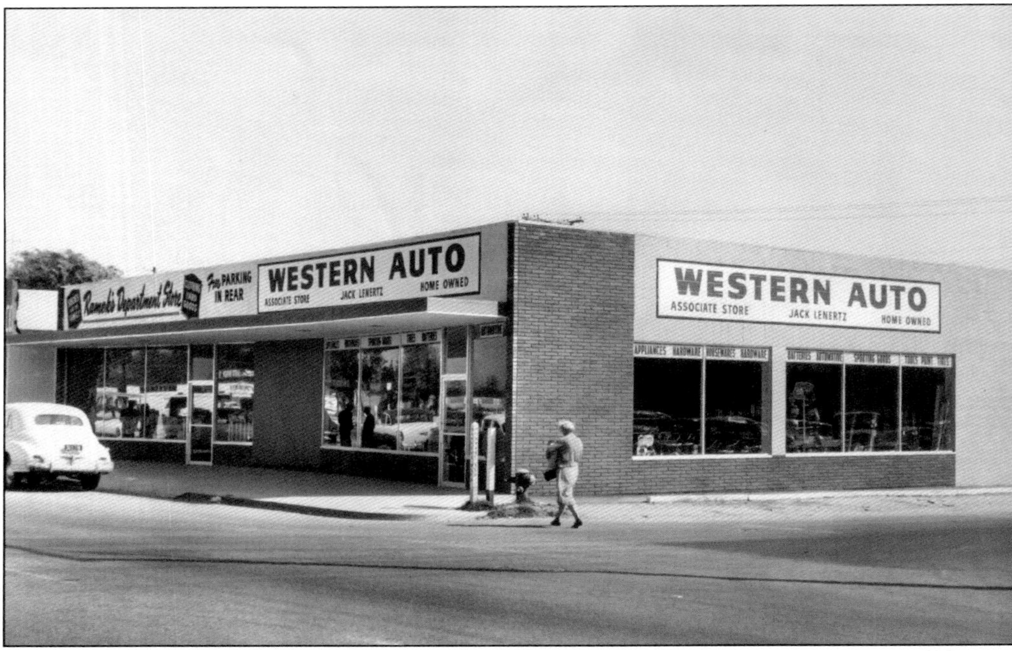

RUBIDOUX BUSINESSES, C. 1955. The above photograph shows Western Auto, a well-known business in downtown Rubidoux. It was located at the corner of Pontiac Avenue and Mission Boulevard. The image below shows the Rexall Center, which included a Rexall Drugstore and the Rubidoux Laundramatic. It was located near the corner of Packard Avenue and Mission Boulevard next to the Stater Brothers Market. While the businesses have long since disappeared, both buildings are still located in Rubidoux. (Courtesy Riverside Metropolitan Museum.)

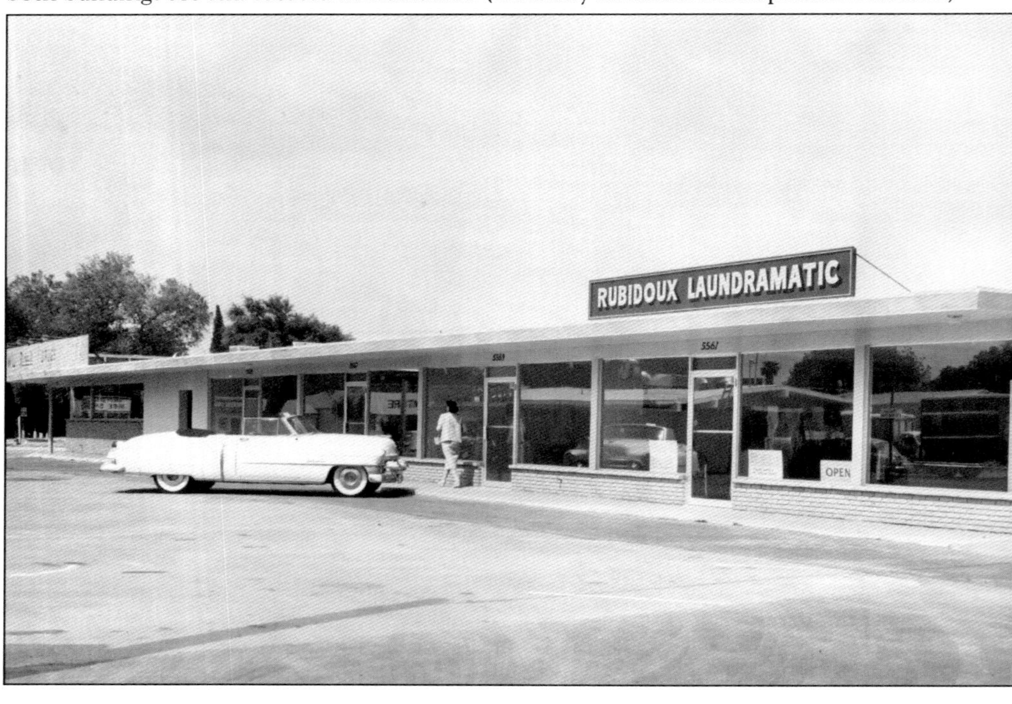

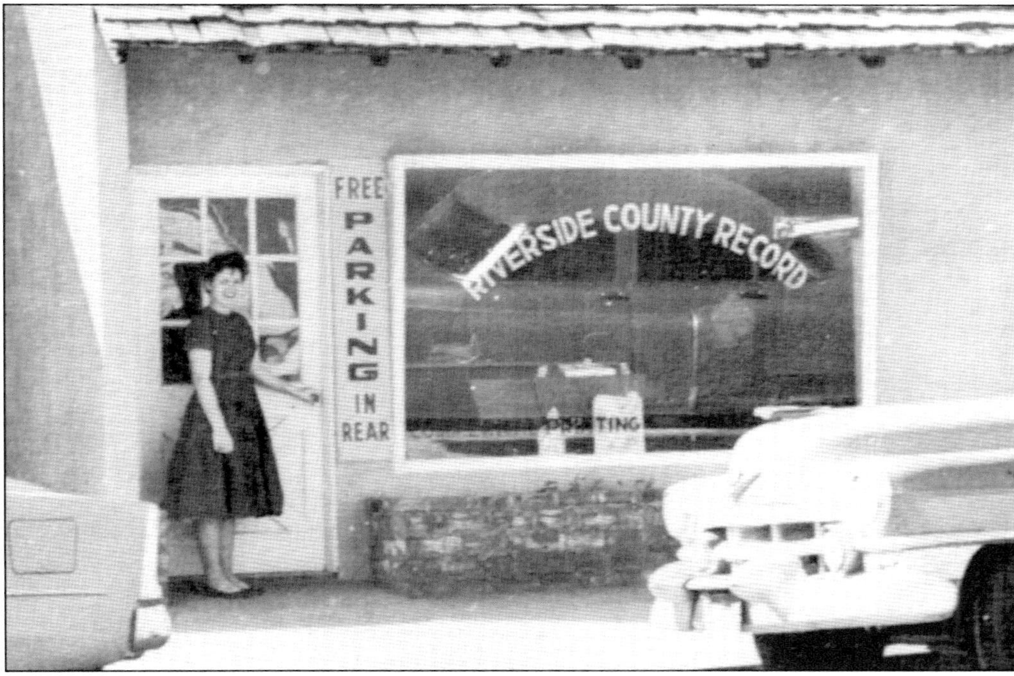

RIVERSIDE COUNTY RECORD. This 1960 photograph shows the offices of the *Record* newspaper, founded in 1955. The office was located on the south side of Mission Boulevard between Rubidoux Boulevard and Fort Drive. This weekly newspaper is still publishing the news of the Jurupa area. (Courtesy Norton family.)

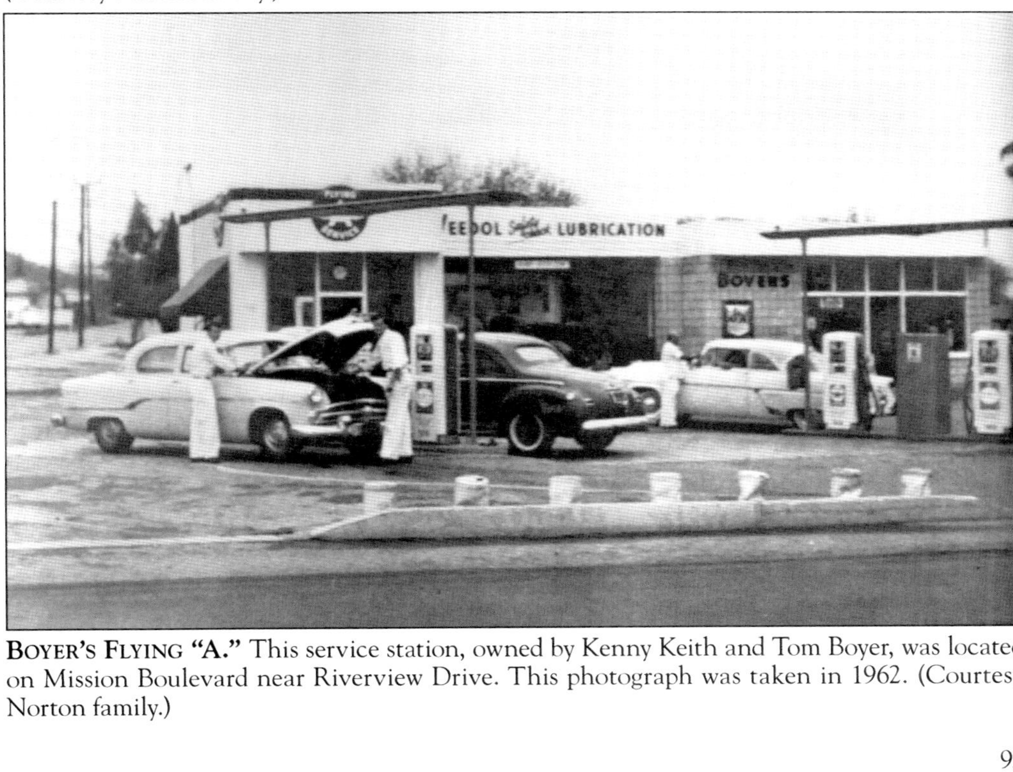

BOYER'S FLYING "A." This service station, owned by Kenny Keith and Tom Boyer, was located on Mission Boulevard near Riverview Drive. This photograph was taken in 1962. (Courtesy Norton family.)

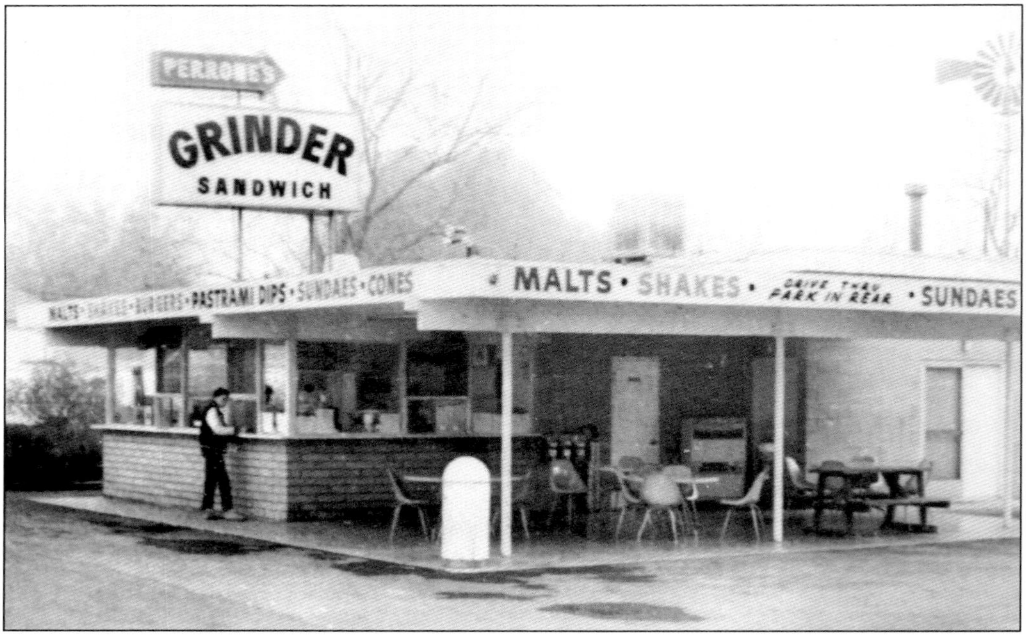

PERRONE'S GRINDER. Perrone's Grinder, located on the south side of Mission Boulevard between Pacific Avenue and Riverview Drive, opened in 1964. The owners, Tony and Helen Perrone, bought an old chicken ranch and had the restaurant built. Perrone's is still in its original location, under different ownership. (Courtesy Norton family.)

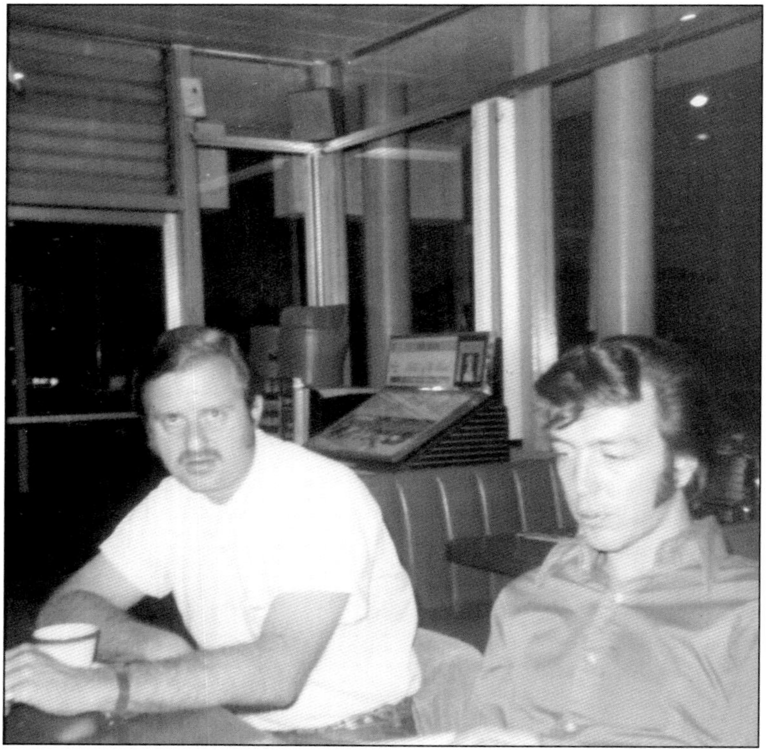

TIFFINY'S RESTAURANT. This 1969 photograph shows customers sitting at the counter of Tiffiny's Restaurant, located at Mission Boulevard and Pontiac Avenue. The restaurant is still there under a different name. (Courtesy Tiny Monfils.)

Six

Home Life

The story of home life in Rubidoux began as an isolated rancho home known for its hospitality and located at a crossroads for many travelers in inland Southern California. It slowly evolved as more and more people settled in the area. The area was always more rural, with many folks building their homes with their own hands. It wasn't unusual for adobe to be used, even in the 1920s and 1930s. Home life began to change in Rubidoux in the 1920s when subdivisions began dividing the land along Mission Boulevard, bringing many more people to Rubidoux. Outside of downtown Rubidoux, people usually owned larger plots of land, and farming was used to supplement the family income.

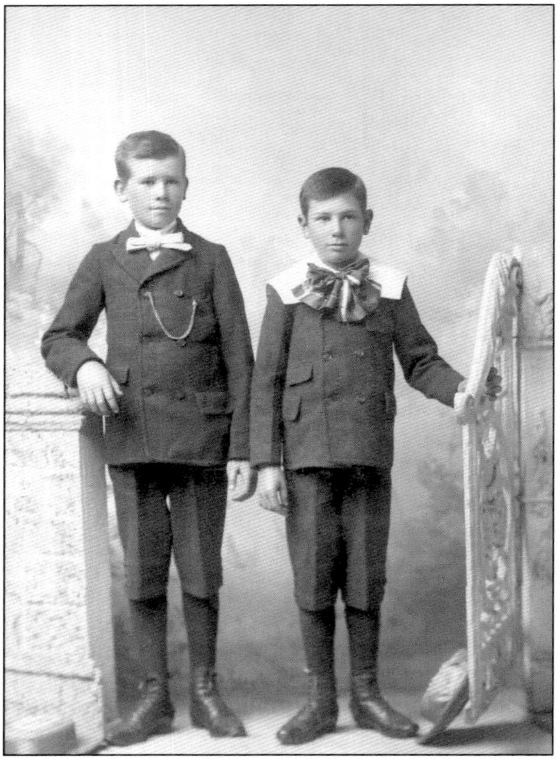

PARKS BOYS, C. 1897. Wallace Russell Parks (left) was born in 1886, and Archibald Gusdorf Parks was born in 1889 at the family home in Rubidoux. They were the children of Heber and Ida Parks. Their father was the son of early Rubidoux pioneer Arthur Parks. (Courtesy Riverside County Regional Park and Open-Space District.)

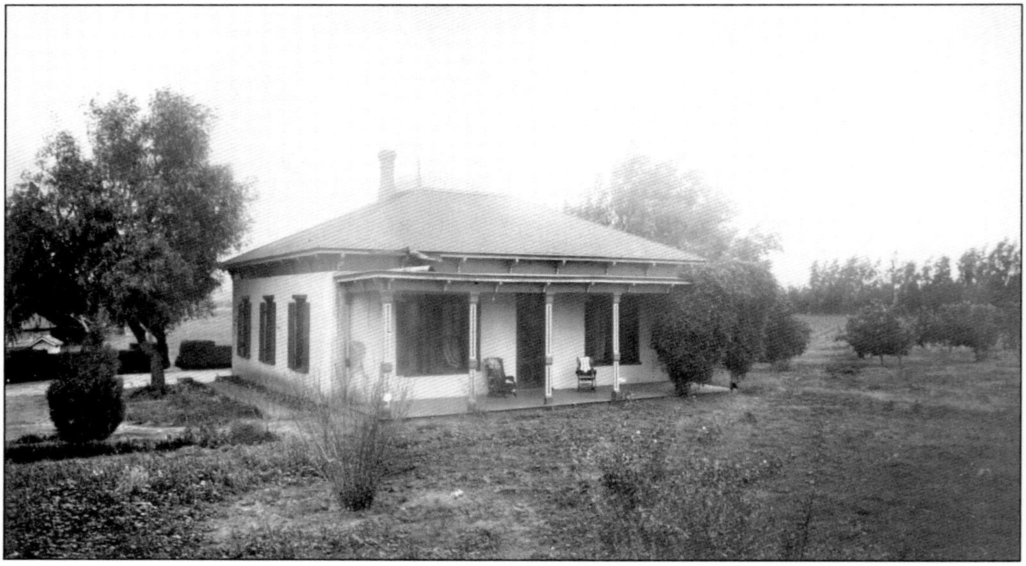

JOHN JENSEN HOME. John Jensen, the ninth child of Cornelius and Mercedes Jensen, married Emily Crowder in 1900. He built this wood-framed house on what is now Forty-second Street. During his lifetime, Forty-second Street didn't exist in that area. A dirt driveway from Riverview Drive accessed John's home. Later, when apartments were proposed for that property, John's home was moved to the Jensen-Alvarado Historic Ranch and Museum where it serves as the caretaker's home. (Courtesy Jensen family.)

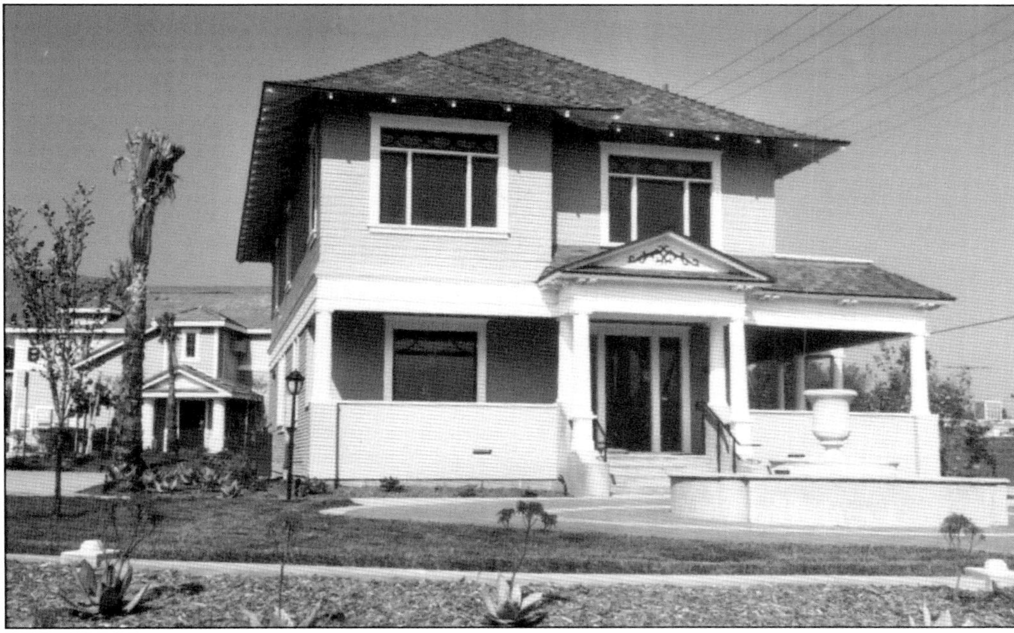

MISSION BOULEVARD HOME. G. Stanley Wilson is said to have built this home at 5841 Mission Boulevard in 1905. Wilson is famous for later being the architect of the Mission Inn Rotunda. The home has been preserved as part of the Mission Palms Apartments, a senior apartment complex. (Courtesy author.)

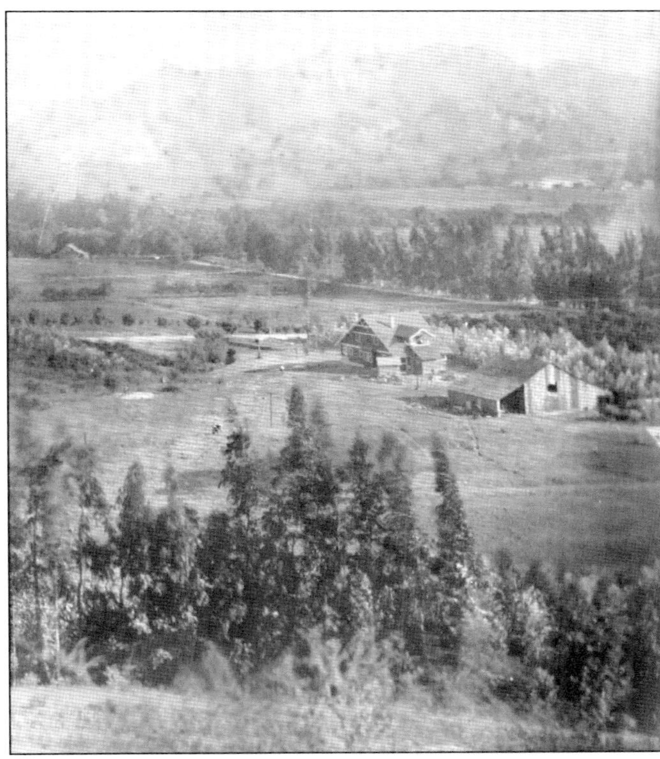

HEBER AND IDA PARKS RESIDENCE, C. 1909. The Parks family built this house in 1908. It is still located at the corner of Avalon and Alta Streets. This view is of the rear of the home, taken from the slope of Rattlesnake Mountain. In the distance is Mount Rubidoux and what would later become downtown Rubidoux. (Courtesy Riverside Metropolitan Museum.)

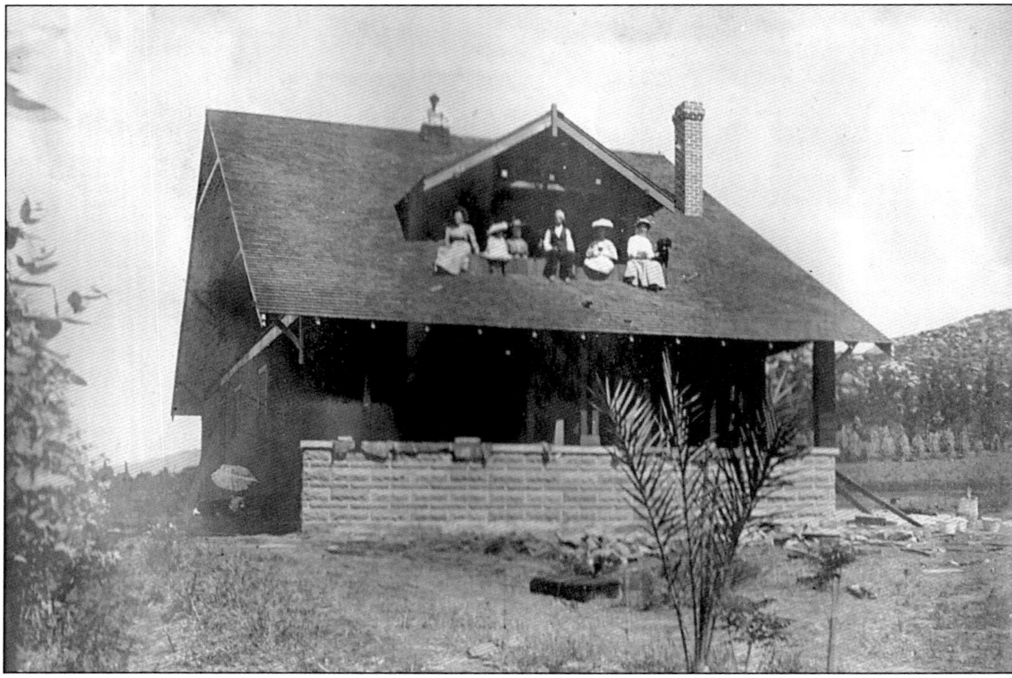

Parks Residence, 1909. This photograph was found in a Parks family scrapbook with no explanation why everyone was on the roof! (Courtesy Riverside Metropolitan Museum.)

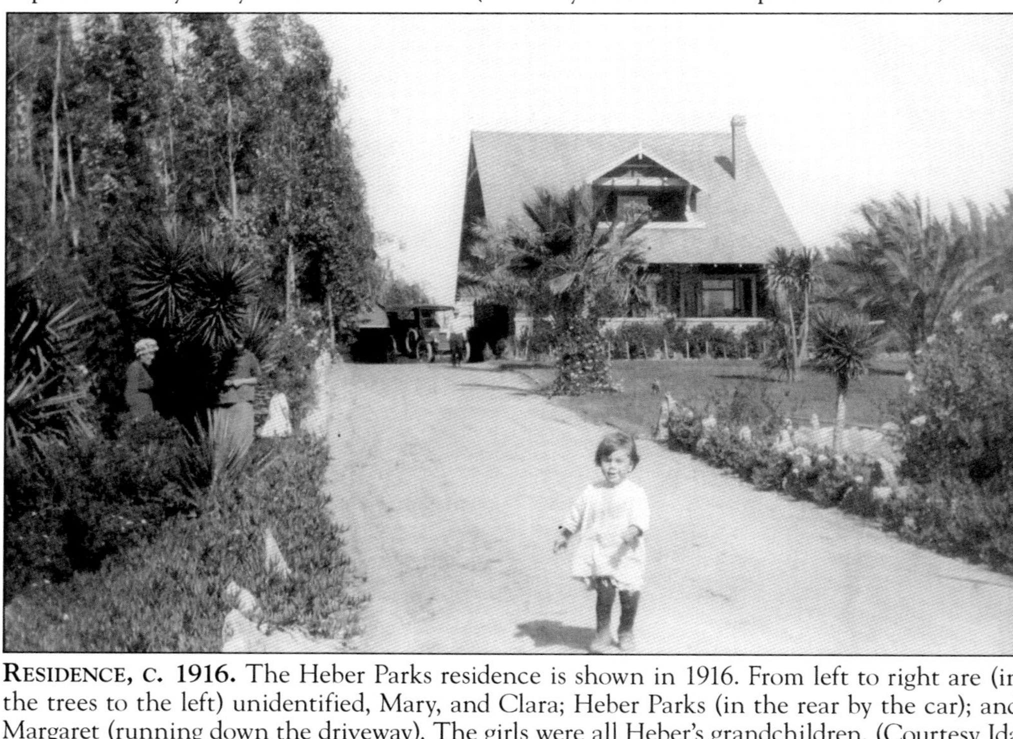

Residence, c. 1916. The Heber Parks residence is shown in 1916. From left to right are (in the trees to the left) unidentified, Mary, and Clara; Heber Parks (in the rear by the car); and Margaret (running down the driveway). The girls were all Heber's grandchildren. (Courtesy Ida Parks Condit family.)

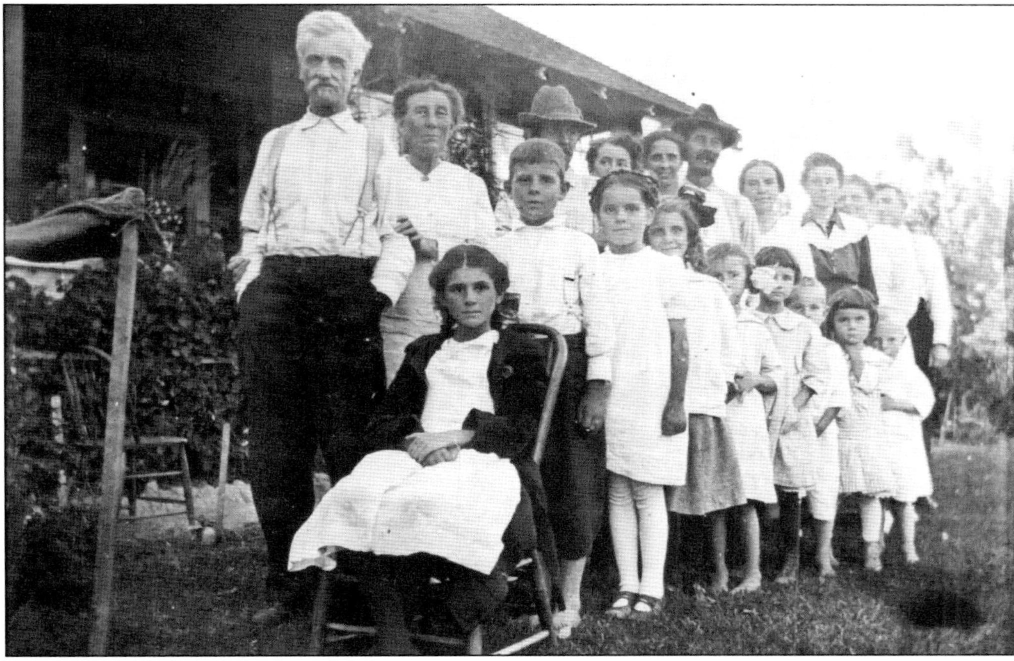

PARKS FAMILY, 1917. Heber and Ida Parks are shown in the back row with their children. The front row includes the grandchildren. Pictured from left to right are (first row) Dorothy, Arthur, Ida, Gladys, Clara, Hazel, Myron, Margaret, and George W.; (second row) Heber, Ida, George, Gertrude, Lula, Elmo, Ethel, Mary S., Mary W., and Frank Paddock. (Courtesy Riverside Metropolitan Museum.)

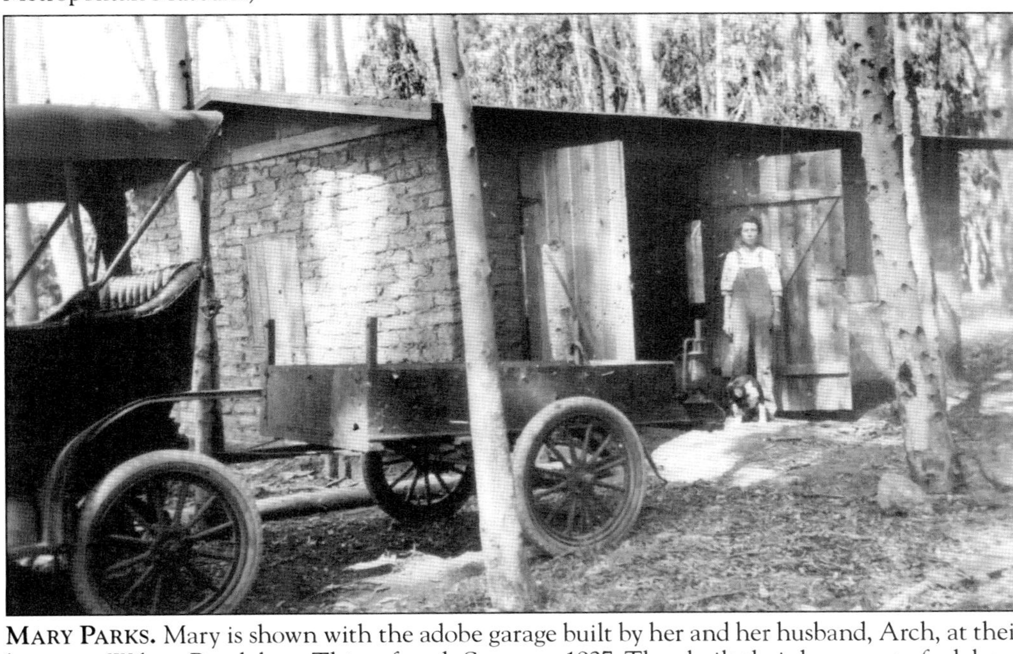

MARY PARKS. Mary is shown with the adobe garage built by her and her husband, Arch, at their home on Wilson Road, later Thirty-fourth Street, *c.* 1927. They built their home out of adobe as well. (Courtesy Richard Nyman.)

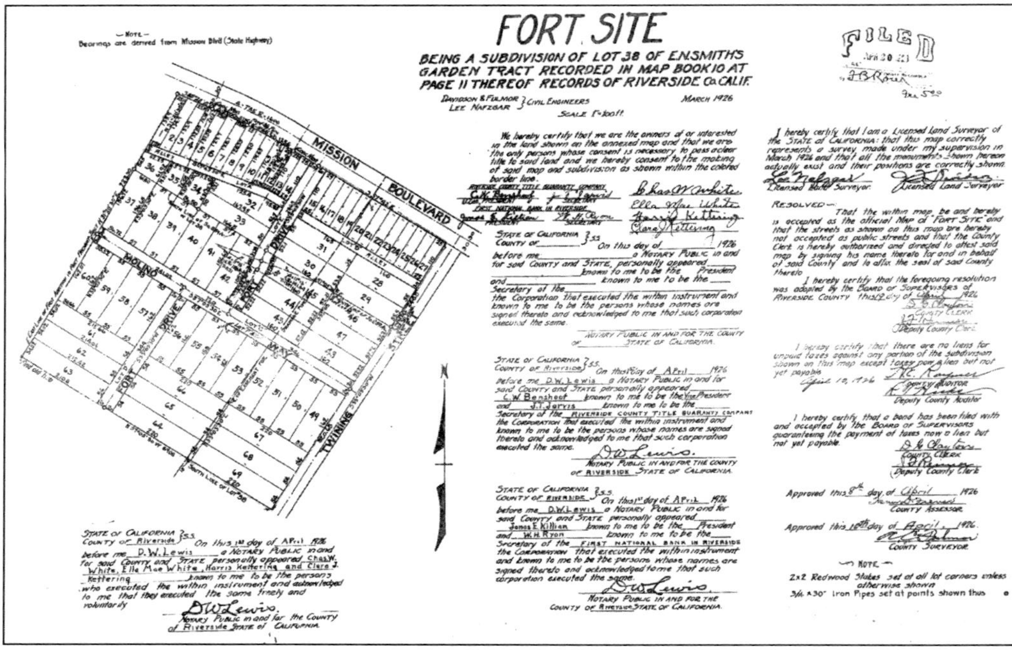

Early Rubidoux Subdivisions. These are two of the earliest residential subdivisions in downtown Rubidoux, resulting in that area changing from a large-lot agricultural area to a small-lot business and residential area. Rubidoux's location near downtown Riverside made it an ideal place for people who wanted a less expensive building site. The Fort Site subdivision was on the south side of Mission Boulevard and was filed in April 1926. The Wilcox Square subdivision was on the north side of Mission Boulevard and was filed in April 1927. (Courtesy author.)

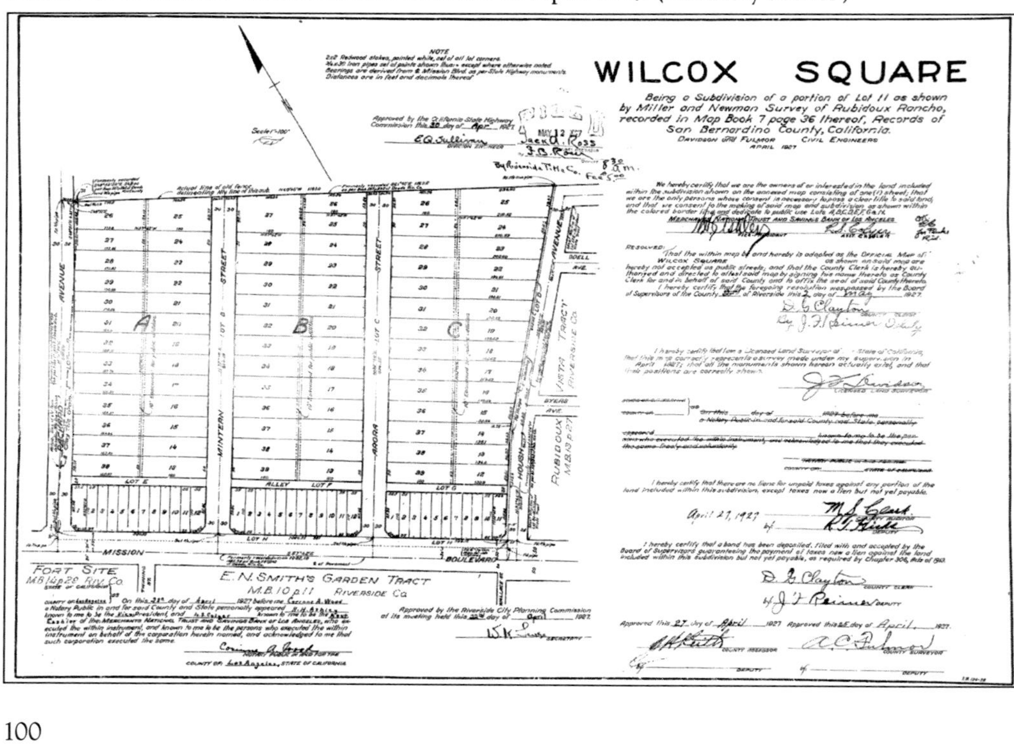

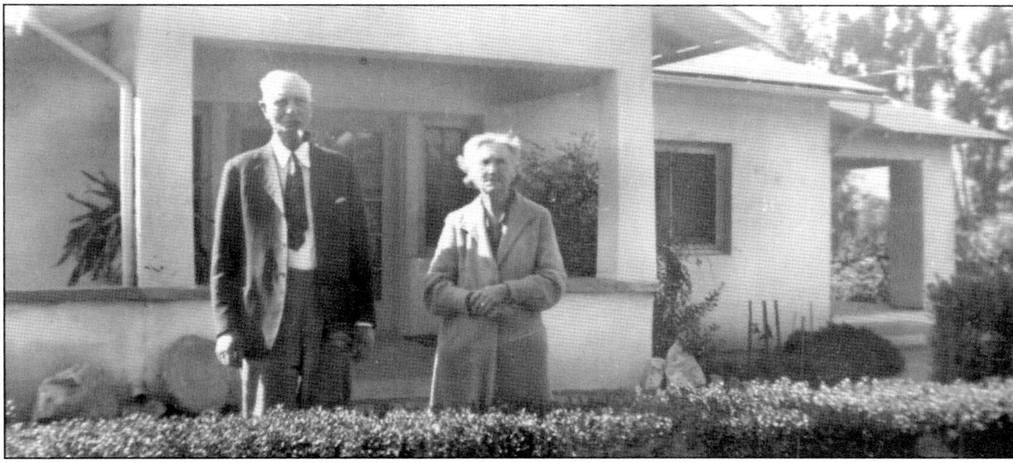

Fairbanks Avenue Home. John and Sarah Walker are shown in front of their adobe home on Fairbanks Avenue. This photograph was taken in February 1942. (Courtesy Anita Walker Blount.)

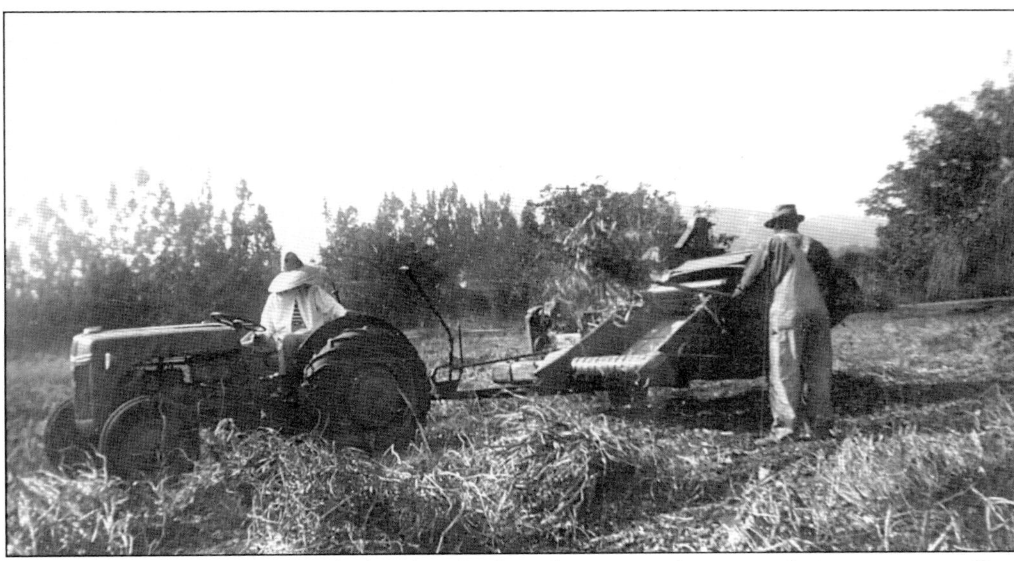

Harvesting Beans. Inez and Theodore Peck are harvesting beans on their property on Opal Street in 1944. Many people in the Rubidoux area had large lots where they could grow crops and/or keep animals to supplement the family income. (Courtesy Don Peck.)

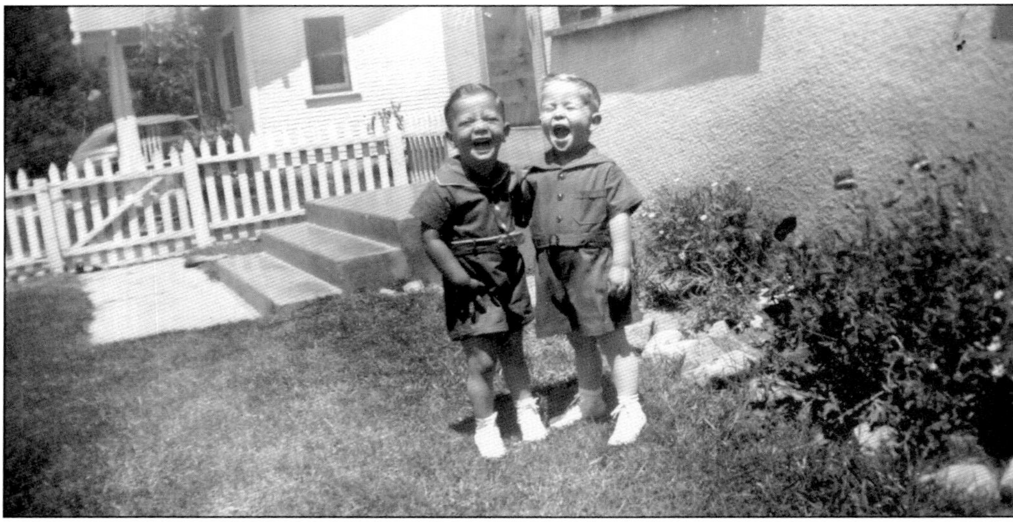

HAPPY BOYS. Toby Dickinson (left) and his cousin Tinky McClure are shown in the front yard of Toby's house on Twinning Street in 1945. (Courtesy Ruby Dickinson.)

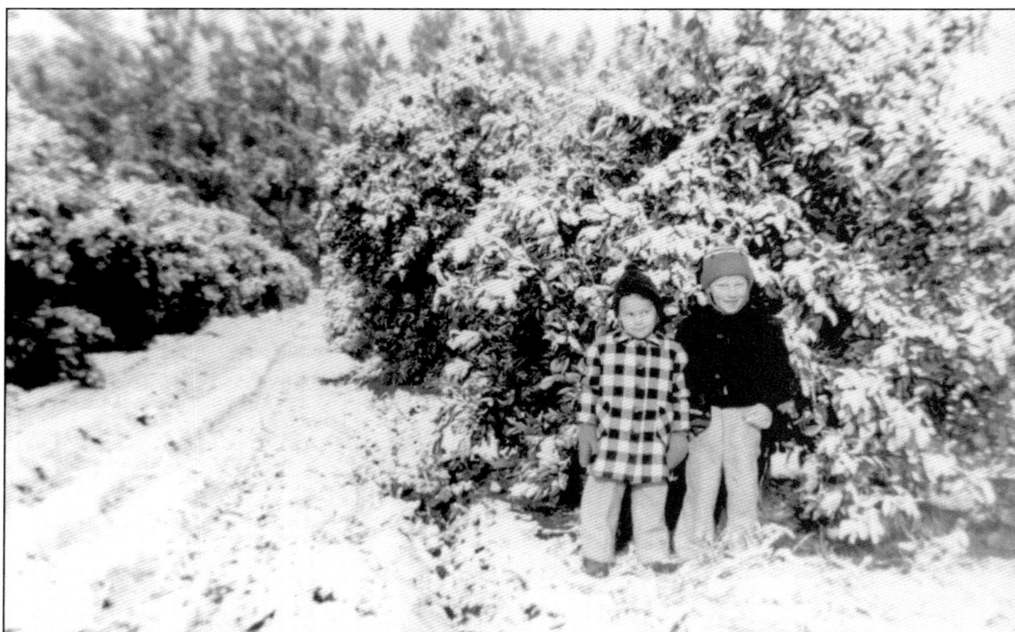

SNOWY ORANGE GROVE. Martha and Don Peck are standing in the family orange grove on Opal and Forty-fifth Streets in January 1949 during a rare Rubidoux snowstorm. The orange grove was already planted when the family bought the property and probably dated to the early 20th century. (Courtesy Don Peck.)

THE ARBUCKLES. J. E. and Ina Arbuckle are shown in the front yard of their home on Mintern Street in Rubidoux. Ina, a longtime teacher in the Jurupa area, is the namesake for a Rubidoux elementary school. (Courtesy Ina Arbuckle School.)

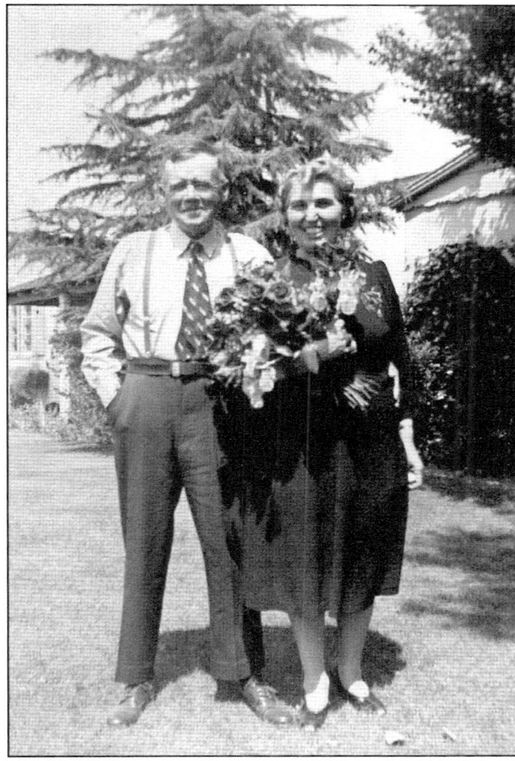

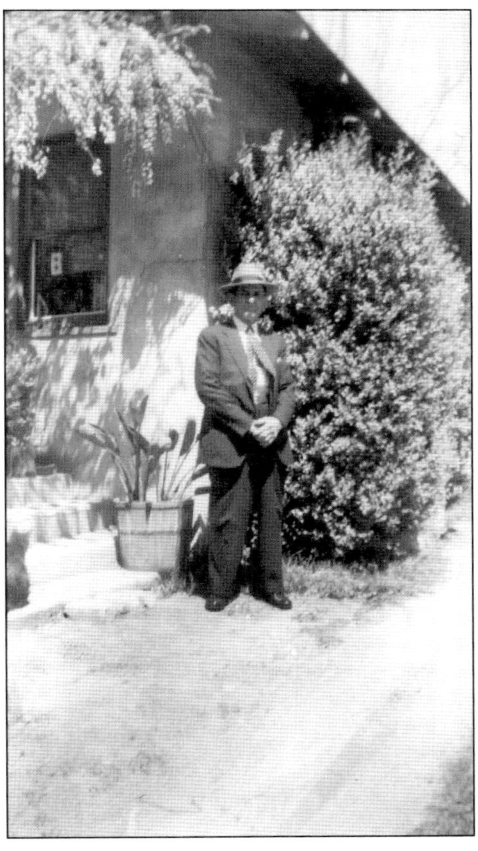

BLUE STAR FATHER. William Engelauf is shown in front of his home on Thirty-fourth Street during World War II. Hanging in the window to the left is a small white flag. During the war, families hung these flags in their windows to show how many sons they had serving in the war. The Engelaufs had two sons serving, so their flag had two stars. (Courtesy Engelauf/Flowers families.)

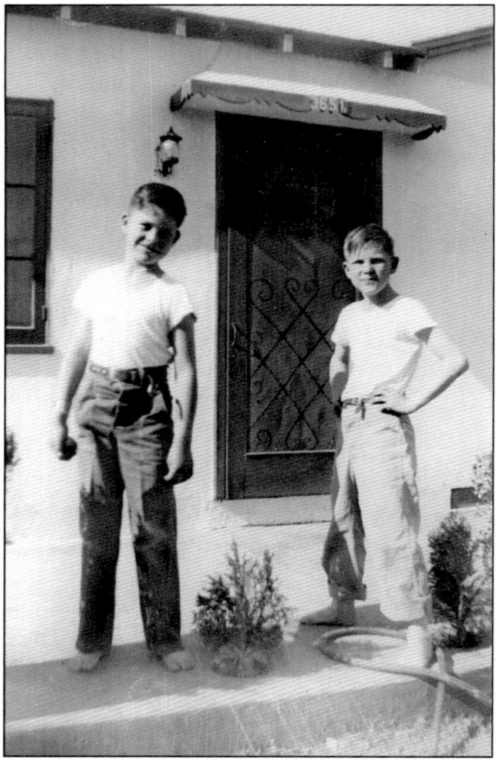

TWO BROTHERS. Cois (left) and John Mack Byrd are shown outside their home on Mintern Street, *c.* 1940s. (Courtesy Byrd family.)

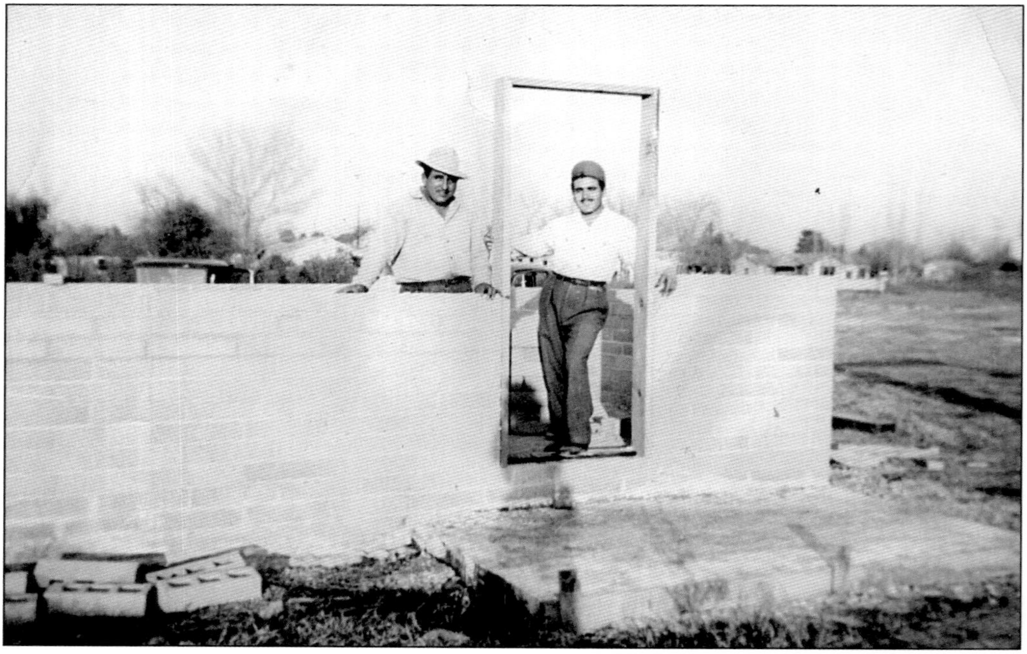

BUILDING A HOME. Tony (left) and Abbie Chavez are building Abbie's home in 1947 on a piece of property he bought from Flavio Madariaga at Flabob Airport. Abbie and his wife, Alice, still live in their home on property completely surrounded by Flabob Airport. (Courtesy Chavez family.)

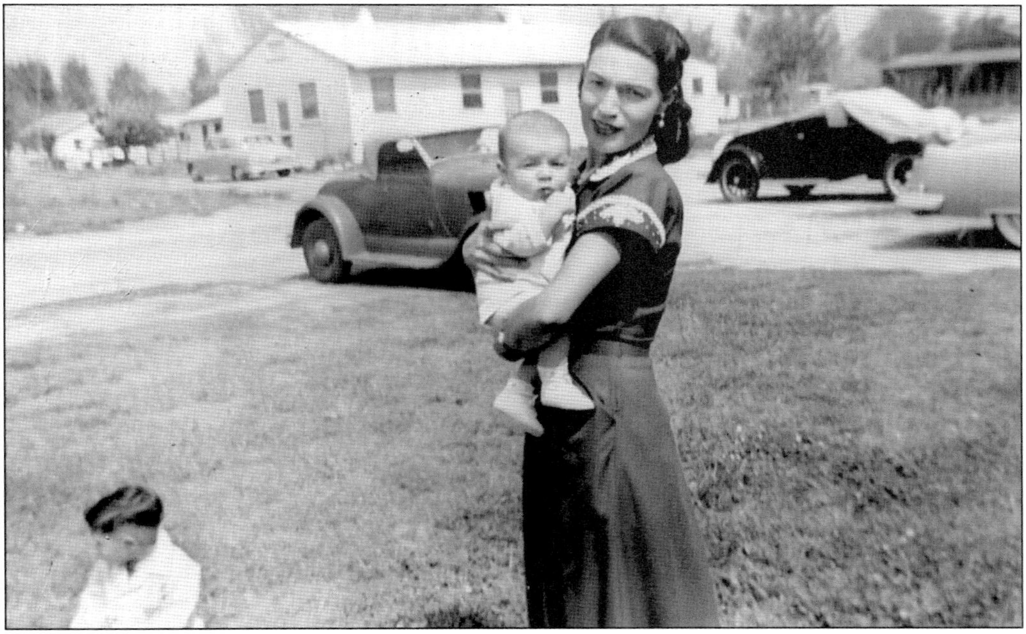

ALICE AND MARIO CHAVEZ. Alice and her son Mario are standing in the front yard of their home on Forty-second Street. Across the street are old army barracks that were moved onto property owned by Flabob Airport and turned into apartments. The barracks came from Camp Haan, which was located next to March Field during World War II. (Courtesy Chavez family.)

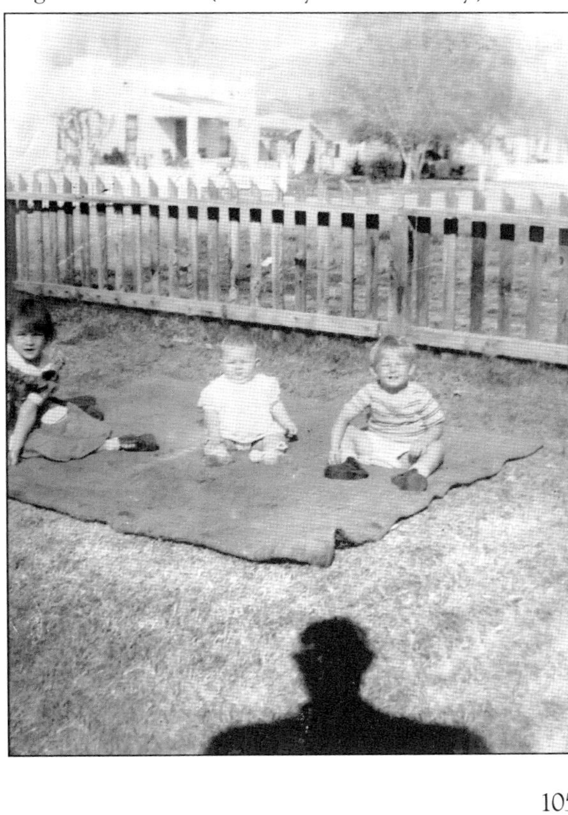

SCHAFFER CHILDREN. From left to right, Carol, Lolly, and Clyde Schaffer are in the front yard of their home on Fort Drive in Rubidoux in 1949. Their father built the home in 1942. (Courtesy Lolly Miller.)

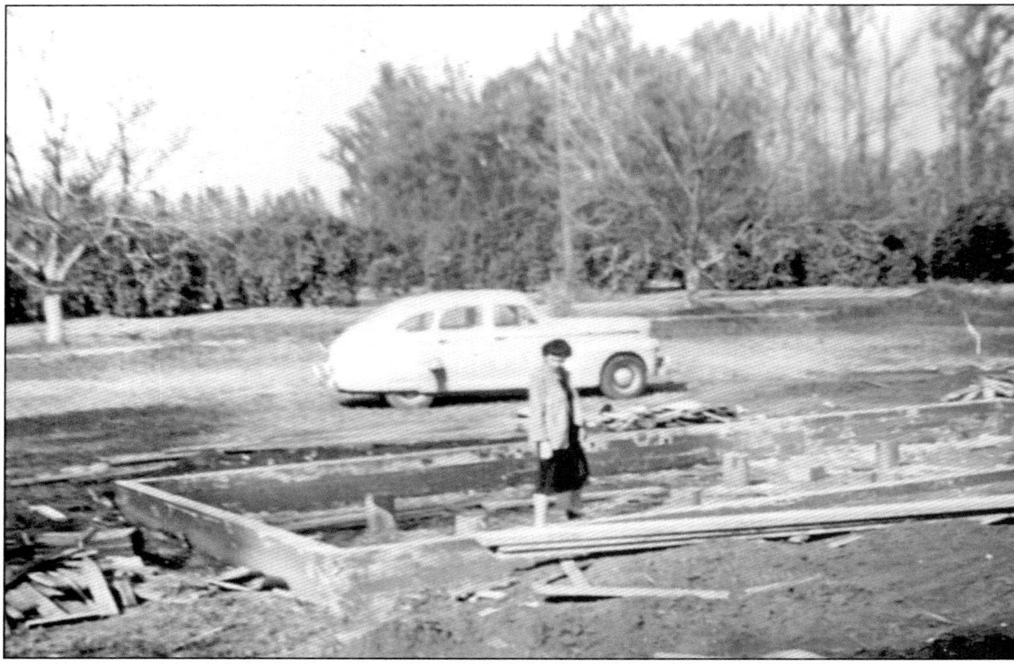

CONSTRUCTING HOME. This shows the construction beginning on the Thorson home on Opal Street. Because of the shortage of construction materials after World War II, Mr. Thorson worked on the home when he had the opportunity. (Courtesy Dorothy Thorson Evans.)

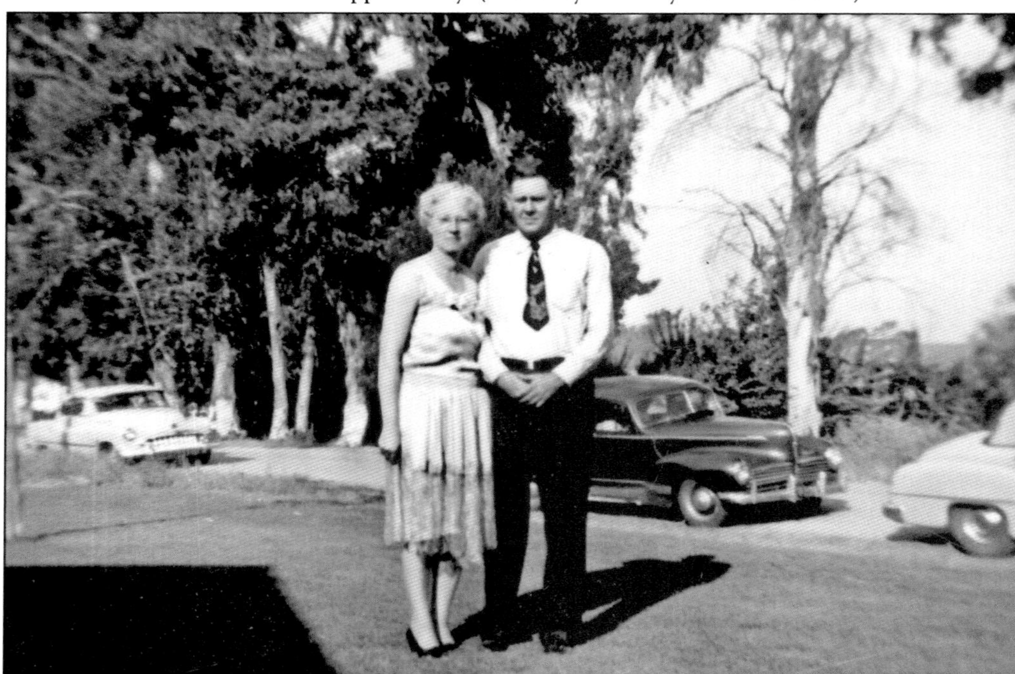

THEODORE AND INEZ PECK. The Pecks are shown on their front lawn in 1952. Behind them is Opal Street before it was widened and improved in 1955. (Courtesy Don Peck.)

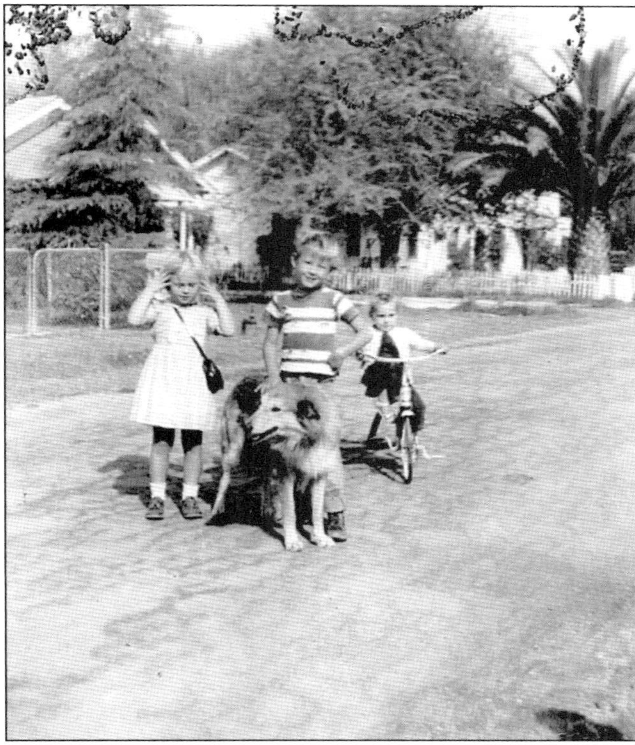

FORT DRIVE, 1955. Lolly (left) and Clyde Schaffer, their family dog, and a neighborhood child (right) are shown on Fort Drive in downtown Rubidoux. This photograph is looking toward Mission Boulevard. (Courtesy Lolly Miller.)

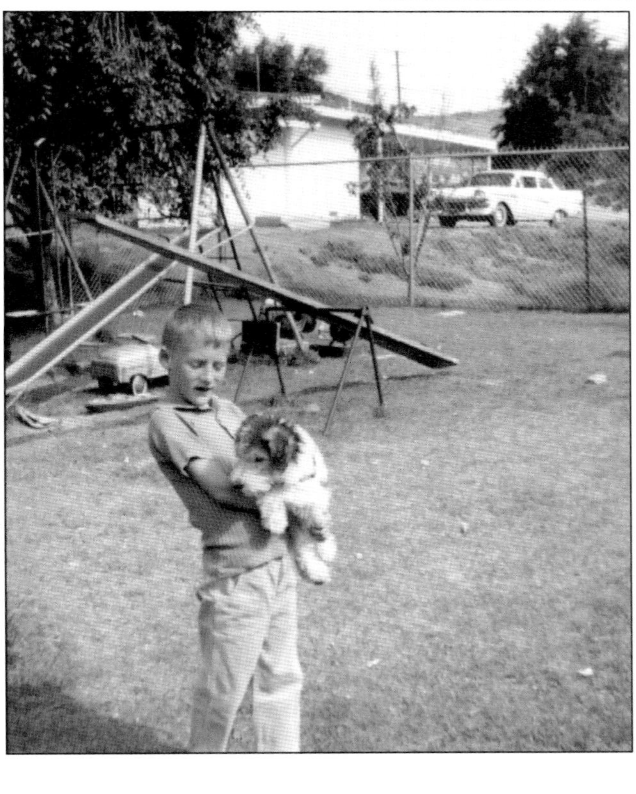

VILLA VISTA AVENUE. Dan Weaver and dog Princess are in the backyard at his family's home on Villa Vista Avenue. This view looks north toward the homes on Lemon Grove Avenue. The homes in this tract were built in the late 1950s and have a distinctive, flat-roofed architecture. (Courtesy Weaver family.)

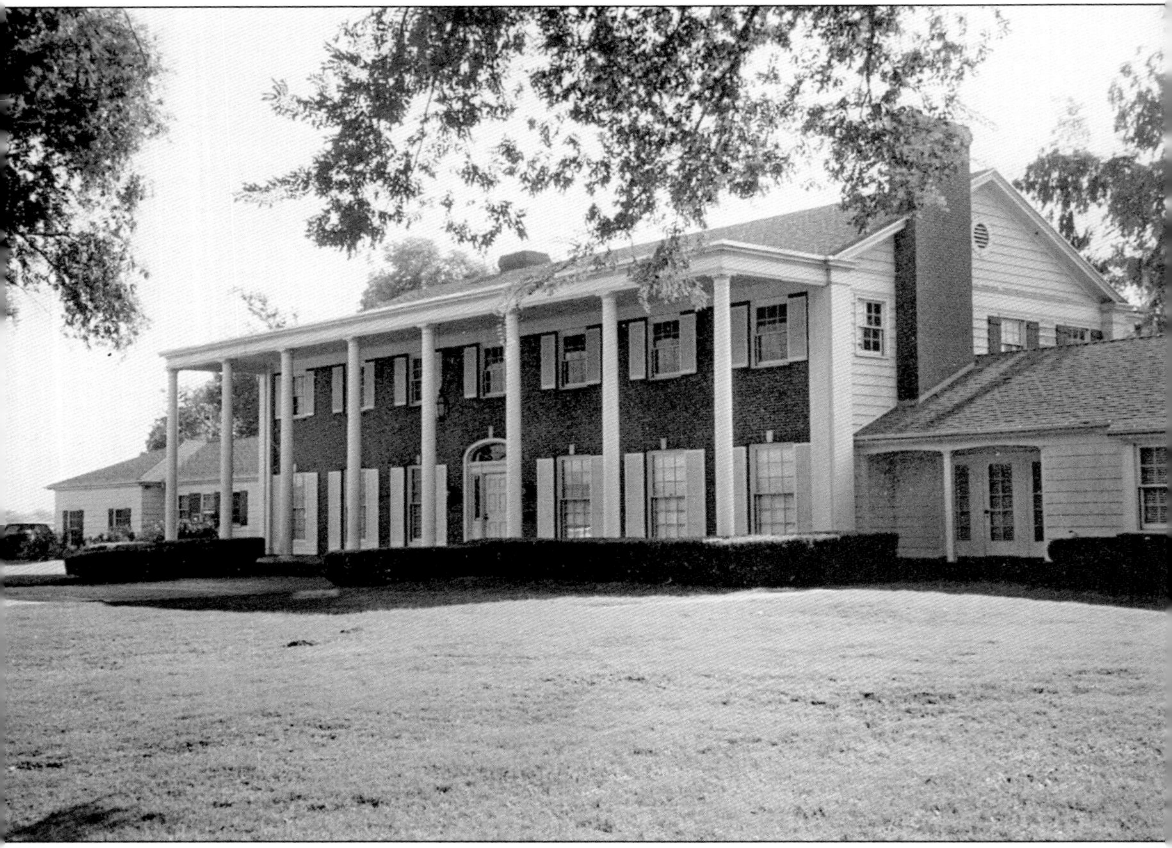

TINY NAYLOR HOUSE. Naylor was a well-known Los Angeles restaurant owner and Thoroughbred-racing enthusiast. He bought land on Mission Boulevard next to the Santa Ana River for a Thoroughbred farm. Around 1956, he built a Southern-style mansion on the property. The housewarming party is still remembered because of Naylor's famous guests including bandleader Harry James and his wife, Betty Grable. Because of health reasons, Naylor himself never lived in the house, although his children did. The house now has a Crestmore Road address and is the headquarters for the Riverside County Regional Park and Open-Space District. (Courtesy Riverside County Regional Park and Open-Space District.)

Seven

Belltown

The story of Belltown began in 1907 with the first Belltown subdivision map. But it was not until the 1920s, when a new subdivision with smaller lots was created, that the population of Belltown really began to grow. The subdivision was called "Ciudad Mexicana de Alvarado" to appeal to Mexican immigrants moving into the area after fleeing the Mexican Revolution. Belltown had no commercial development to speak of, so its residents traveled to nearby Rubidoux for shopping. Belltown's community life revolved around the Catholic church, which was built in 1927. The little Belltown School was also built in the 1920s, and until it closed in the 1950s, it also provided a community focal point.

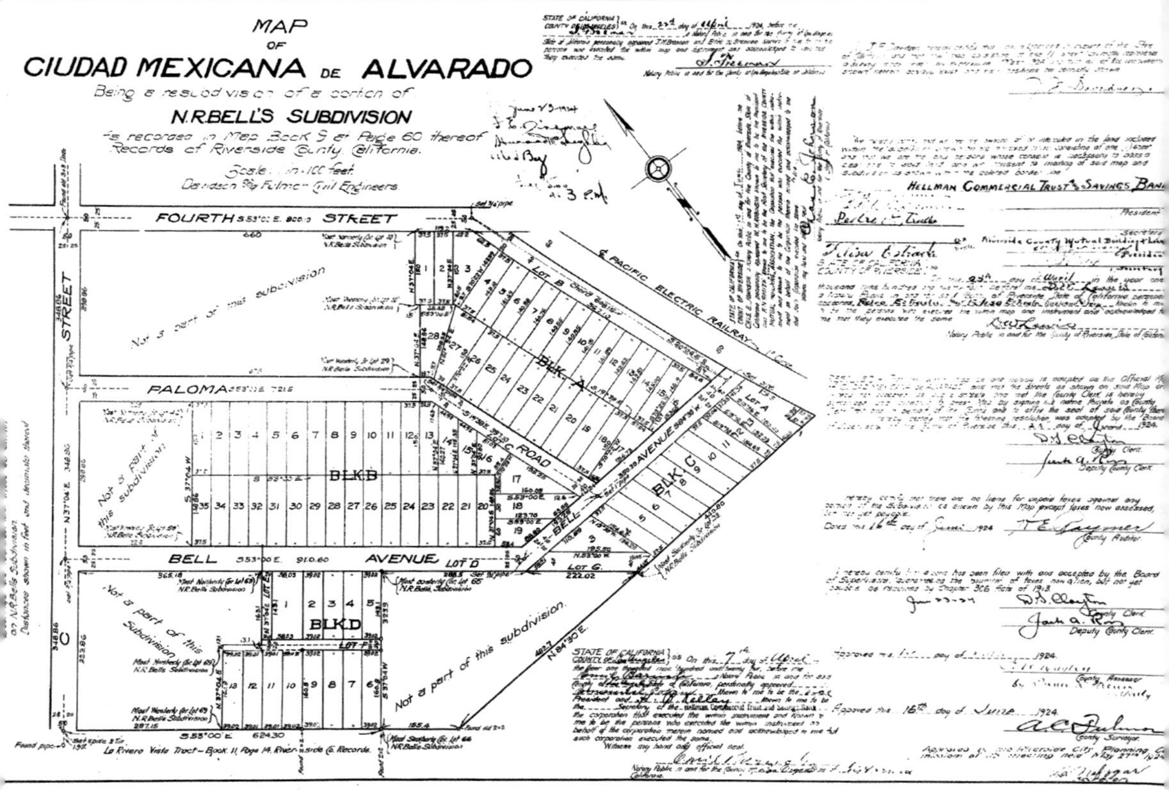

BELLTOWN SUBDIVISION. This is a 1924 subdivision map for Ciudad Mexicana de Alvarado, which shows the Belltown area much as it is today. (Courtesy author.)

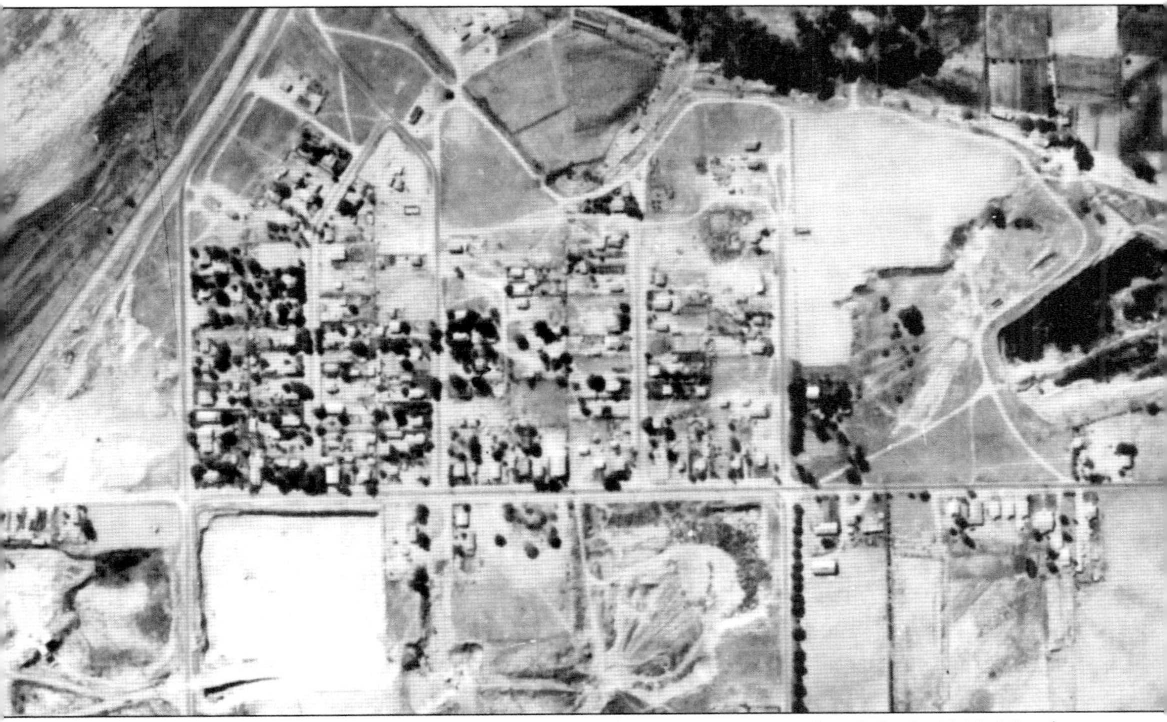

Aerial Photograph. This photograph of the Belltown area was taken July 8, 1948. North is to the left of the image. Hall Avenue is in the lower center of the photograph running north to south. It shows that the most concentrated area of development was in the area at the top of the photograph bounded by Hall Avenue, Twenty-fourth Street, and Paloma Road. (Courtesy Riverside County Flood Control and Water Conservation District.)

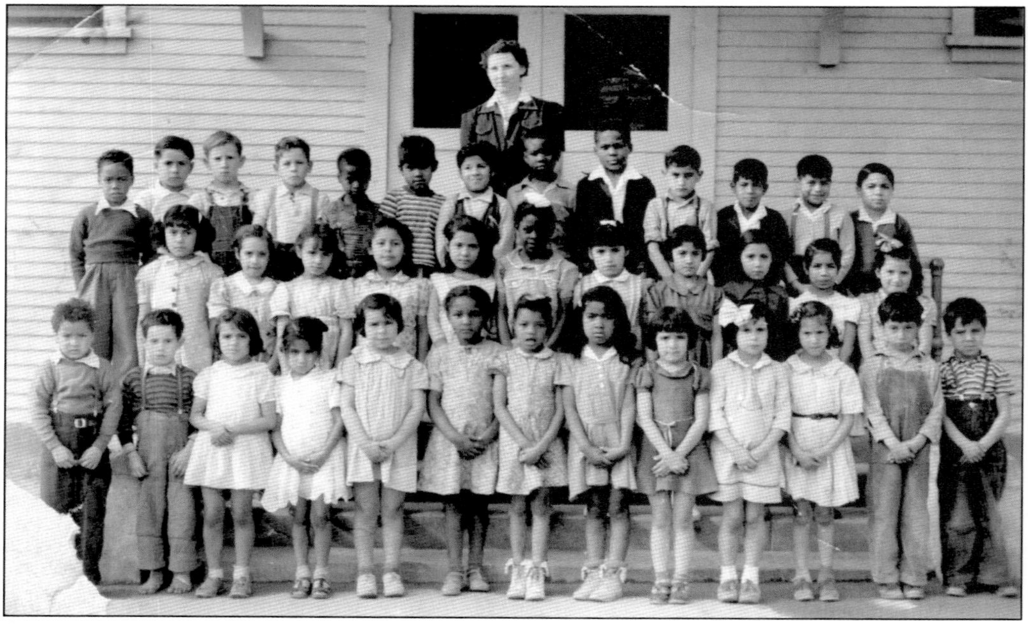

BELLTOWN SCHOOL CLASS, C. 1941. Belltown School, located on Hall Avenue across from the Our Lady of Guadalupe Catholic Church, was built in 1920. It was a small, three-room school designed to serve just the Belltown area. Each room at the school held two grades of students. It was closed in 1956, and its students were moved to the new Ina Arbuckle School in Rubidoux. This class photograph was taken in front of the school. (Courtesy Roberts family.)

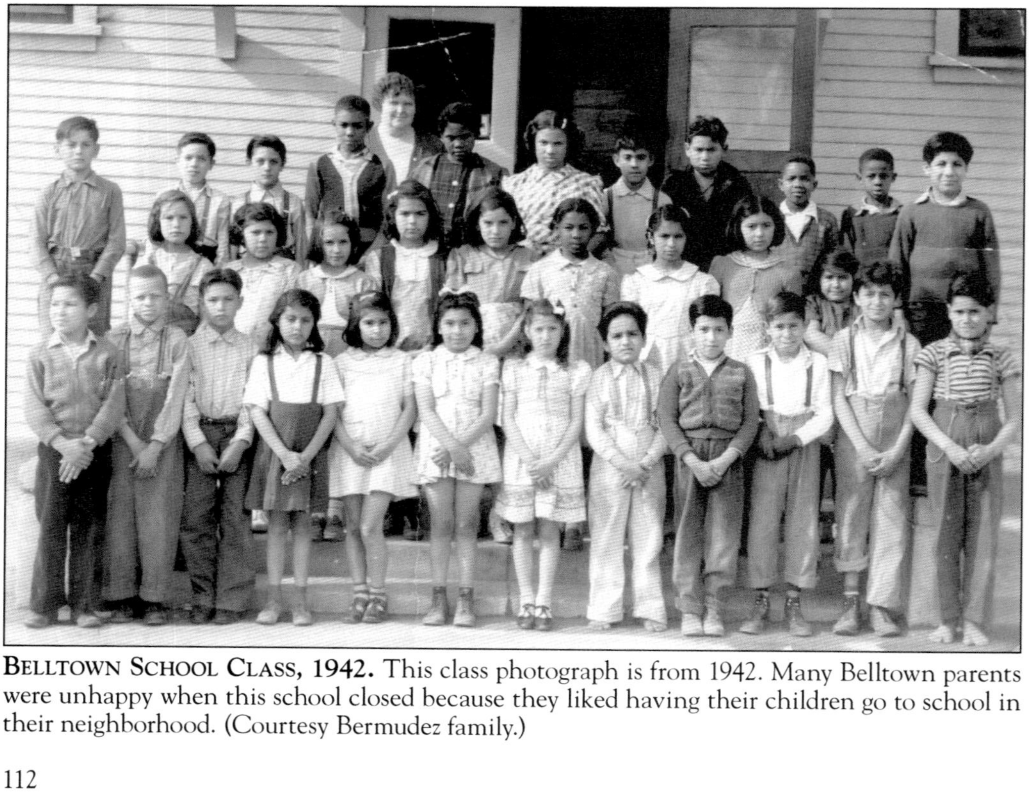

BELLTOWN SCHOOL CLASS, 1942. This class photograph is from 1942. Many Belltown parents were unhappy when this school closed because they liked having their children go to school in their neighborhood. (Courtesy Bermudez family.)

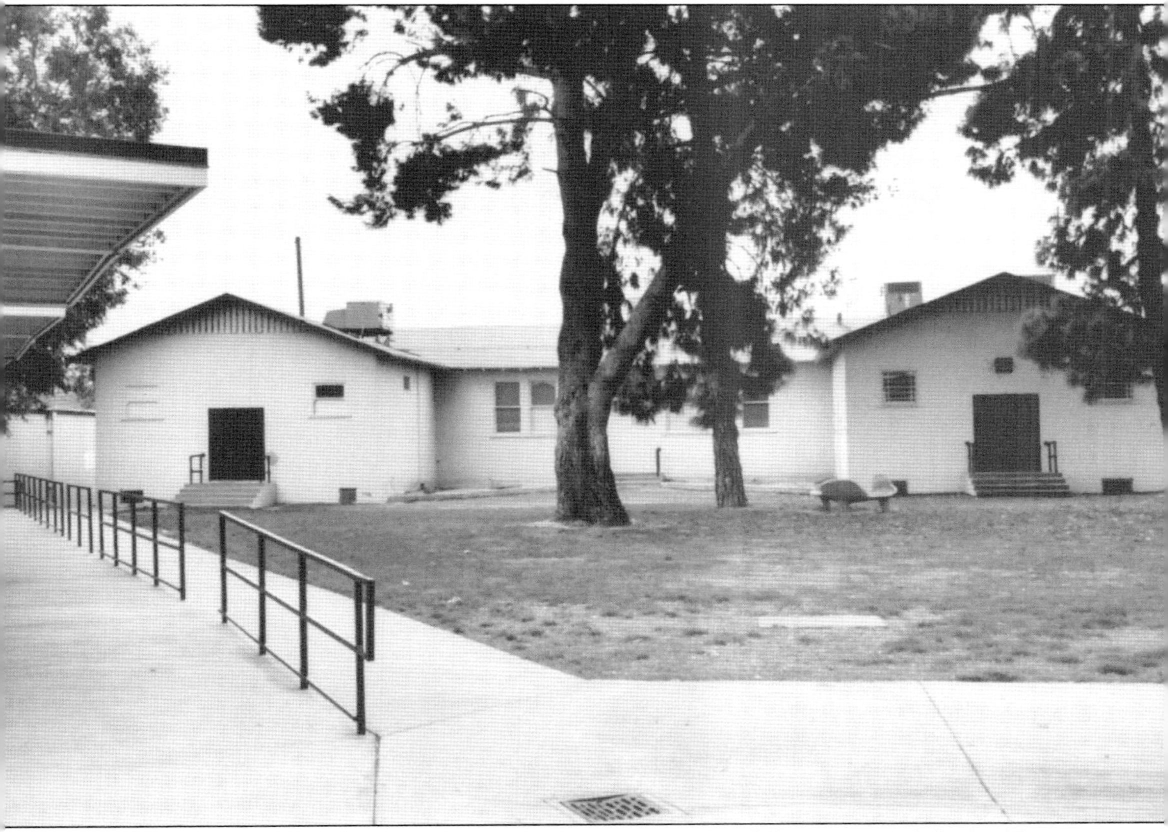

BELLTOWN SCHOOL TODAY. After the school closed, the school district moved the building to district property at the rear of West Riverside School. There it has served many uses through the years. This photograph shows the rear of the school, which is basically unaltered from its days serving the students in Belltown. (Courtesy author.)

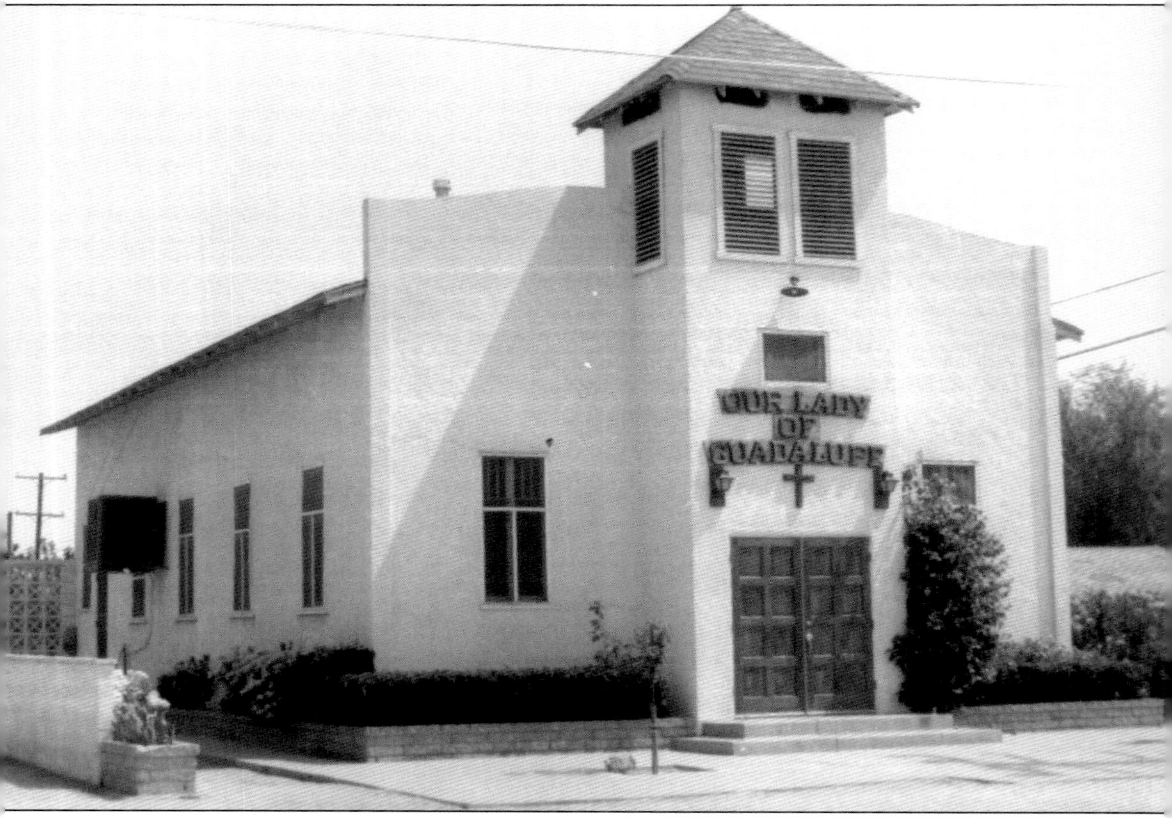

OUR LADY OF GUADALUPE CHURCH. Our Lady of Guadalupe Church on Hall Avenue in Belltown was founded in 1927. At that time, the Catholic Diocese was responding to an influx of Mexican immigrants who came to the area after the Mexican Revolution. A total of three churches were built all named Our Lady of Guadalupe. The three churches were located in Belltown, Highgrove, and Riverside's Eastside. The Belltown church remains an active mission church. (Riverside County Regional Park and Open-Space District.)

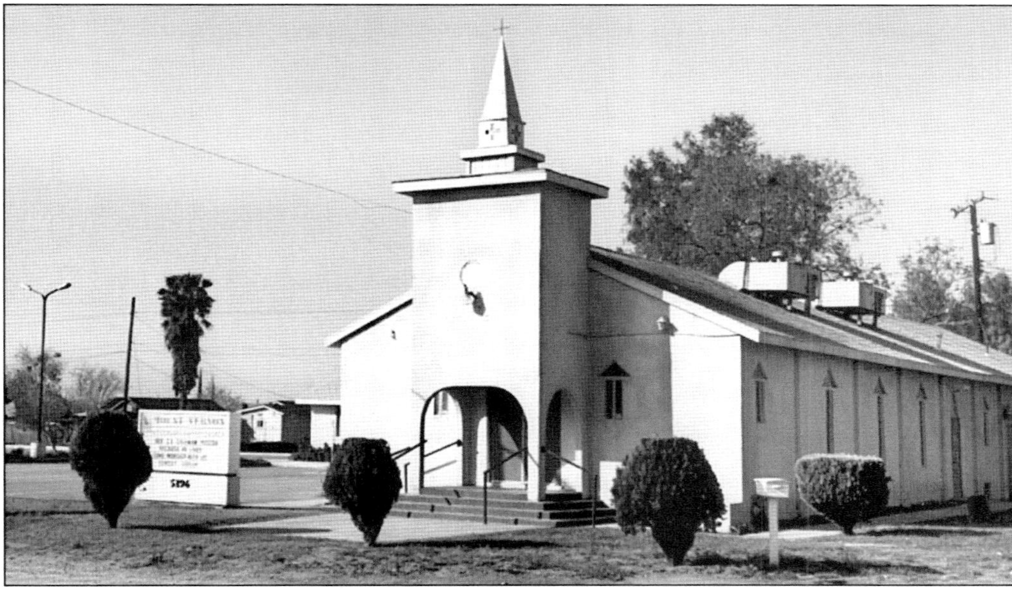

MOUNT VERNON BAPTIST CHURCH. On March 18, 1945, community members, including Eddie Dee Smith, organized Sunday school classes for the children of Belltown, which were held at Belltown School. Smith saw that too many children in the Belltown area were not able to go to church on Sundays because the closest African American church was in Riverside. From this Sunday school grew Mount Vernon Baptist Church, which is located on Twenty-fourth Street in Belltown. (Courtesy author.)

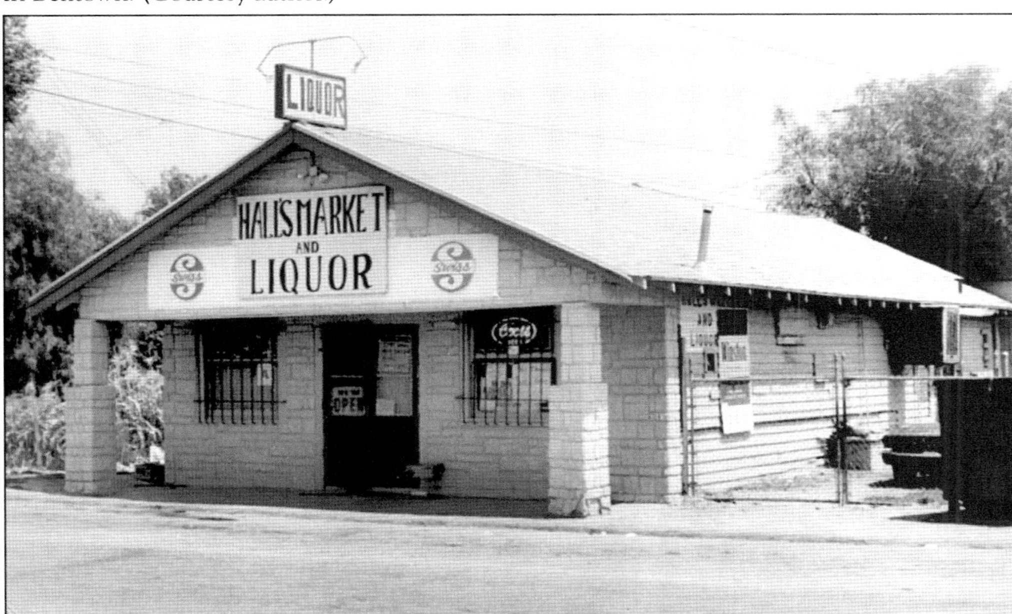

HALL'S MARKET. Originally a bungalow-style home on Hall Street in Belltown, *c.* 1926, it was later converted to a market. It became important to the residents of Belltown who didn't have any other stores close by. The market is still in business today. (Courtesy Riverside County Regional Park and Open-Space District.)

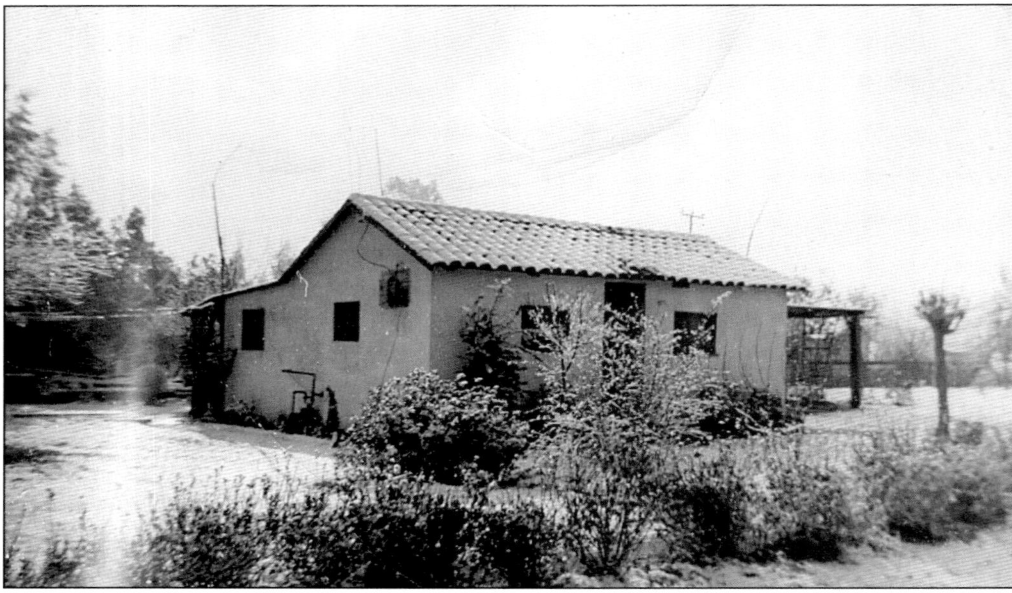

Perez House. The Belen Perez house in Belltown is shown in the 1930s. This picture was taken because it snowed that day! (Courtesy Bermudez family.)

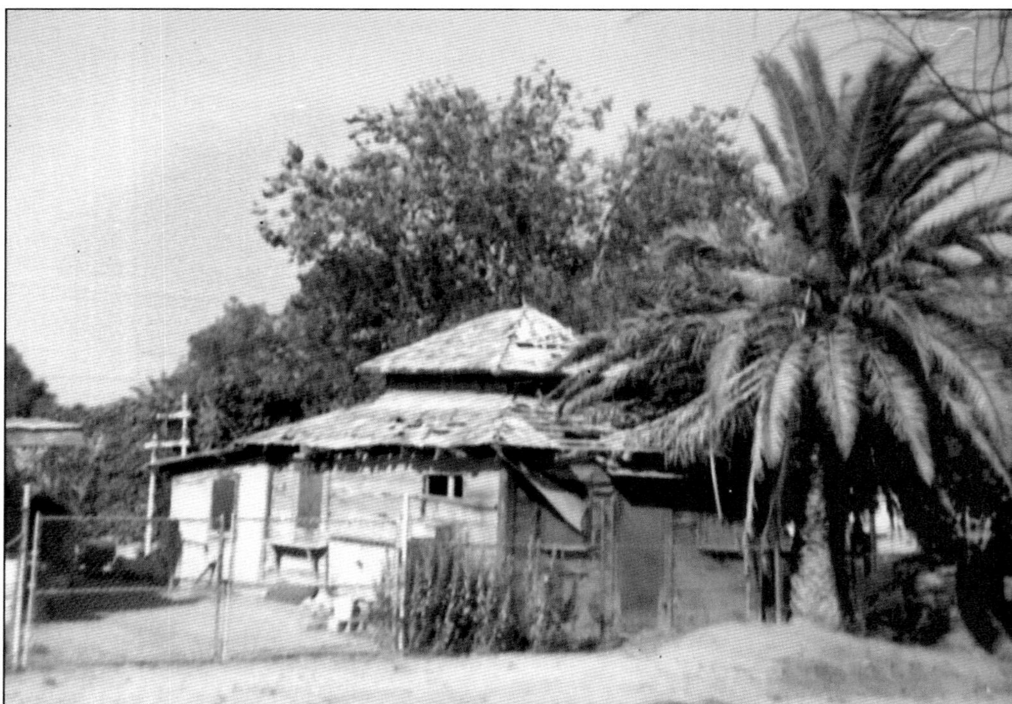

Belltown House. Many people remember this unique house that was located on Hall Avenue next to Hall's Market. (Courtesy Bermudez family.)

ROSIE ROBERTS. This photograph was taken in the 1930s at the farm owned by Rosie and her husband, Carter. The Robertses' property was on Hall Street approximately where the 60 Freeway is today. There the family raised truck crops, which they sold to area grocery stores. (Courtesy Roberts family.)

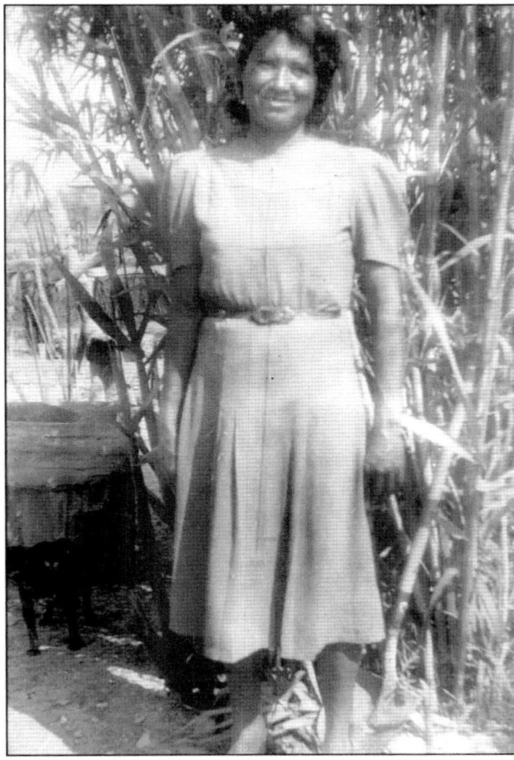

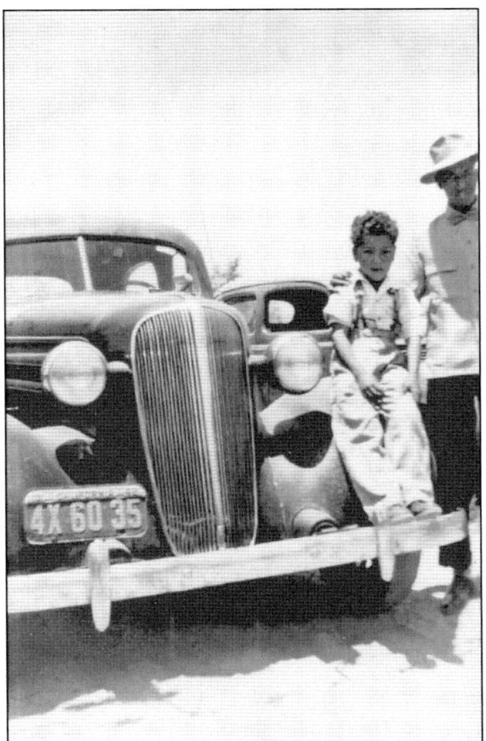

BOB AND WILLIE ROBERTS. Bob Roberts is shown with his uncle Willie, *c.* 1940, at the family farm. (Courtesy Roberts family.)

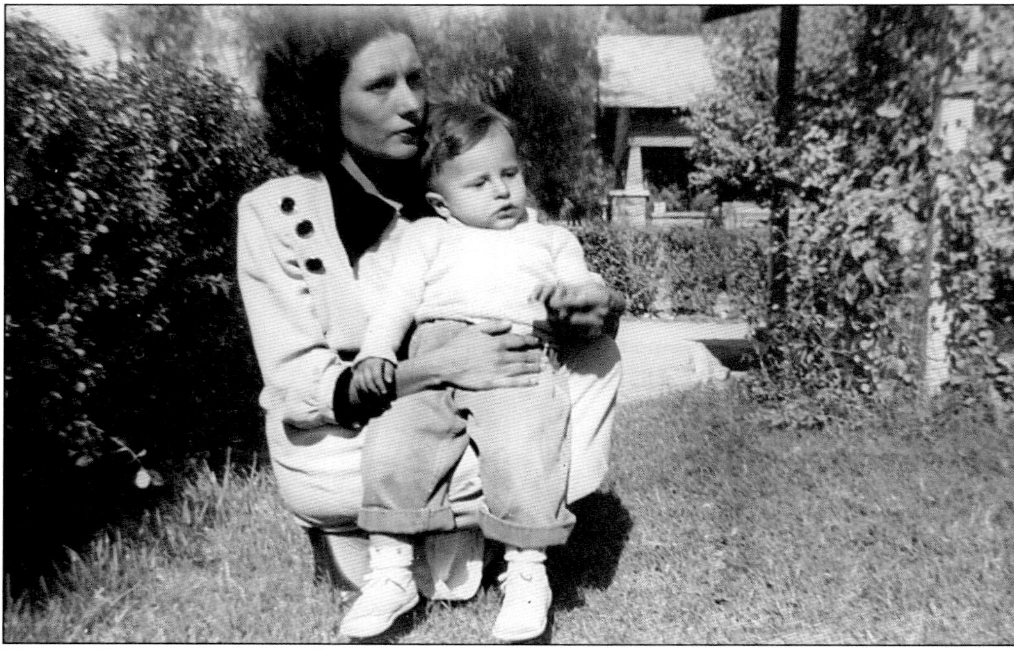

ESTHER BERMUDEZ, 1949. This photograph of Esther Bermudez and her nephew Arthur Duron was taken at the Duron home on Hall Avenue. (Courtesy Bermudez family.)

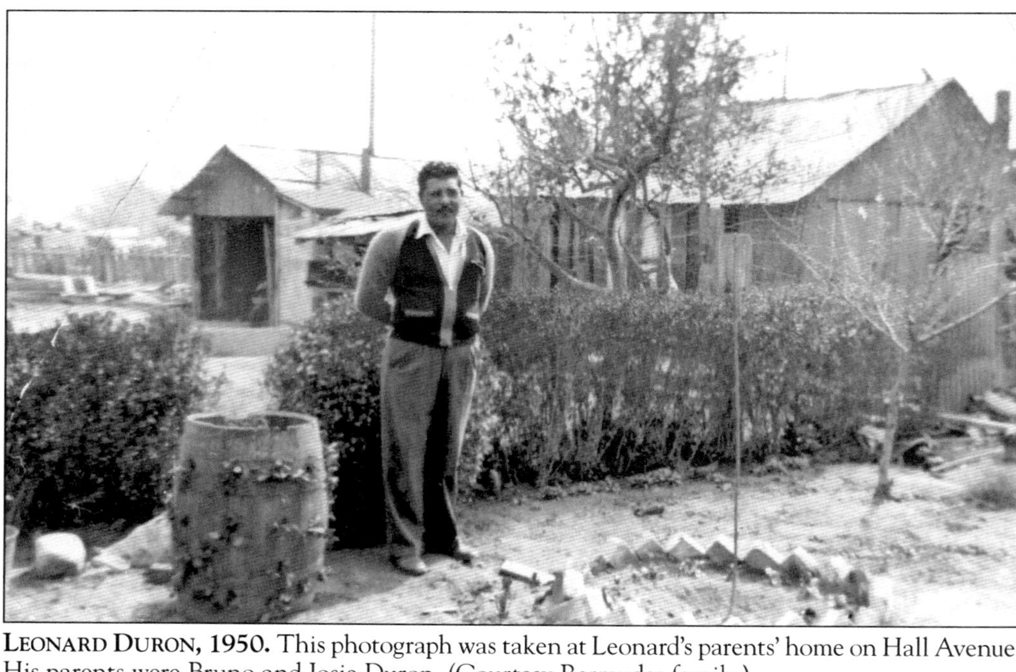

LEONARD DURON, 1950. This photograph was taken at Leonard's parents' home on Hall Avenue. His parents were Bruno and Josie Duron. (Courtesy Bermudez family.)

Eight

Crestmore

The story of Crestmore is about a small community that was built right next to the county line, in the hills above Rubidoux Boulevard. Subdivided in the 1920s, the homes are an eclectic mix of styles that reflect the decades in which they were built, mainly the 1920s to the 1960s. The large lots allow animal keeping, something many residents take advantage of. With no shops, markets, schools, or churches of its own, Crestmore maintained close ties with Rubidoux. Crestmore's story also includes the large cement plant and mining operation, which are still just across Rubidoux Boulevard from this small housing development. This landmark business, which began in 1906, provided jobs to residents of Crestmore and Rubidoux.

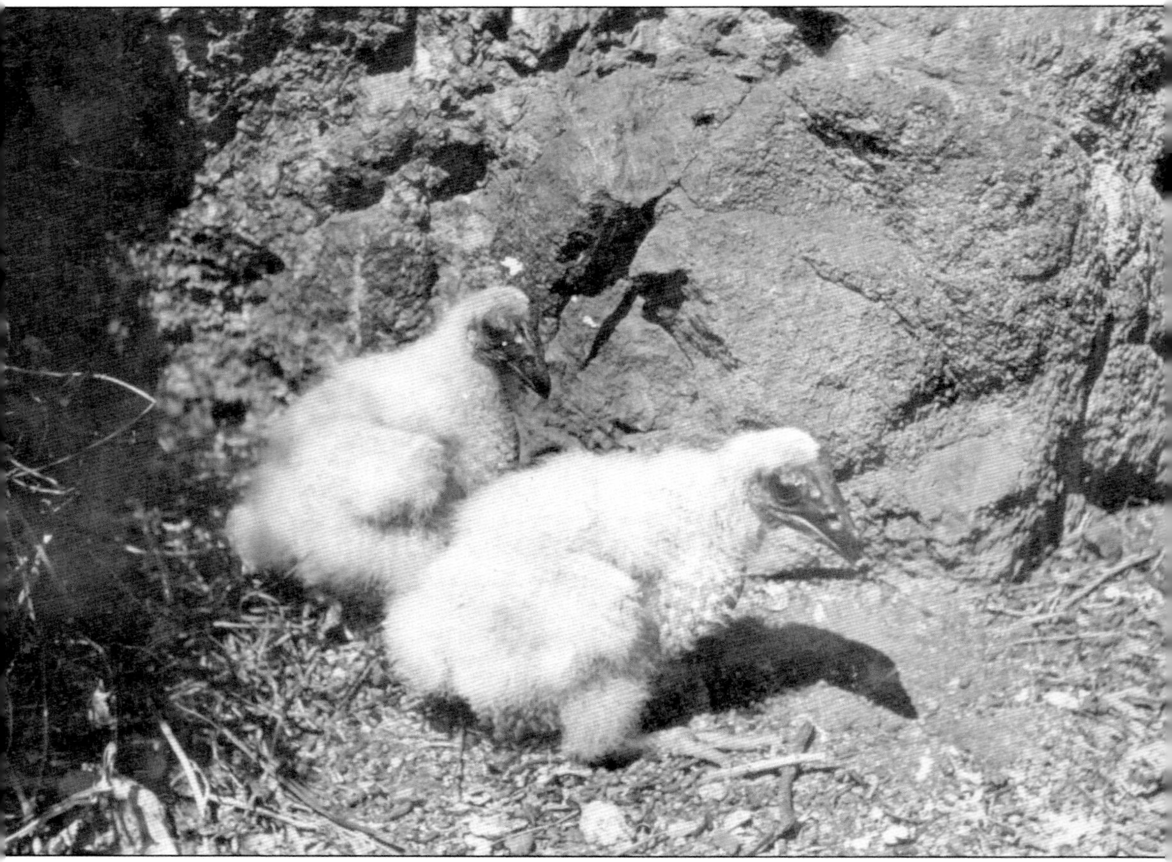

VULTURES. This photograph of young vultures in their nest was taken on Crestmore Hill around 1900. (Courtesy Riverside County Regional Park and Open-Space District.)

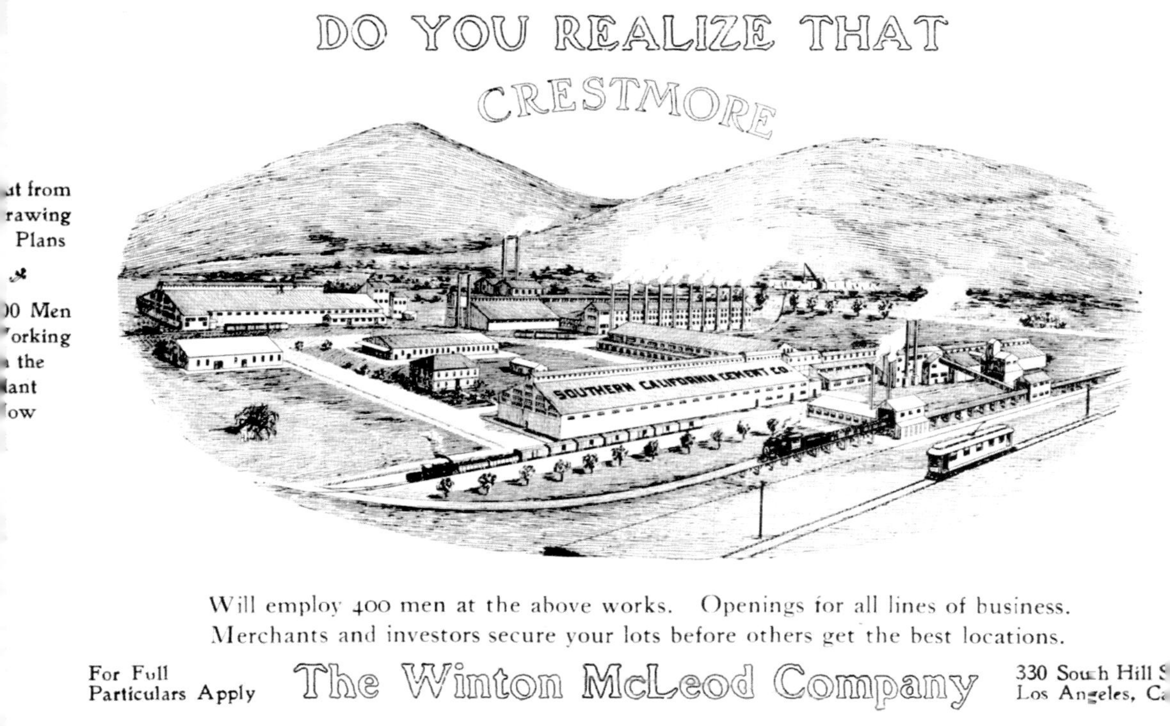

SOUTHERN CALIFORNIA CEMENT COMPANY. This advertisement appeared in the May 24, 1907, *As You Like It* magazine. It is advertising both the cement plant and the adjacent subdivision/town site of Crestmore. While the cement plant was in Riverside County, the subdivision was actually in San Bernardino County, just across the county line from the cement plant. (Courtesy Riverside Metropolitan Museum.)

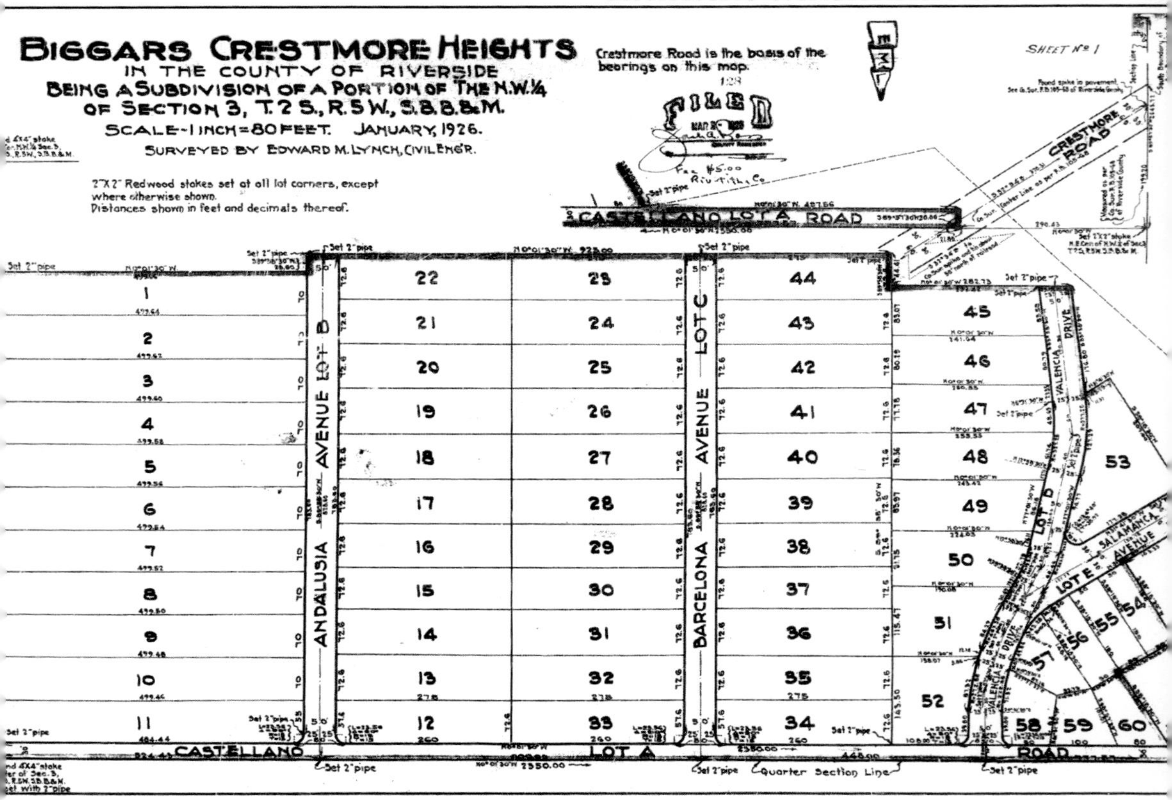

CRESTMORE HEIGHTS. In 1926, Irvine and May Keith Biggar filed a subdivision map for Biggar's Crestmore Heights. It was located just south of the Riverside/San Bernardino County line and west of today's Rubidoux Boulevard. Just north of this subdivision, in San Bernardino County, was the 1907 subdivision of the city of Crestmore, which is where the Biggars got the idea for the name. (Courtesy author.)

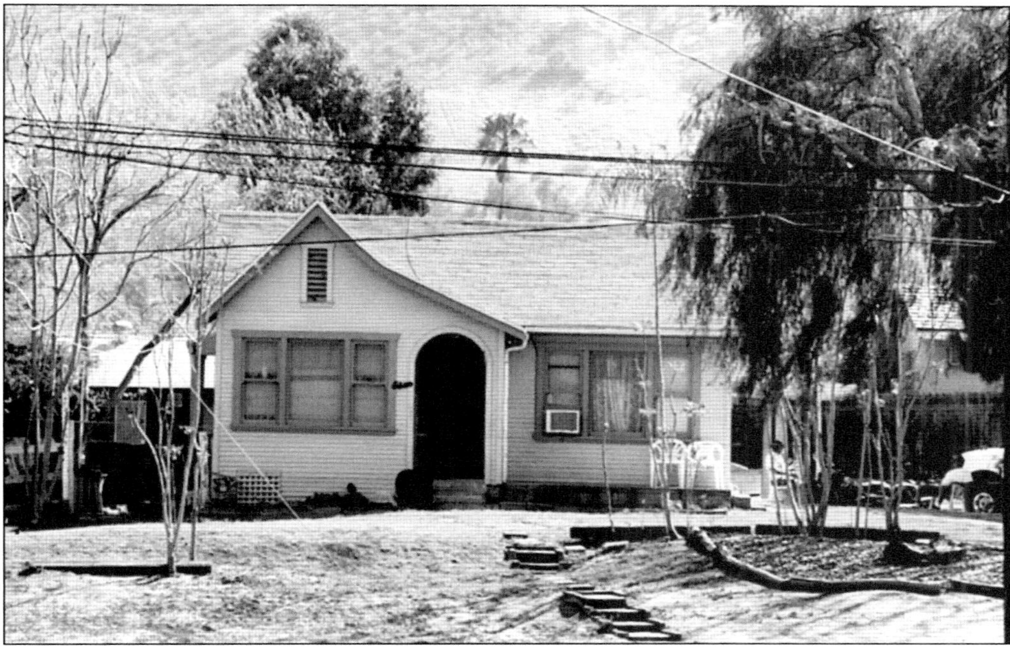

CRESTMORE HOMES. The Crestmore Heights subdivision was a land division only. The lots were sold to individuals who built the home of their choice on the property. Here are two examples of the types of early homes that can be found in the Crestmore area. The above house is Tudor revival with clapboard siding, dating to the 1930s. The home below is Spanish-eclectic style, *c.* 1920s. (Courtesy author.)

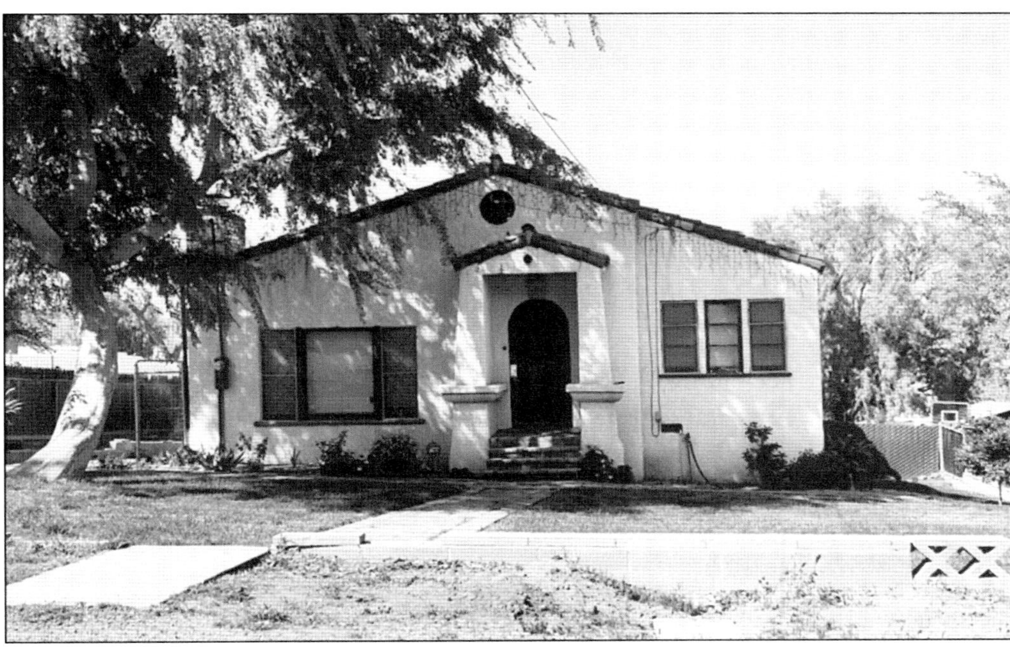

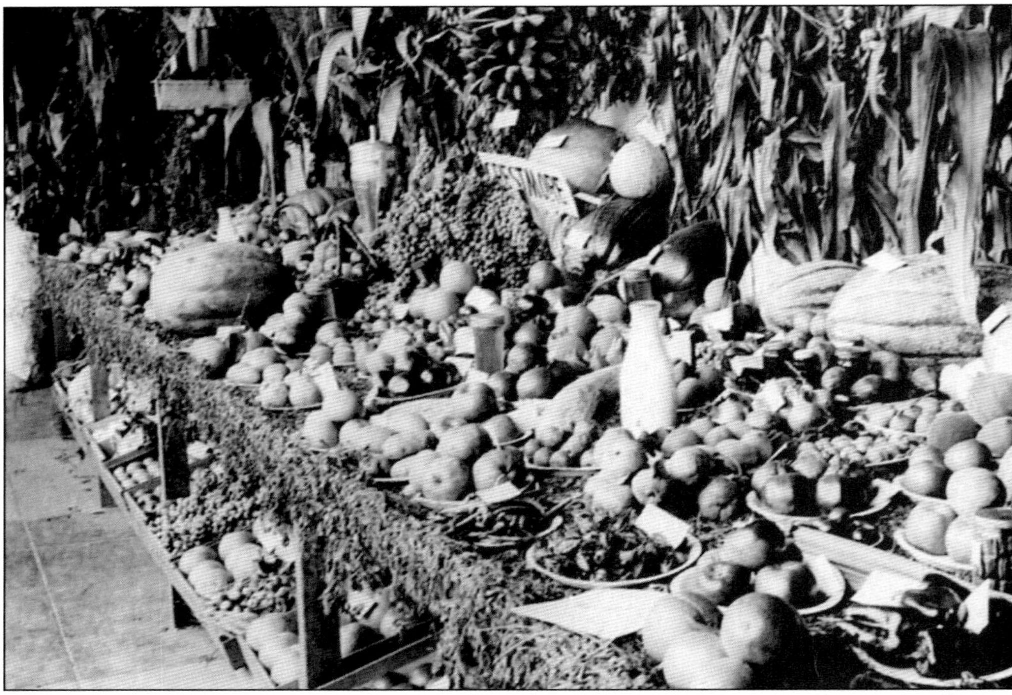

HARVEST FESTIVAL EXHIBIT. Beginning in the early 1930s, the Harvest Festival was a fair that was put on in the Jurupa area. Each community in Jurupa would have a display of items raised in their area. This is the Crestmore display from the early 1930s. (Courtesy Ida Parks Condit family.)

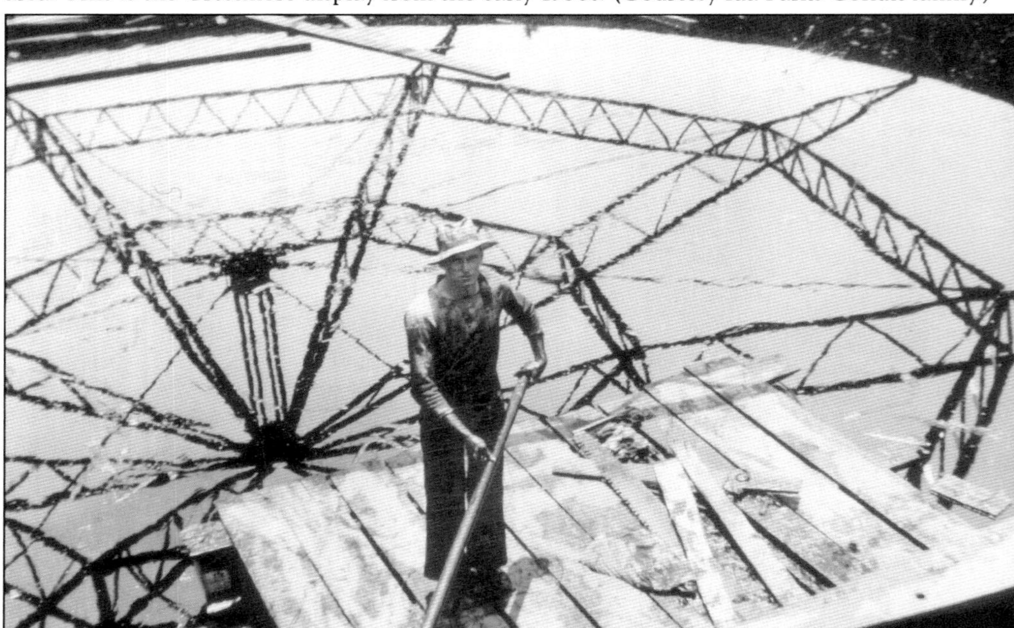

OIL TANK, C. 1941. This large tank of oil sat near Rubidoux Boulevard at the cement plant site. The man in the photograph is standing on what looks like a raft floating on the oil. (Courtesy Byrd family.)

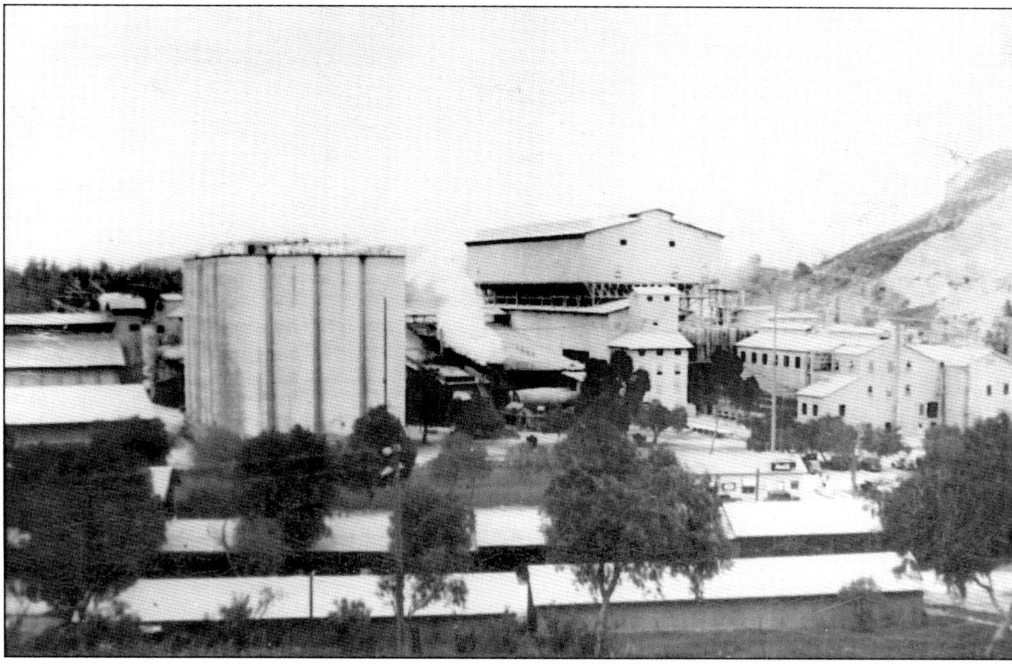

Cement Company. This photograph is looking east at the plant site, *c.* 1941. Crestmore Hill is in the background at the right of the photograph. (Courtesy Byrd family.)

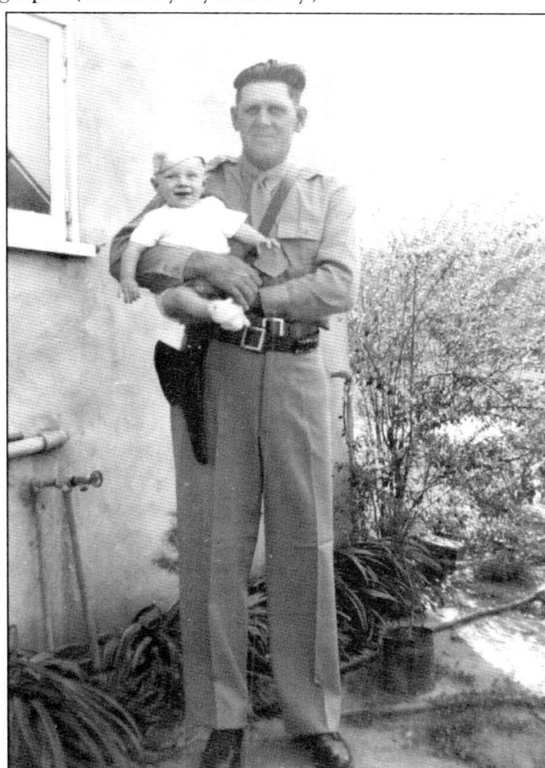

Plant Watchman. Theodore Peck is shown in April 1944 with his young son Don. Theodore, a resident of Rubidoux, was a watchman at the Riverside Cement Company. He is wearing his watchman's uniform. (Courtesy Don Peck.)

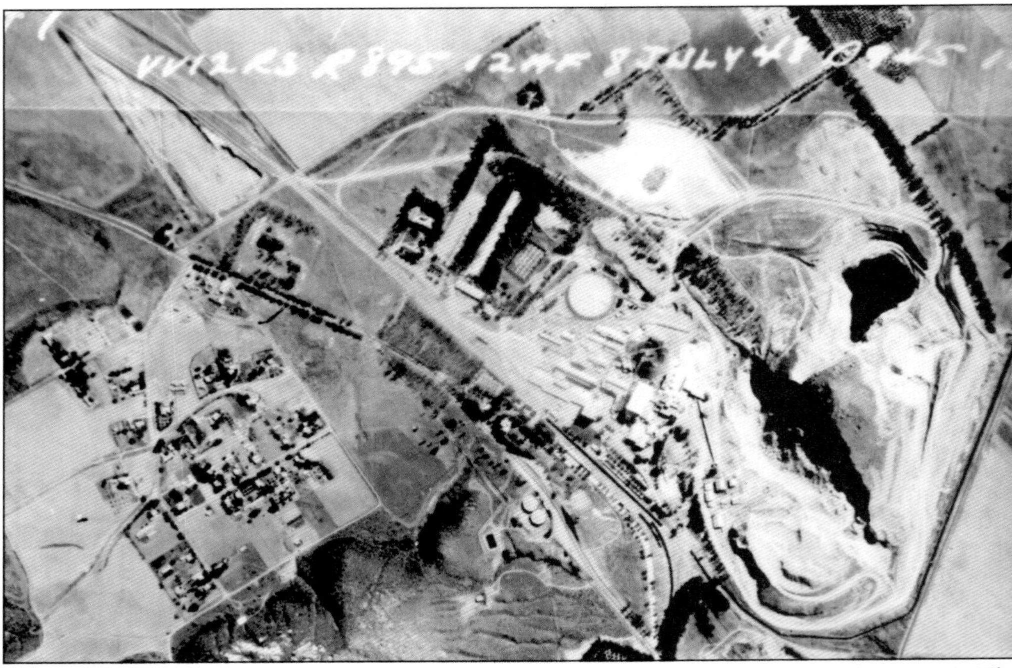

AERIAL PHOTOGRAPH. This photograph of the Crestmore area was taken July 8, 1948. The small Crestmore residential area is to the left of the photograph, and the cement plant is to the right and includes the large, round tank. (Courtesy Riverside County Flood Control and Water Conservation District.)

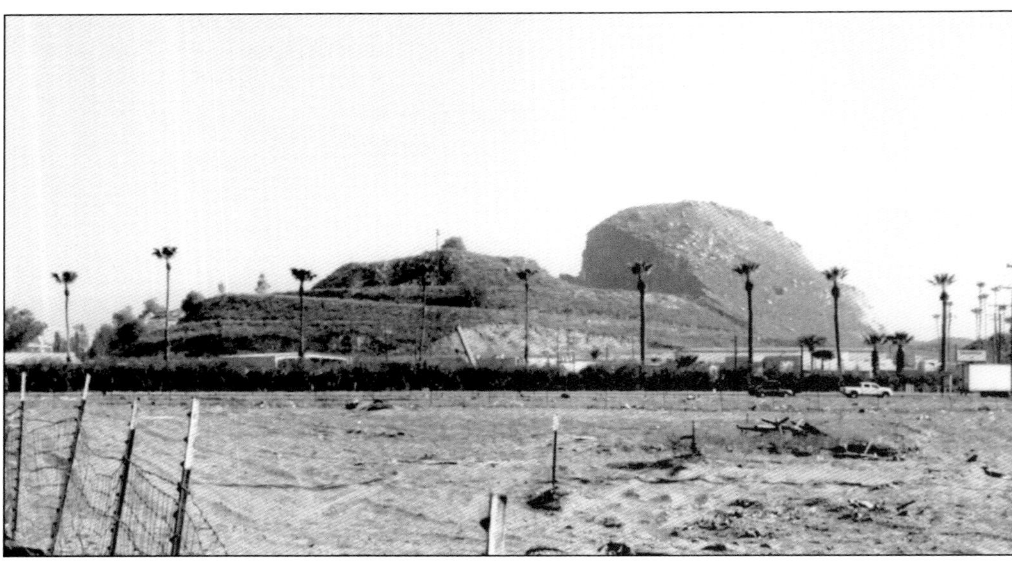

CRESTMORE HILL TODAY. Visible from many parts of Rubidoux, Crestmore, and Belltown are the remnants of Crestmore Hill. This hill was mined for many years for the raw materials needed to make cement and concrete. (Courtesy author.)

BIBLIOGRAPHY

Condit, Ida Parks. *Jurupa Peace and Friendship*. Riverside, CA: self-published, 1984.

Gunther, Jane Davies. *Riverside County, California, Place Names*. Riverside, CA: self-published, 1984.

Johnson, Kim Jarrell. *Jurupa*. Charleston, SC: Arcadia Publishing, 2005.

Kurz, Don. *Robidoux Rancho on the Jurupa*. Riverside, CA: self-published, 1972.

Lech, Steve. *Along the Old Roads*. Riverside, CA: self-published, 2004.